REASONS AND THE GOOD

In *Reasons and the Good* Roger Crisp answers some of the oldest questions in moral philosophy. Claiming that a fundamental issue in normative ethics is what ultimate reasons for action we might have, he argues that the best statements of such reasons will not employ moral concepts. He investigates and explains the nature of reasons themselves; his account of how we come to know them combines an intuitionist epistemology with elements of Pyrrhonist scepticism. He defends a hedonistic theory of well-being and an account of practical reason according to which we can give some, though not overriding, priority to our own good over that of others. The book develops original lines of argument within a framework of some traditional but currently less popular views.

Roger Crisp is Uehiro Fellow and Tutor in Philosophy, St Anne's College, Oxford.

Reasons and the Good

ROGER CRISP

CLARENDON PRESS · OXFORD

OXFORD

UNIVERSITY PRESS

Great Clarendon Street, Oxford OX2 6DP

Oxford University Press is a department of the University of Oxford.
It furthers the University's objective of excellence in research, scholarship,
and education by publishing worldwide in

Oxford New York

Auckland Cape Town Dar es Salaam Hong Kong Karachi
Kuala Lumpur Madrid Melbourne Mexico City Nairobi
New Delhi Shanghai Taipei Toronto

With offices in

Argentina Austria Brazil Chile Czech Republic France Greece
Guatemala Hungary Italy Japan Poland Portugal Singapore
South Korea Switzerland Thailand Turkey Ukraine Vietnam

Oxford is a registered trade mark of Oxford University Press
in the UK and in certain other countries

Published in the United States
by Oxford University Press Inc., New York

© Roger Crisp 2006

The moral rights of the author have been asserted
Database right Oxford University Press (maker)

First published 2006
First published in paperback 2008

British Library Cataloguing in Publication Data
Data available

Library of Congress Cataloging in Publication Data
Crisp, Roger, 1961–
Reasons and the good / Roger Crisp.
p. cm.
Includes bibliographical references and index.
ISBN-13: 978–0–19–954869–9 (Pbk.) (alk. paper)
ISBN-10: 978–0–19–929033–8 (Hbk.) (alk. paper)
1. Ethics. 2. Practical reason. I. Title.
BJ1012.C75 2006
170′.42—dc22 2006016460

Typeset by Laserwords Private Limited, Chennai, India
Printed in Great Britain
on acid-free paper by
Biddles Ltd., King's Lynn, Norfolk

ISBN 978–0–19–929033–8 (Hbk.)   978–0–19–954869–9 (Pbk.)

1 3 5 7 9 10 8 6 4 2

For Catherine

Acknowledgements

During the writing of this book many people have assisted me with insightful comments, discussion, and advice. Some of these people, to whom I am especially grateful, have read and commented on complete or nearly complete drafts: Robert Audi, Jonathan Dancy, Stephen Gardiner, Brad Hooker, Matthew Liao, Andrew Mason, Derek Parfit, Michael Ridge, John Skorupski, Larry Temkin, Jeremy Watkins, and David Wiggins.

Alan Thomas invited me to present drafts of chapters at a series of research seminars at the University of Kent, Canterbury, and I wish to express thanks to him and to participants in these seminars, especially Jonathan Friday, Edward Harcourt, Simon Kirchin, Richard Norman, Sean Sayers, Tony Skillen, Murray Smith, Julia Tanney, and Robin Taylor. John Tasioulas organized at Corpus Christi College, Oxford, a colloquium on a draft of the book under the auspices of the Oxford Centre for Ethics and the Philosophy of Law. I am indebted to him, to Robert Audi, Krister Byvkist, Jonathan Dancy, Joseph Raz, and Susan Wolf, who provided commentary on individual chapters, and to other participants: James Griffin, Brad Hooker, Douglas Maclean, Jonas Olson, and Onora O'Neill.

Others who have helped me, often substantially, include Robert M. Adams, Gustaf Arrhenius, Elizabeth Ashford, Lawrence BonJour, Nigel Bowles, John Broome, Benoît Castelnérac, Paul Coates, Michael DePaul, Timothy Endicott, Joshua Gert, Bernward Gesang, John Greco, Lorenzo Greco, Bashshar Haydar, Nils Holtug, Desmond King, James Levine, Kasper Lippert-Rasmussen, Noboru Maruyama, Adrian Moore, Andrew Moore, Kevin Mulligan, Stuart Opotowsky, Michael Otsuka, Catherine Paxton, Ingmar Persson, Thomas Petersen, Vasilis Politis, Robert Pulvertaft, Andrew Reisner, Daniel Robinson, Guy Robinson, Paul Robinson, Mark Rowlands, Jesper Ryberg, Julian Savulescu, Tim Scanlon, Bart Schultz, Robert Shaver, Daniel Star, Philip Stratton-Lake, Gabriele Taylor, Valerie Tiberius, Mark Timmons, Pete Tramel, Adrian Viens, Robert Wardy, Ralph Wedgwood, Andrew Williams, Nick Zangwill, and Michael Zimmerman. There are no doubt others I should have mentioned, and to them I apologize for my poor memory. I wish to thank audiences at the following: the Reading Philosophy Graduate Seminar;

a workshop at the Dept. of Philosophy, University of Copenhagen; the Oxford Jurisprudence Discussion Group; the Trinity College Dublin Philosophy Colloquium; the University of Hertfordshire Philosophy Research Symposium; the University of Northampton Philosophy Society; the University of Bristol Philosophy Research Seminar; and the University of Stockholm Philosophy Colloquium.

Without the support of a Leverhulme Trust Major Research Fellowship between 2003 and 2005 I would have been unable to write this book or indeed any book. I am greatly indebted to the Trustees. For allowing me to take the necessary leave, I am grateful to the Principal and Fellows of St Anne's College, and to the Board of the Faculty of Philosophy at the University of Oxford. Peter Momtchiloff at Oxford University Press has combined his characteristic patience and wisdom with appropriate degrees of exhortation and encouragement. I am grateful also to Jacqueline Baker and Rupert Cousens at OUP, and consider myself lucky to have had Laurien Berkeley as my copy-editor. My continuing connection with the Uehiro Foundation on Ethics and Education has remained a source of pride and pleasure.

Some of the book is based on earlier articles of mine. I thank the Royal Institute of Philosophy, Oxford University Press, the International Phenomenological Society, Chicago University Press, and editors of *Philosophy, The Stanford Encyclopedia of Philosophy, Philosophy and Phenomenological Research*, and *Ethics* for permission to use material from the following, details of which will be found in the Bibliography: 'Does Modern Moral Philosophy Rest on a Mistake?'; 'Well-being'; 'Hedonism Reconsidered'; 'Sidgwick and the Boundaries of Intuitionism'; 'Equality, Priority, and Compassion' (© 2003 by the University of Chicago. All rights reserved). Material from 'The Dualism of Practical Reason' is used by courtesy of the Editor of the Aristotelian Society: © 1996. I wish to reiterate here the thanks recorded in the original versions of these articles.

R.S.C

Oxford
April 2006

Contents

Introduction

> If there is such a thing as the truth about the subject matter of
> ethics—the truth, we might say, about the ethical—why is there
> any expectation that it should be simple? In particular, why should
> it be conceptually simple, using only one or two ethical concepts,
> such as *duty* or *good state of affairs*, rather than many? Perhaps we
> need as many concepts to describe it as we find we need, and no
> fewer.
>
> (Bernard Williams, *Ethics and the Limits of Philosophy*)

Williams is right. And it is in some ways regrettable that reflection
on ethical concepts is now significantly less common than it was in
the days of 'linguistic philosophy'. Many ethical concepts have quite
particular evolutionary, social, and cultural histories which it must
surely be a mistake to ignore if one is at all inclined to follow through
an implication of one interpretation of Williams's suggestion—that
we should avoid using concepts for which we have no need. In this
book I begin by trying to see the wood for the trees in ethics, and the
wood I describe is—as a reader for the Press put it—'a stark shape of
close-packed conifers in an empty landscape'. I know that few readers
will share my perspective. But I stand by Williams's principles, and ask
these readers to describe to me what it is in the ethical landscape that I
am missing.

The book opens with the suggestion that a—perhaps *the*—fundamental question in philosophical normative ethics concerns what
each of us has reason to do. That leads one immediately into the issue of
whether we have *moral* reasons to act, in the sense of ultimate or non-
derivative reasons the correct description of which makes ineliminable
use of the moral concepts—right, wrong, good, bad, virtuous, kind,
cruel, and so on. Drawing an analogy between morality and law as social

phenomena, I claim that there is a strong case for thinking that morality in itself provides no such reasons, though there may well be derivative reasons for doing what some actual morality or other prescribes. If I am right, then the correct theory of reasons for action should be stated without using the moral concepts.

In the hope of offering such a theory, in the second chapter I discuss the notion of a reason for action. I begin by distinguishing epistemic from practical reasons, and suggest that all practical reasons must be grounded in well-being. I go on to distinguish, within the domain of practical reasons, between explanatory (including motivating) reasons, and normative reasons. Normative reasons I define as properties of actions that count, for the agent in question, in favour of the performance of those actions by that agent. I then categorize normative reasons as either grounding or justificatory, the former being those of primary interest in ethics. My view of reasons is that they are, to use Williams's term, 'external' and I spend some time in defending the external view against his objections, and then realism about reasons against Humean and Kantian critiques. The chapter concludes with discussions of the relation between reasons and values and a defence against the arguments of G. E. Moore and T. M. Scanlon that the concept of well-being cannot be central to ethics.

An obvious question to ask of anyone who claims that we have some reason or other to act is how we are supposed to know what they are. In Chapter 3 I defend ethical intuitionism as the most plausible account of our knowledge of certain basic normative principles. The example I take is the principle that each of us has a reason to promote our own well-being, the strength of which reason is in direct proportion to the degree of promotion. The intuitionism I advocate is relatively modest, the essential components of the idea being that human beings have a capacity for grasping certain a priori truths, that such truths include truths about normative reasons, and that a grasp of such a truth can in itself provide justification for accepting it, in some cases sufficient justification for knowledge. After some discussion of issues concerning universality I defend the analogy between ethical principles and mathematics which has been standard in the rational intuitionist tradition. Intuitionists are often thought to be dogmatists. But I make no claims to infallibility and indeed in the final section of the chapter argue that the degree of disagreement in ethics shows that we know very little and should therefore adopt what amounts to a modest Pyrrhonist attitude in philosophical debate.

Well-being has already played an important role in my claims about the grounding of reasons and about value and self-interest. In the fourth chapter I approach the question of the best account of well-being, making a case for a historically significant but, in philosophy at least, currently unpopular view: hedonism. Having clarified the scope of the theory I wish to defend, I argue for another traditionally popular but now largely rejected view—that enjoyment is a felt quality common to every enjoyable experience. The chapter concludes with a development of Mill's distinction between the quality and quantity of pleasures, intended as a way of avoiding the objection that hedonists reduce all enjoyment to a 'common denominator', and some responses to the argument that hedonism must be rejected on the ground that it requires us to plug into an 'experience machine'.

So far in the book I have expressed support for the claim that each of us has a reason to promote her own well-being. If that were the only reason we had, then egoism would be true. In Chapter 5 I begin by discussing the nature of self-interested reasons themselves, agreeing with Derek Parfit that what matters is not personal identity. Rather, I suggest, what matters to each of us is the hedonic quality of the experiences realized by the exercise of any capacity for conscious experience we now have or any such capacity in future which emerges from our present capacity (thus allowing for division of capacities, between which other things being equal we should be impartial). But is an egoism based on this view correct? In the rest of the chapter I argue that the well-being of others can ground reasons for each of us to act, sometimes to the detriment of our own individual well-being. The well-being of others is to be assessed impartially in the sense that no intrinsic weight is to be attached to relationships with others, so that my view may accurately be described as a version of the 'dualism of practical reason'. Reasons are either self-interested or impartial and must be weighed against one another in particular cases. How strong a reason might we have to sacrifice ourselves for the sake of the good of others? I argue that there is a threshold beyond which reason cannot require any further sacrifice.

The notion of a threshold reappears in the final chapter. Given my rejection of special relations as grounds for reasons, it might seem likely that I shall claim that the impartial principle to counter self-interest is act-utilitarianism. But act-utilitarianism ignores the idea that distribution of goods can matter independently of pure aggregation. I reject two theories of such distribution—egalitarianism and the 'priority view'—before arguing for the view that there is a certain threshold—that at which an individual has 'enough'—such that the well-being of those below that threshold grounds reasons of a strength that varies in proportion to the distance from the threshold.

1

Morality

1. QUESTIONS AND CONCEPTS

Philosophy books usually seek to answer several questions, of which some are more fundamental than others. A book on knowledge, for example, might contain a chapter about the kind of justification required for a true belief to count as knowledge. But an earlier chapter might well have answered the prior question whether knowledge should be understood as justified true belief in the first place. And earlier still there may have been some discussion about whether we need the concept of knowledge in epistemology at all.

This is a book of moral philosophy. A fundamental concern of moral philosophy, it might be assumed, is what one ought, morally, to do. There is significant disagreement about that in certain cases, so it might seem at first sight that a fundamental question in moral philosophy must be which of the many different moral views available is correct. Indeed some philosophers seem to have thought like this. In the first paragraph of his *Foundations of Ethics*, for example, Sir David Ross says:

I propose to take as my starting-point the existence of what is commonly called the moral consciousness; and by this I mean the existence of a large body of beliefs and convictions to the effect that there are certain kinds of acts that ought to be done and certain kinds of things that ought to be brought into existence.[1]

Ross goes on to outline his favoured 'method of ethics', which he claims to be endorsed by Socrates, Plato, Aristotle, and Kant. It consists in examining these moral beliefs, comparing them with one another, and clearing up any ambiguity. Those that remain we may assume to be justified.

---

[1] Ross, *Foundations of Ethics*, 1.

It may be that Ross's use of the term 'method' here is intended to imply a contrast with the view of Henry Sidgwick, in whose *Methods of Ethics* we read:

we conceive it as the aim of a philosopher, as such, to do somewhat more than define and formulate the common moral opinions of mankind. His function is to tell men what they ought to think, rather that what they do think... though he is expected to establish and concatenate at least the main part of the commonly accepted moral rules, he is not necessarily bound to take them as the basis on which his own system is constructed. Rather, we should expect that the history of Moral Philosophy... would be a history of attempts to enunciate, in full breadth and clearness, those primary intuitions of Reason, by the scientific application of which the common moral thought of mankind may be at once systematised and corrected.[2]

The contrast, then, might seem to be between those, such as Ross, who begin with unreflective common-sense morality and end with reflective, and those, such as Sidgwick, who claim to base their views on rational intuitions which are themselves independent of common-sense morality. Any difference here, however, is if anything one of subtle degree rather than of kind. Ross approvingly quotes Aristotle's famous statement of his 'dialectical' method of ethics:

As in our other discussions, we must first set out the way things appear to people, and then, having gone through the puzzles, proceed to prove the received opinions about these ways of being affected—at best, all of them, or, failing that, most, and the most authoritative. For if the problems are resolved, and received opinions remain, we shall have offered sufficient proof.[3]

Often, Aristotle is guided by this dialectical principle, as for example in the discussion of incontinence (*akrasia*) following the passage just quoted, in which he sets out competing positions on the influence of knowledge on action and seeks a plausible compromise. But equally often he engages straightforwardly in philosophical argument on the basis of what might well be described as 'primary intuitions of Reason' such as that the human good is to be understood in the light of

---

[2] Sidgwick, *The Methods of Ethics*, 373–4.

[3] Aristotle, *Nicomachean Ethics* 7. 1, 1145^{b}2–7 (the line references are to *Ethica Nicomachea*). It might be claimed that there is a vast difference between the Aristotelian view that practical knowledge is exemplified in knowing how to live and the modern conception that it consists in having the right ethical theory: see e.g. Joachim, *Aristotle: The Nicomachean Ethics*, 1. But it would be easy enough for Ross to distinguish between having the right theory and knowing how to live in accordance with it.

characteristic human activity, leaving for later the checking of his conclusions against common sense or the views of other philosophers.[4] Ross often proceeds in the same way. Nor does Sidgwick believe that philosophers should aim to answer the fundamental questions of ethics in complete isolation from common-sense moral beliefs. Those beliefs have sufficient epistemic weight at the very least to remove any claim to the 'highest degree of certainty' of an alleged ethical principle with which they are inconsistent.[5]

Nevertheless, Sidgwick is more prepared than Ross not to assume the correctness of common-sense morality but to seek a grounding for much of that morality in rational intuition about conduct. In that sense this book is more in the spirit of Sidgwick than of Ross.[6] Though I shall indeed begin with 'the moral consciousness', this is a beginning merely in the sense of a starting point rather than of a foundation. The mere fact that we use some moral concept or hold some moral belief unreflectively[7] should not be taken to count strongly in its favour, and any such reliance on what one has been taught should be especially troubling given the large moral differences that have existed and continue to exist among human beings.[8] Nevertheless, like Sidgwick I believe that abstract rational intuition will quickly validate many common-sense moral rules. This should not itself be taken to count in favour of such intuition, however, since the intuition is itself insight into the reasons behind those rules. The rules of common-sense morality are not, I shall suggest, in themselves statements of ultimate reasons and hence have no grounding or justificatory weight; the reasons for the rules are knowable by intuition, and cannot be assumed to exist merely because of the existence of the rules. So in that

---

[4] Aristotle, *Nicomachean Ethics* 1. 7, 1097^{b}22–5; 1. 8, esp. 1098^{b}9–12.

[5] *Methods*, 338, 341–2.

[6] As Sidgwick fully realized, the rational intuitionist tradition in ethics, broadly construed, stretches back at least to Plato.

[7] Reflection can provide justification, as I shall argue in Ch. 3. But I see no need for any notion of 'reflective equilibrium' between principles and considered convictions about particular cases (see e.g. Rawls, *A Theory of Justice*, 18–19 and *passim*). If I have a considered conviction about some particular case worth taking into account in my ethical theory, then I should be able to give a reason for that conviction which can itself be expressed in the form of a principle. For more on ethical method, see Ch. 3, esp. Sect. 4.

[8] There is of course also a good deal of convergence, much of which may be explained by the social role of morality as described in the text below. But such convergence results also from some grasp of at least some of the correct ultimate normative principles to be elucidated later in my argument.

sense my position perhaps puts less weight on any dialectical appeal to common-sense morality than does the Aristotelianism of Ross and Sidgwick.[9]

Earlier I suggested that the question of what one ought morally to do might plausibly be held to be fundamental in philosophical ethics. But we should not begin by assuming that there *is* something we ought morally to do. A version of egoism according to which morality is a sham, for example, should not be ruled out *ab initio*. Nor should we start with the idea that if there are things that we ought morally to do, then doing these things is all we have reason to do. The view which became popular in the 1950s and 1960s that morality consists in whatever we have overriding reason to do is liable to confuse.[10] The concern of philosophical ethics is how we should live, and in particular how we should act, where these 'shoulds' are not to be taken as equivalent to 'morally ought to' but to 'have reason to'.

The kind of reasons philosophical ethics should be most concerned with are *ultimate* or *non-derivative* in nature. I have a reason to catch the bus, because I have a reason to visit the dentist, because I have a reason to avoid suffering, because I have a reason to advance my well-being. That final reason is *ultimate*, in the sense that there is no further normative reason for advancing my well-being, and it is the normative force of that reason which is inherited by the actions in the rest of the chain described. That is, I have a reason to catch the bus, other things being equal, only in so far as catching the bus is the action which will advance my well-being.[11]

A fundamental question of philosophical ethics, then, and perhaps *the* fundamental question of practical or normative ethics as opposed to metaethics, is: What does one have ultimate reason to do?[12] Nevertheless, the question whether we have ultimate moral reasons is a significant part

---

[9] At *Methods*, 341–2, Sidgwick appears to attach epistemic significance to consensus, thus allowing what might be seen as an element of coherentism into his ethical epistemology.

[10] Hare, *Freedom and Reason*, 168–9. Sidgwick also fails to draw a sharp distinction between what is right on the one hand, and what is rational or what we have reason to do on the other. See Frankena, 'Sidgwick and the History of Ethical Dualism', 193–6.

[11] A complete account of my reason to visit the dentist will include reference to each of the various factors here mentioned. See Sect. 2.4, esp. on 'buck-passing', and my 'Value, Reasons and the Structure of Justification: How to Avoid Passing the Buck'.

[12] Cf. e.g. Scanlon: 'I take the reason-giving force of judgments of right and wrong as the starting point of my inquiry' (*What we Owe to Each Other*, 3). Scanlon's first chapter is entitled 'Reasons'.

of answering that fundamental question, and requires me to go into the nature of morality itself.

2. MORALITY AND LAW

Philosophical ethics is like the philosophy of religion or jurisprudence, in that it emerges out of a set of social practices with their own particular place in our lives. Without religion or law there would be no philosophy of religion or jurisprudence; and without morality there would be no ethics. Nearly every human society that we know of has possessed some form of what I shall call a

> *Positive Morality.* A set of cognitive and conative states, including beliefs, desires, and feelings, which leads its possessors among other things to (*a*) view certain actions as wrong (that is, morally forbidden) and hence to be avoided, (*b*) feel guilt and/or shame as a result of performing such actions, and (*c*) blame others who perform such actions.

Note that this definition is intended to capture the 'core' of positive morality as we understand it. We might imagine a set of action-guiding states consisting only in beliefs about ideals, and involving as sanctions only 'carrots' rather than 'sticks'—what Hume calls in the conclusion to his *Enquiry* 'the peaceful reflection on one's own conduct', and praise rather than blame. Our own morality of course contains such elements, but it is hard to see them as essential elements of any positive morality. Attributions of wrongness, and the sanctions of guilt, shame, and blame, however, are central components of morality understood as a social phenomenon.

Those familiar with the philosophy of law will already have guessed that I chose the name 'positive morality' advisedly, to correlate with the term 'positive law' as used to refer to those laws that have been created within some legal system or other, as opposed to 'natural law', which is not created by human beings and is independent of legal systems understood in positive terms.[13] For I now want to suggest that there are

---

[13] The classical source of the distinction is Aristotle, *Ethics* 5. 7. The idea that the law can be understood as independent of morality in various ways is a version of legal positivism, and that is not an uncontroversial doctrine. I am inclined to think, however, that a broadly positivist understanding of the law is perhaps the most attractive to

important analogies between positive law and positive morality. This
is not a new view. Locke, for example, in his *Essay concerning Human
Understanding* wrote:

> The *laws* that men generally refer their actions to, to judge of their rectitude,
> or obliquity, seem to me to be these three. 1. The *divine* law. 2. The *civil* law.
> 3. The law of *opinion* or *reputation*, if I may so call it. By the relation they bear
> to the first of these, men judge whether their actions are sins, or duties; by the
> second, whether they be criminal, or innocent; and by the third, whether they
> be virtues or vices.[14]

The divine law, Locke continues, is 'the only true touchstone of
moral rectitude', whereas 'these names, *virtue* and *vice*, in the particular
instances of their application, through the several nations and societies
of men in the world, are constantly attributed only to such actions, as
in each country and society are in reputation or discredit'. The civil law
and the law of opinion, then, are both human laws.

So what are the analogies between positive morality and positive
law? Let me mention three. First, they are *functionally* analogous. Both
morality and law serve as socially instantiated mechanisms for guiding
human action towards similar kinds of goals.[15] Often these goals are

---

most people who consider the issue, and I suspect that it is the dominant view in the
philosophy of law. Partly for these reasons, but also for reasons of shape and space, I have
decided not to attempt any independent defence of legal positivism in this book, other
than the evolutionary arguments in the text. But my hope is that those arguments will
be sufficient for many, and that my overall position is broadly compatible with a variety
of positivist theories of law, including the simple command theory (see e.g. Austin, *The
Province of Jurisprudence Determined*), Hart's view, in which weight is attached to both
the customary basis of law and the internal perspective of participants within a legal
system (see esp. *The Concept of Law*), and Raz's 'sources thesis', according to which the
existence and content of a law can be identified with reference to social facts alone, and
the account of authority on which it is based (see e.g. 'Authority, Law, and Morality').
One important point to note is that I am not putting any great weight on the claim in
the text below that we can easily see through law to the reasons behind it. It may be that
the internal perspective of participants, including their view of authority, is itself to be
understood in terms of the kind of 'error theory' which I use in the main text below in
my analysis of positive morality.

[14] *Essay*, 2. 28. 7 (capitals and spelling changed). The law–morality analogy is
characteristic of the British empiricist tradition. See also e.g. Mill, *Utilitarianism*, 5.
12–15, esp. 5. 12.

[15] It is important to note that, though the social function I discuss here seems
especially significant, I am not assuming that law or morality has only one function. A
related point is that my focus is primarily on criminal law rather than, say, civil law. But
other areas of law do involve the kind of sanctions typical of the criminal law, as I explain
in the text below.

broadly unobjectionable. Both morality and law, for example, can serve to place limits on the harms done to one individual by another in pursuit of her self-interest. Indeed the two systems frequently operate together. A condemned murderer will receive not only a judicial sentence, but the moral opprobrium of others in her society. Morality can also be called upon in support of certain legal ordinances designed purely to resolve coordination problems. Only once there is a well-promulgated law requiring drivers to keep to a particular side of the road will those found driving on the wrong side be blamed. Sometimes, however, the goals of morality and law are open to objection, as for example in racist societies where racist laws and moral principles are promulgated by the dominant group in order to preserve their dominance.

Second, morality and law are *structurally* analogous. Both centrally involve the forbidding of certain actions, and the infliction of sanctions on those who perform these actions. This is seen most clearly in the case of the criminal law, where the same action may be forbidden by both law and morality. But in the case of, say, contract, the penalty for default can be seen as a deterrent punishment. A good deal of law, such as the law of marriage or commercial law, is designed to facilitate individual or joint projects. But even here deviations from the prescribed norms can be costly. And indeed morality provides its own resources in the same spheres, in the form of the institution of promise-making, which allows individuals to create new obligations.

Finally, and most importantly, law and morality have a similar *origin*. One might expect this anyway, given the functional and structural analogies noted above. But in recent years a good deal of research has been published on the possible origin of morality, and the accounts given can usually be carried across to law.[16] According to one plausible view, put forward by the anthropologist Christopher Boehm, the development of morality into its current stage took place at the very latest about 100,000 years ago, with the emergence of so-called Anatomically Modern Humans.[17] Boehm's argument is based partly on certain primatological data but mainly on evidence concerning existing nomadic foraging bands whose lifestyle is similar to those of our Palaeolithic ancestors. These bands are without exception politically egalitarian, in that any attempt at domination is prevented by social sanctions

---

[16] For an excellent philosophical introduction to the issues, see Singer, *The Expanding Circle*.

[17] 'Conflict and the Evolution of Social Control'. See also *Hierarchy in the Forest*.

such as gossip.[18] The reasons for this are straightforward. The group will function less well if valuable resources are wasted on internecine conflict, and there is also, especially in the case of big game, a need for a system to ensure roughly equalized food distribution. What Boehm calls 'morality' consists essentially in social pressure applied by the group to deviant—that is, in this case, power-seeking—behaviour.[19] Originally the emotions involved would have been simply the anger of the group and the fear of the deviant individual, but as language and gossip developed the emergence of more sophisticated and self-conscious emotions and attitudes became possible. Boehm does not discuss this in detail, but one strong possibility is that guilt and blame are especially closely related to fear of the anger of an internalized other and of distancing from that other (in particular the parent, who has power over the bond between herself and the child as well as the power to inflict punishment); whereas the development of shame went hand in hand with a growing awareness by individuals within the group of the importance of trusting relationships to their survival, and the emergence of a sense of oneself as a being whose status and membership of the group depended on being viewed with trust and respect by others, which again provides a link with the fear of exclusion, not on the basis of anger but merely through lack of status.[20]

Note also that Boehm's account allows for morality to take on a life of its own. Once a method of social control was in place, it could be put to uses other than the maintenance of equality within the group. Indeed morality might itself be used as part of a strategy for gaining power. Further, it is easy to see how the development of the moral emotions might allow, with the emergence of language, for the attribution of wrongness to certain actions. Boehm's account can explain the origin of law as well as that of morality, thereby accounting also for their functional and structural similarities and especially their overlapping scope. And, as already mentioned, even if one doubts the details of his

---

[18] This is to say not that deference to age or experience is ruled out, merely that such deference does not extend to the granting of power beyond the sphere of knowledge in question. For further insightful discussion of such spheres, see Walzer, *Spheres of Justice*.

[19] For a discussion of how group selection favours the development of non-self-interested or 'altruistic' punishment, see Boyd and Richerson, *The Origin and Evolution of Cultures*, ch. 13.

[20] For insightful discussions of guilt and shame, see e.g. Freud, *Civilization and its Discontents*, sect. 7; Taylor, *Pride, Shame, and Guilt*, chs. 3–4; Williams, *Shame and Necessity*, endnote 1.

argument, it does seem likely that any plausible account of the origin of either morality or law will carry across to the other system.

With these analogies between positive morality and law in mind, let me now return to the question whether there are specifically moral ultimate reasons. If there are such reasons, then a full statement of them will make ineliminable use of certain moral concepts. These concepts include that of being immoral or forbidden by morality itself, in which case our question concerns the following claim:

(I) The property any action has of being immoral gives an agent ultimate reason not to perform it.

Or consider wrongness, where the question concerns:

(W) The property any action has of being wrong gives an agent ultimate reason not to perform it.

The moral concepts as I understand them include those which are more specific, such as unkindness or cruelty, the central normative element in which, when it is employed within a positive morality, is usually supplied by moral prohibition.[21] Cruelty, that is to say, consists centrally in a specifiable kind of action which is morally wrong. Here the claim under consideration would be:

(C) The property any action has of being cruel gives an agent ultimate reason not to perform it.

I now wish to approach these and similar questions through an analysis of law. It will be easiest to focus on a case where there is clear overlap between law and morality:

> *Inheritance.* I am so poor that I am made miserable by my inability to pursue various projects that mean a great deal to me. I know that when my uncle Jack dies I shall inherit from him a large amount of money. I happen to know that Jack is in the habit of taking a late-evening walk by some deserted cliffs and that it would be quite easy for me to kill him by pushing him off at a certain point where the path is particularly narrow.

---

[21] I am thinking here of what Bernard Williams calls 'thick' moral concepts (*Ethics and the Limits of Philosophy*, 129 and *passim*). There may now be or have been positive moralities in which cruelty is or was considered admirable or morally neutral. Such moralities are certainly imaginable.

Does the law capture any of my ultimate reasons in this case? Criminal law of course prohibits me from killing Jack, and if I am caught I am likely to be severely punished. But the sheer fact of this legal prohibition does not seem to provide any ultimate reason for me to obey it, just as the sheer fact that the Town Police Clauses Act 1847 forbids the shaking of carpets in the street does not provide me with an ultimate reason not to do just that if I so wish. In *Inheritance* the law is best seen as providing derivative or non-ultimate reasons in the sense that if it is worth obeying it is so only for ultimate reasons that are themselves independent of the law and lie behind it. On the face of it I appear to have an ultimate reason grounded in self-interest to kill Jack. The law serves to place a limit on my pursuit of that self-interest by providing a self-interested reason for me not to kill him; and if the law is justified it is because I have reasons independent of the law for not killing him.

At this point, morality may well be said to provide an ultimate reason not to kill Jack. That is to say, the fact that it is wrong itself justifies the deliverance of the law on homicide in this case. But I now want to suggest that positive morality is like law in providing only non-ultimate or derivative reasons, and that this is exactly what we should expect given the analogies between the two systems outlined above. There certainly are ultimate reasons for me not to kill Jack, such as that I shall by doing so decrease his well-being and that of his friends and relations. But these are the same reasons that justify the law's forbidding me to kill.

There is an issue here concerning positive morality analogous to a standard problem that arises for divine command theories of ethics. On one version of divine command theory, we have ultimate reason not to kill merely because God says we should not. But this seems to make morality arbitrary, and to pass over all the reasons for killing which are independent of God's command. So it is tempting then to say that God's command *adds* a further ultimate reason not to kill. But quite how such a command can add an ultimate reason is hard to grasp. It is more plausible to claim that we have derivative reason to obey God because, being omniscient, he has knowledge of the correct moral principles. Now consider a positive morality like our own that contains a principle forbidding killing. There appear in many cases to be some strong ultimate reasons against killing that can be stated without using narrowly moral terminology. But someone might want to claim that, though our positive morality forbids killing because of these non-moral reasons, that very forbidding constitutes wrongness, and wrongness is surely a *further* ultimate reason against killing, and this time a moral one.

But again the force of this reason is hard to understand, and it is more plausible to conclude that the only reasons against killing are non-moral. The mere fact that some action is forbidden, either by God or by a positive morality, does not seem sufficient to ground an ultimate reason.

There is an obvious objection to my claim that moral wrongness is like legal wrongness in providing only non-ultimate reasons. Law, it may be said, is a purely human institution, and there is no non-positive law, independent of human judgement, against which particular positive laws can be judged. Of course, over the centuries, some have claimed that there is indeed a natural law, originating on certain views from God. But strict divine command versions of this position face the Euthyphro dilemma, and anyway most natural law theories are best understood as involving principles that are not really legal but rational or moral. Morality, the objection continues, is different. There are indeed positive moralities, just as there are positive laws. But when someone says that my killing Jack is wrong, they are not claiming something like: 'According to the positive morality in which we have both been brought up and which is almost universally accepted in our society, your killing Jack is wrong'. Rather they are claiming that my killing Jack is wrong in itself, and would be wrong regardless of the views taken in any positive morality of such behaviour. In other words, while there is no natural law, there is a 'natural morality', and it can be stated in the form of that set of principles, independent of human judgement, which state the truth about wrongness and rightness as ultimate reasons for action.

There is indeed an important difference between law and morality. I have said that when there is a reason to obey the law we can see through its prescriptions to the ultimate and non-legal reasons that lie behind it. Law might function perfectly well even if everyone were to see it in this way. Indeed, when asked why we should obey the law, few would say that we should obey because the law says we should, or that some action's being illegal itself provides an ultimate reason not to do it. Rather, appeal is usually made to *moral* principles, based on ideas of contract and consent, fairness, utility, democracy, or whatever. Morality is different. For it to function most effectively requires that those who obey it should take it to be ultimately reason-giving.[22] This is clear when we reflect upon the fact that, unlike the moral sanctions, legal penalties can be viewed merely as costs imposed in the currency of well-being. Guilt and moral shame usually involve the thought that the wrongness

---

[22] See Mackie, *Ethics*, ch. 1; Joyce, *The Myth of Morality*.

of what the agent did itself constituted an ultimate reason not to act in the way she did. Expressions of blame can be made quite dispassionately, as a way of affecting the behaviour of the party blamed. But even this strategy is most likely to succeed when the blamed agent feels that the wrongness of what she has done was itself an ultimate reason. The feeling of blame is like guilt and moral shame, in that it is hard to imagine feeling that someone is genuinely blameworthy without also feeling that they had a reason not to perform the action because it was wrong.

So it is only to be expected that we who have been brought up to accept a positive morality should tend to believe that morality itself provides reasons. And it seems somewhat unparsimonious to postulate genuine properties of wrongness, understood as intrinsically reason-giving, when their attribution by human beings can be fully explained without reference to them.

Further, the Euthyphro dilemma constructed above for positive morality arises as well for any 'natural' or ideal morality. What extra reason against, say, killing in certain circumstances is provided by that killing's being forbidden by some set of special principles? It may be objected that the view I am taking of wrongness, and other moral concepts involving prohibition, requirement, and so on, is mistaken. Wrongness is a way of referring not to some additional reason against acts such as killing, but to the form in which the reasons that count against killing do so count. My reason not to kill may be seen as unconditional, absolute, or pre-emptive in some way, and the reaction of blame, indignation, resentment, and so on, to such acts particularly appropriate given the nature of the reasons against them.

This position does avoid the Euthyphro dilemma. But it is an open question whether we need to postulate these special categories of reason. My inclination is to think that this view is an attempt to retain in one's account of reasons some of the central ideas of morality, and given that our concept of morality has emerged through the evolution of positive morality itself we should at least be initially sceptical of such a conservative approach. That is to say, we should assume that there are these special categories of reason only if reflection freed of commitment to positive morality suggests them.[23] I believe, after such reflection, that we can do without them.[24]

---

[23] I shall say more about such reflection in the following section.

[24] The same goes for views such as Scanlon's, according to which we have reasons to stand in relations of mutual recognition with others, to feel indignation or guilt or to

I am, then, aiming to 'debunk' the idea that we have ultimate reasons which to be stated require essential reference to moral properties as reason-giving in themselves. But why, it may be asked, should we accept that morality has been debunked merely because some evolutionary account has been given of its origins? Mathematics has evolutionary origins, perhaps in practices of sharing food, but accepting that does not debunk it. And I myself have already mentioned the principle that each person has a reason to advance their own well-being. Why should law and morality be treated any differently from mathematics or self-interest?

What makes for a successful debunking argument is a difficult question, the answer to which depends on the kind of arguments under discussion. In the case of mathematics, what is central is the contrast between practices or beliefs which develop because that is the way things are, and those that do not. The calculating rules developed as they did because $2 + 2 = 4$, $7 + 5 = 12$, and so on, and the rules reflect mathematical truth.[25] The functions of law and morality, however, are to be understood in terms of the promotion of well-being, and there seems no reason to think that had human nature involved, say, different motivations then different practices would not have emerged.[26] Imagine a community of rational beings who are benevolent to the point where there is no need for the sanctions of law and morality to guide their behaviour, though they may perhaps have certain rules for the purposes of coordination and cooperation. If they know nothing of law and morality, it does not seem that they are missing something—in particular the idea that certain actions are wrong, and that this wrongness provides reasons for action; whereas an entirely unmathematical community does seem fundamentally ignorant. The same sort of claim seems true in the case of self-interest. Let us imagine a rational being faced with some agonizing and avoidable ordeal, who

make amends when recognition has not been shown, and so on. (See *What we Owe*, esp. chs. 1, 4–6.) I say more about the status of moral responses such as blame below.

[25] Here I am relying on Platonism as the most natural and widely accepted account of mathematical objects. Just as my argument about the status of morality would not persuade natural lawyers, so my position on debunking arguments will not persuade formalists, intuitionists, and other non-Platonists in the philosophy of mathematics. Again we reach bedrock, and I want here to be understood not to be making some dogmatic assertion, but in effect reporting the way things appear to me. See Sect. 3.4 below.

[26] I am suggesting not that mere contingency is enough to demonstrate irrealism, merely that such contingency makes such irrealism more plausible.

has no conception of her having any ultimate reason to avoid it. On reflection I find myself unable to accept the idea that my belief that she has such a reason is a mere result of the effectiveness of that belief in motivating action to advance my own well-being; while I find myself perfectly able to accept a debunking view of morality, the functions of which are so specific to the human condition.

There is, however, another potential disanalogy between law and morality which may be pressed by the proponent of morality as a source of ultimate reasons for action. The sanctions of law can be understood, somewhat simplistically but nevertheless usefully, as the imposition of costs on 'offenders' in terms of their own well-being. Morality is different in that it involves what we might call the 'emotions' of guilt, shame, and blame (the 'feeling' that someone is blameworthy). The experience of any particular emotion in any particular situation can be assessed for its reasonableness. Consider this from C. D. Broad:

> Some kinds of emotional quality are *fitting* and others are *unfitting* to a given kind of epistemological object. It is appropriate to cognise what one takes to be a *threatening* object with some degree of *fear*. It is inappropriate to cognise what one takes to be a fellow man *in undeserved pain or distress* with *satisfaction* or with *amusement*.[27]

Ronald de Sousa provides further useful examples:

> it is bizarre to experience intense amusement at the perfectly familiar taste of potatoes... and it is altogether unintelligible... to be told that someone experienced excruciating remorse at the thought of having once smiled at a child.[28]

The same sort of account might be provided for, say, blame. In considering some array of different courses of action open to me at a certain time I may decide that some of them would be blameworthy in the sense that there would be a reason for others to feel the blame-feeling if I were to perform them. Further, I may also think that there is reason for me to act in the light of what there is reason to feel or not to feel.[29] Consider anger. If I have mortally offended a colleague, I might well conclude that he has not only a reason to feel anger, but a reason, say, to complain to me and to raise his voice in so doing. Analogously, I may

[27] 'Emotion and Sentiment', 209.

[28] *The Rationality of Emotion*, 143; see also Greenspan, *Emotions and Reasons*, 3; Nussbaum, *Love's Knowledge*, 79.

[29] Cf. Skorupski's 'Feeling/Disposition Principle', in 'Reasons and Reason', 358.

think that the property some action has of being blameworthy and in that sense wrong gives me an ultimate reason not to perform it.

Do we have reasons to feel or not to feel emotions? There is a complex system of norms for assessing the appropriateness of feelings.[30] If I am reading something hilariously funny, then I have a reason to feel amusement; if I am eating chips, then I do not. I am tempted to think that these norms are contingent in the following way. Consider fear. It is hard to believe that fear did not evolve as a mechanism for directing attention to threats and motivating avoidance of them.[31] Now consider a world in which the role of the *feeling* of fear is filled by the feeling of, say, anger or pity, but in which that feeling functions as effectively as does fear in threat-avoidance: the feeling continues to occur alongside the thought 'This is to be avoided', and that thought issues in action in appropriate circumstances.[32] My view is that this world is no less 'rational' than our own. Which feeling is attached to which thoughts, that is to say, is something that has emerged by selection pressure rather than through human development tracking any genuine rational norms for feeling in a certain way.

But in fact even if these norms are non-contingent, the disanalogy with law is insufficient to provide a direct route to the conclusion that morality is a source of ultimate reasons. This is because we should not assume that, if we *do* have some reason to feel some emotion, we *thereby* have a reason to act in some way or other. Often of course one will have a reason to act as one is prompted to act by emotion—fear is the obvious example. But one's reason to avoid something one fears is best seen as grounded in the nature of the threat to one's well-being itself rather than in one's emotional response to it. There can be reasons to 'listen' to one's emotions, either as a practice or in individual cases. And there can be reasons to resist certain emotions in particular cases or to initiate strategies that will result in one's feeling or not feeling certain emotions to some degree or other.[33] But again these reasons relate ultimately to one's own well-being and perhaps that of others.[34]

---

[30] See Greenspan, *Emotions and Reasons*; Skorupski, 'Reasons and Reason'.

[31] See Fessler, 'The Evolution of Human Emotions'; Panksepp, *Affective Neuroscience*, ch. 11.

[32] The view that emotions are to be identified with judgements and not feelings is well criticized in Robinson, *Deeper than Reason*, chs. 1–3.

[33] De Sousa, *The Rationality of Emotion*, 11.

[34] In the following chapter I shall claim that a reason is a property of an action that counts, for the agent, in favour of the performance of that action. So in that sense I am

In other words, whether we have reason to act on the blame-feeling or other moral emotions is a matter independent of the appropriateness or inappropriateness of those emotions themselves. So even if some action is genuinely blameworthy, how we should act in the light of that is a question that depends on well-being, not on the intrinsic rationality or otherwise of the blame-feeling.

3. AVOIDING THE MORAL CONCEPTS

I began this chapter by asking what ultimate reasons we have, and have been attempting to provide some considerations in favour of thinking that morality, narrowly construed, provides us with none. I mean this in the sense that, since morality provides only non-ultimate reasons, any ultimate reasons we have should be statable without using narrowly moral concepts. So it would be a mistake to think that we can immediately conclude that, if there are no moral reasons, there is no reason to do anything, or to conform to positive morality in some form, or that there is reason to do whatever one wishes, or to pursue one's maximal self-interest. As far as ultimate reasons are concerned, a large amount is still up for grabs.

Since morality provides only non-ultimate reasons, we should avoid the terminology of morality as far as possible in our account of ultimate reasons. There are at least two reasons for this. First, since the fundamental question we are addressing in practical ethics is what normative reasons for action we have and since there are no ultimate moral reasons, there is no immediate need for us to consider those many philosophical views which postulate them. It may be that considering these views turns out to be of indirect benefit, in that we find that they point us in the direction of genuine ultimate reasons. But we should try to do without them to begin with and see how we get on.

A second reason to avoid moral terminology is a hermeneutic one related to the considerations raised at the close of the previous section. Because morality and the moral emotions often involve the erroneous thought that morality is a source of ultimate reasons, we may be misled

ready to accept that there may be a reason to feel an emotion—if, say, feeling it promotes the subject's well-being. But these 'reasons' are irrelevant to that branch of philosophical ethics which is concerned with the fundamental matter of reasons for acting, and in particular reasons for trying to act.

into thinking that because some moral quality can plausibly be ascribed to some action (such as that it is wrong, or cruel), we have, just because of this, ultimate reasons resting on that quality. We have been brought up from an early age to live by a positive morality according to which certain actions are forbidden, permitted, or encouraged. The sanctions of that morality consist mainly in the moral emotions of guilt, shame, and blame, and its functioning involves many other emotions, such as admiration, benevolence, pity, or a sense of righteous indignation. If we are going to try to go beyond that morality to any reasons that lie behind it, we should try to avoid the risk of allowing our moral emotions to cloud our judgement. Consider someone who has been brought up to accept a code of honour and who believes that he must fight a duel to the death over some trivial matter. If he is asked to reflect upon his decision in moral terms, it is not unlikely that as soon as he sees that his refusal to fight would be dishonourable his emotions will be engaged and he will conclude that he has a reason to accept the challenge. But if he is asked to reflect upon the matter in less heated terms, it may be that he will see through the concept of dishonour to the rational emptiness behind it. The same goes for us. Consider the following case:

> *Blindness.* On Monday I blind a stranger to prevent his buying the last copy of a CD I want to buy. I buy the CD. On Tuesday I buy another CD, knowing that I could have given the money to Sight Savers International and prevented the blindness of at least one person.[35]

Ask yourself how you would respond to hearing that I have performed these actions. According to the morality of common sense, though the outcome for the individuals concerned is largely the same, the blinding is forbidden, whereas the failure to prevent blindness is permissible. This kind of morality is what we would expect to have emerged from the evolutionary process. It is clear that a group cannot function well if its members are permitted to harm one another, whereas the survival value of a prohibition on allowing others to suffer is more dubious. Given that such reactions have been contingently engendered in us by evolution, we should not endanger the rationality and impartiality of our normative theory by allowing them to interfere with our judgement. This is to say not that common-sense morality is mistaken in the weight

[35] For further information on Sight Savers International, see <http:www.sightsavers. org.uk>.

it places on this distinction between killing and letting die, merely that the distinction should be held up to the light of reason and not allowed to go through by default.

In seeking to avoid the influence of the emotions, I appear to be swimming against a strong current in contemporary ethics. Writers such as Bernard Williams, Martha Nussbaum, Lawrence Blum, Michael Stocker, and several others have mounted arguments in favour of allowing the emotions to play a significant role in ethics.[36] Here is a typical statement of the general position, from the first page of Nussbaum's *Upheavals of Thought*:

> If emotions are suffused with intelligence and discernment, and if they contain in themselves an awareness of value or importance, they cannot, for example, easily be sidelined in accounts of ethical judgment, as so often they have been in the history of philosophy. Instead of viewing morality as a system of principles to be grasped by the detached intellect, and emotions as motivations that either support or subvert our choice to act according to principle, we have to consider emotions as part and parcel of the system of ethical reasoning. We cannot plausibly omit them, once we acknowledge that emotions can be true or false, and good or bad guides to ethical choice.

Nussbaum claims that the emotions may provide us with an awareness of genuine value or importance which would be missed by an attempt at understanding value through employing 'the detached intellect', or reason. What kind of value or importance does she have in mind? Here is an example from another of her works:

> 'Here is a case where a friend needs my help': this will often be 'seen' first by the feelings that are constituent parts of friendship, rather than by pure intellect. Intellect will often want to consult these feelings to get information about the true nature of the situation. Without them, its approach to a new situation would be blind and obtuse.[37]

Now consider this case:

> *Blindness 2.* I am about to make a donation of my only spare cash to Sight Savers International, enough to save several people from blindness. Just at that moment a friend asks me for exactly this

---

[36] See e.g. Williams, 'Morality and the Emotions'; Blum, *Friendship, Altruism, and Morality*; Stocker, 'How Emotions Reveal Value and Help Cure the Schizophrenia of Modern Ethical Theories'; Nussbaum, *Love's Knowledge*.

[37] *Love's Knowledge*, 79.

amount for her train-fare home. Without the money, she will have to walk.

My emotional attachment to my friend may lead me in the direction of thinking that what I have strongest reason to do here is to give the money to my friend. But one should not assume that the deliverances of an emotional response which has arisen quite contingently through biological and social evolution are correct.

There might be some doubt as to whether emotions, as emotions, involve any kind of cognition or awareness.[38] But there is a more basic problem with the claim that the emotions should be given a fundamental role in the construction of our ethical theories. Nussbaum herself does not believe that the emotions are always to be trusted.[39] But once it is admitted that the emotions are not always a reliable guide, which of our faculties are we to use to discriminate between reliability and unreliability? It can only be the 'detached intellect'. In other words, Nussbaum's view that friendship gives us special obligations is one that she has arrived at on the basis of rational reflection and in that way her position is on an epistemological par with impartial theories according to which the emotions of friendship are unreliable.

I accept that certain emotions or the capacity for them may well play an important epistemic enabling role and in that sense the intellect may not be entirely 'detached'.[40] If partialism is true, for example, then perhaps only those individuals who have the emotional capacity for friendship can recognize it; likewise, if impartialism is true, then perhaps only those who can respond with the emotions characteristic of sympathy for others can recognize it.[41] What is important, however,

---

[38] For an insightful defence of the claim that emotions do not involve judgements, see Peacocke, *The Realm of Reason*, 252–65. Robinson (see n. 24 above), on the basis of empirical evidence from psychology and neurology and some helpful examples, plausibly suggests that emotions should be understood not in terms of judgements but as 'non-cognitive appraisals', rough-and-ready automatic assessments of salient features of the environment with concomitant physiological changes, assessments which may subsequently be assessed by reason. On the tendency to 'over-intellectualize' the emotions, see e.g. Goldie, *The Emotions*, 3; Pugmire, *Sound Sentiments*, 14.

[39] *Upheavals*, 2.

[40] As Gallagher points out (*How the Body Shapes the Mind*, 151), 'there is an emerging interdisciplinary consensus about the importance of emotions in cognition', including perception. On emotion and reason in ethics, see e.g. Solomon, *In Defense of Sentimentality*, esp. 29–31; Lacewing, 'Emotional Self-Awareness and Ethical Deliberation'.

[41] Nichols claims that the evidence on psychopathy suggests that the capacity for moral judgement in them is disrupted because of 'an emotional deficit rather than

is that what does the bulk of the work in constructing one's normative theory, whatever it is, is reason not emotion. And, given the dubious origin of the emotions and their lack of any claim to universal reliability, the sensible strategy is to be suspicious rather than welcoming towards them.

Nor, it is important to remember, must views which are more sceptical of the reliability of the emotions be committed to 'cold' or unemotional ideals of moral agency. It is not uncommon among contemporary advocates of the emotions in ethics to fail to notice the important distinction between ethics understood as that set of principles which captures the truth about which normative reasons we have (what we might call a 'normative ethics') and ethics as what constitutes an agent's 'decision procedure' broadly construed, the most obvious example here being a positive morality.[42] Many versions of the views in opposition to which the advocates of the emotions set up their own position can allow for the same emotion-based decision procedures as are recommended by Nussbaum and others.[43]

Michael Stocker objects that such 'split-level' theories are 'schizophrenic':

> Those theories misunderstand, and often do not allow for, large and important parts of human life, including such important goods as love and friendship. For here, motivation and value must come together if the goods are to be actualized: if I do not act for your sake, then no matter whether what I do is for the best, I am not acting out of friendship.[44]

An impartialist—a utilitarian, for example—might claim here that her motivation to help her friends is the same as Stocker's. It is based on natural and spontaneous concern for their interests. Nevertheless, Stocker may point out, that concern is out of line with the utilitarian conception of impartiality, according to which no one matters more than any other. But that is a view at the level of normative ethics. Exactly how much concern one should feel for particular individuals is a matter

---

any rational shortcomings' (*Sentimental Rules*, 71; see ch. 3 and *passim*). But another explanation is that a capacity for certain emotions *enables* the exercise of a cognitive capacity to grasp certain reasons, so the emotional deficit results in a rational deficit.

[42] See e.g. Williams's claim that impartial theories provide agents with 'one thought too many', 'Persons, Character and Morality', 18.

[43] See e.g. Railton, 'Alienation, Consequentialism, and the Demandingness of Morality'; Crisp, 'Utilitarianism and the Life of Virtue'.

[44] 'How Emotions Reveal Value', 173. See also 'The Schizophrenia of Modern Ethical Theories'.

of what that utilitarian normative ethical principle says about what goes on in our minds when we act—our 'decision procedures'. The utilitarian agent does not have to 'pretend' that her friend matters more than others 'from the point of view of the universe', to use Sidgwick's phrase.[45] She merely has to act on her emotions, and in so doing she may well produce the best state of affairs.

Let me now return to the matter at hand: the avoidance of the moral concepts. Which concepts do I have in mind? At the most general level there are, as I have already suggested, the concepts of 'right' and 'wrong', where wrongness may be understood in terms of what is 'required', 'demanded', or 'forbidden', and rightness in terms of what is 'permitted'. Another 'thin' moral concept which has received a great deal of attention in philosophy during at least the last fifty years is 'ought', and I shall say more about that in the next section. 'Duty' should not be used, nor notions related to supererogation, such as 'going beyond the call of duty' or 'the morally praiseworthy'. The concept of the moral 'must' is also to be avoided, as are notions of what is 'morally good' or 'morally bad'. More specific, thicker moral concepts include that of 'moral value', and particular alleged moral values such as 'fairness', and the concepts of 'virtue' and 'vice' and of individual virtues such as 'justice' or 'generosity'.

Earlier I claimed that using moral concepts may skew our judgement when we are considering which account of our normative reasons for action is correct. The example I gave was the deeply inculcated tendency all of us have to view causing a certain amount of suffering in certain circumstances as forbidden, and allowing the same amount of suffering in similar circumstances as permissible. It might now be objected, however, that I am skewing normative theory in the opposite direction, away from theories which require statement in moral language (such as perhaps so-called 'deontological' theories or virtue ethics) to theories which do not (perhaps broadly 'consequentialist' theories). But this objection is incorrect, and to this extent the first-order position I shall outline later in this book does not follow directly from the methodological constraints I am seeking to impose. It is true that act-utilitarianism can fairly easily be translated out of moral language from

Moral Utilitarianism. It is wrong not to maximize utility.

---

[45] *Methods*, 382.

to

> *Normative Utilitarianism.* Any agent has ultimate reason only to maximize utility.

But the same strategy can be applied to paradigmatic 'deontological' theories such as that of Ross:

> *Rossian Deontology.* Any agent has the following prima facie duties: fidelity, reparation, gratitude, justice, beneficence, self-improvement, non-maleficence.

> *Normative Rossianism.* Any agent has the following ultimate reasons: to abide by her contracts; to provide certain goods to those whom she has treated in particular ways detrimental to them; to express thanks for benefits; to distribute well-being according to certain rules concerning the status of possible beneficiaries; to increase the degree to which she possesses intelligence and certain traits of character; not to cause decreases in the overall well-being of others.

Even Kantian ethics may not need as much restatement as might be expected, since, though many Kantian arguments use the concepts of positive morality, in its essential form the position is couched in non-moral language:

> *Kantianism.* Any agent has ultimate reason to act only on that maxim by which she can at the same time will that it should become a universal law.[46]

To take one final example:

> *Traditional Virtue Ethics.* Any agent should act as the virtuous person would act, that is, the person with courage, justice, generosity, etc.

> *Normative Virtue Ethics.* Any agent has ultimate reason only to act as the person would act with character traits that enable her to control her fear when she has reason to, distribute goods in the ways she has reason to distribute them, and so on, and, if she lacks the dispositions to feeling and action characteristic of such a person, to engage in strategies to shape her own dispositions accordingly.

---

46 See *Groundwork for the Metaphysics of Morals*, 2. 25 [4: 421].

Of course, explaining and providing arguments for utilitarian, Rossian, Kantian, or virtue ethics without using moral terminology will be hard; but it is essential if we are to avoid postulating ultimate reasons where there are none as well as the risk of being led to our normative theory by emotion rather than reason.

Let me end this section by dealing with two objections. The first is that my recommendation to 'sanitize' the language of ethics is without point, since we can be swayed as much by claims expressed in non-moral language as by moral claims. Compare for example 'She is selfish' with 'She doesn't care about anyone but herself'. I accept the general point here, but would suggest that in the case of any attempted restatement of an ethical view we examine the phrasing to see whether it employs language typically used in the everyday positive and negative evaluations, prescriptions, and so on that constitute our positive morality. Both of the phrases mentioned by the objector clearly do and indeed play an almost equivalent role. But that is not true of those I used in my restatement of utilitarianism and the other views above.

A second objection that has been voiced to my proposal is that it makes it impossible in certain cases for us to say what we want to say. All I could say about Hitler, for example, might be that he had a reason (albeit a very strong reason) not to do many of the things he did. In fact that is all, philosophically, I think one needs to say. And again one must not forget that avoiding the moral concepts in philosophical reflection can sit quite happily with making the strongest moral condemnations in the world outside philosophy.

4. ANSCOMBE AND THE MYTH OF OBLIGATION

In a famous paper, 'Modern Moral Philosophy', Elizabeth Anscombe also argued for the conclusion that we should avoid using the notion of 'ought', claiming that—once we have an adequate account of the psychology of human action—we should use instead the language of the virtues.[47] I have recommended that we eschew the language of the virtues as well, but it might be thought that my argument is merely an extension of hers or that her argument could provide further resources for my approach. Since some of her central arguments do indeed focus

---

[47] This section draws on material from my 'Does Modern Moral Philosophy Rest on a Mistake?'

on a legalistic interpretation of modern morality, further examination of her position is called for.

Anscombe's suggestion is that the views of modern moral philosophers (she means those since Butler) are stated using moral concepts such as 'ought' that have now lost the context within which they once made sense. There is a perfectly respectable use of 'ought'—we might call it the 'non-moral "ought"'—which relates straightforwardly to non-moral goodness or badness. For example, 'This engine ought to be oiled' means something like 'Running without oil is bad for this engine'. But such concepts

have now acquired a special so-called 'moral' sense—i.e. a sense in which they imply some absolute verdict (like one of guilty/not guilty on a man) on what is described in the 'ought' sentences used in certain types of context . . . [They] acquired this special sense by being equated in the relevant contexts with 'is obliged', or 'is bound', or 'is required to', in the sense in which one can be obliged or bound by law . . . (30)[48]

This legalistic sense of 'ought', Anscombe suggests, emerged from Christianity's 'law conception' of ethics, that is, a conception according to which 'what is needed for conformity with the virtues failure in which is the mark of being bad *qua* man . . . is required by divine law' (31). I take it that Anscombe would count as a law conception any view according to which there is a divine law governing our action and would not wish to restrict that notion only to conceptions of ethics expressed in terms of the virtues. For her view is that the claim of, say, a modern utilitarian that we ought, morally, to maximize utility may be taken as equivalent to the claim that divine law requires us to maximize utility. And herein lies the problem: most modern utilitarians would not accept the existence of any such law. All that remains is the 'psychological' force of the notion—primarily, presumably, some kind of 'anti-attitude' to those who do what it is believed they ought not. 'Ought' is 'a word retaining the suggestion of force, and apt to have a strong psychological effect, but which no longer signifies a real concept at all' (33). As Anscombe puts it, the modern usage of 'ought' is 'as if the notion "criminal" were to remain when criminal law and criminal courts had been abolished and forgotten . . . where one does not think there is a judge or law, the notion of a verdict may retain

---

[48] All page references in the text are to the version of Anscombe's article cited in the Bibliography.

its psychological effect, but not its meaning' (31, 33). Anscombe takes these claims to apply also to related moral concepts, such as 'obligation', 'duty', 'morally right', and 'morally wrong', and recommends: 'We should no longer ask whether doing something was "wrong", passing directly from some description of an action to this notion; we should ask whether, e.g., it was unjust; and the answer would sometimes be clear at once' (34).

Anscombe supports her argument through a contrast between modern usage and that found in Aristotle's *Ethics* (26–7). In particular, she suggests, the modern sense of 'moral' is nowhere to be found in Aristotle. Aristotle distinguishes between the 'moral' and the 'intellectual' virtues, but the intellectual virtues themselves have what we would describe as a 'moral' aspect in so far as certain intellectual failures are seen by Aristotle as blameworthy. We might want to say '*morally* blameworthy', but

has Aristotle got [the] idea of *moral* blame, as opposed to any other? If he has, why isn't it more central? There are some mistakes, he says, which are causes, not of involuntariness in actions but of scoundrelism, and for which a man is blamed. Does this mean that there is a *moral* obligation not to make certain intellectual mistakes? Why doesn't he discuss obligation in general, and this obligation in particular? If someone professes to be expounding Aristotle and talks in a modern fashion about 'moral' such-and-such, he must be very imperceptive if he does not constantly feel like someone whose jaws have somehow got out of alignment: the teeth don't come together in a proper bite.

Given her view that we should refrain from use of 'ought', and the claim that the problematic notion of obligation is absent from Aristotle's thought, we can understand Anscombe's recommendation that we return to an essentially Aristotelian form of virtue ethics—though, she says, we should begin rather with psychology rather than with straightforward first-order ethics, seeking to understand concepts such as 'action', 'intention', and 'virtue' more clearly than did Aristotle himself (30, 37).[49]

Let me turn then to Anscombe's general position on the moral concepts. An important preliminary point is that, even if Anscombe were right about the special modern sense of 'ought', it would not follow that we should return to any particular first-order ethics, such as one with any close similarity in content to Aristotle's or indeed

---

[49] Anscombe says that she sees 'no harm' in moving towards an Aristotelian conception, as opposed to a law conception, of ethics (40). But later in her article (43–4), she appears to express some doubt about the enterprise. For further discussion, see below.

Anscombe's. For many modern debates—such as those between Rossian intuitionists and utilitarians—could be carried on in the terminology of virtue (is gratitude, say, a self-standing virtue, or is every other alleged virtue to be subsumed under benevolence?). Anscombe's strategy is to suggest that in returning to Aristotle we drop the notions of 'ought', 'right', and 'wrong' entirely and use only thick concepts such as 'injustice' (40).[50] Her hope is that we shall also accept that an action's being unjust is a matter of fact, and always avoid injustice, because on the assumption that the virtues could not conflict we no longer have the conceptual apparatus to ask whether there may be cases in which injustice would be right (40–1). Again, even if Anscombe's history were right, we might wonder whether we could not raise the question in Aristotelian terms whether a virtuous person might not in certain circumstances procure the punishment of the innocent, or whether we might not invent some new moral concept in which this question could be asked. Indeed Anscombe recognizes the former possibility:

It may be possible, if we are resolute, to discard the term 'morally ought', and simply return to the ordinary 'ought', which, we ought to notice, is such an extremely frequent term of human language that it is difficult to imagine getting on without it. Now if we do return to it, can't it reasonably be asked whether one might ever need to commit injustice, or whether it won't be the best thing to do? Of course it can. (43)

Anscombe goes on to repeat her point that we cannot decide such questions at present because 'philosophically there is a huge gap, at present unfillable as far as we are concerned, which needs to be filled by an account of human nature, human action, the type of characteristic a virtue is' (43–4). But this raises the question how Anscombe felt entitled to such certainty herself in this paper about what justice required.

Now consider Anscombe's 'criminal' analogy. What might be going on in the culture in which judicial institutions have been forgotten? There would of course be no place for the use of the term within those very institutions. But it might well be used of those who commit certain actions which were once crimes, such as assault. If so, the most plausible initial interpretation would be not that 'criminal' no longer

---

[50] See n. 21 above. If anything like my account of the moral concepts is correct, it is doubtful whether one could unpack the content of thick *moral* concepts without reference to thin.

had any sense, but that it had changed its sense to become equivalent to something like 'morally bad individual'. So we should ask whether, even if Anscombe is right about the past sense of 'ought', the term might not have taken on some new sense. It is indeed a little surprising to find the Wittgensteinian Anscombe looking not to use but to etymology. A simple 'open question argument'[51] throws the onus directly onto Anscombe: whether 'ought' means 'required by divine legislation' seems an entirely open question, which fact at least suggests that the senses of each are different.

Recall that Anscombe allows for non-moral uses of 'ought', such as 'This engine ought to be oiled', which involve no reference to divine law. As I have said, Anscombe sees this as equivalent to something like 'Running without oil is bad for this engine'. But this seems to leave out any reference to action. That phrase in the standard case is better seen as amounting to something like '[Given that you want this engine to function,] you have a reason to oil it'. That is, it resembles what Kant would have called a hypothetical imperative. So we shall need to ask whether there is space in our conceptual scheme for something like a Kantian categorical imperative, an action-guiding analogue to Anscombe's 'absolute verdict'.

With these thoughts in mind, let me now address the contrast Anscombe seeks to draw between Aristotle and modern moral philosophy. Anscombe asks whether Aristotle has the notion of 'moral blame', as opposed to any other. Her example of non-moral blame is criticism of the workmanship of a product or the design of a machine, but this is problematic, since such blame could well be understood to be moral criticism of the worker or designer, of her lack of conscientiousness or attention to detail perhaps. A better example might be someone's blaming the weather for ruining their holiday. Such blame (if that is what it is) may have certain properties in common with some paradigm cases of moral blame: one may be angry at the weather, for example. But what is missing is the possibility of holding the object blamed responsible on the ground that the object has the capacity to act for reasons and may now have to pay the penalty for not doing so appropriately in this case. Does Aristotle have this idea of moral blame? He certainly does: praise and blame fix the boundaries of the voluntary, which he seeks to elucidate in the first five chapters of the third book of the *Ethics*, and he frequently notes that the excesses and deficiencies of character that

---

[51] Moore, *Principia Ethica*, 15–17.

constitute the vices are to be avoided as blameworthy.[52] It is central to his conception of ethics.

But what of the law conception of ethics? Surely that is not to be found in Aristotle? Anscombe is right that Aristotle does not claim that we must be virtuous because it is required by divine law.[53] But her suggestion that the law conception led to a change in sense of 'ought' such that the word became 'equated in the relevant contexts with "is obliged", or "is bound", or "is required to", in the sense in which one can be obliged or bound by law, or something can be required by law' (30) is less plausible.[54] For that sense can be found in Aristotle. Anscombe suggests that the Greek word *hamartanein* was the one most apt for expressing the concept of being bound. *Hamartanein* means something like 'to miss the mark', but Anscombe fails to consider whether Aristotle may not have had in mind the sense of 'missing the *moral* mark', that is, 'being bound to hit a moral target but failing'. It can be used, in deliberate contrast with *adikein* ('to commit injustice or wrongdoing'), to mean *mere* 'error', but this is not usual: 'any crime or sin can be called "error" in Greek'.[55]

It is true that there is little room in Aristotle's ethics for the notions of being permitted or excused, which Anscombe sees as correlative to 'being bound' and as likewise the 'consequence of the dominance of Christianity' (30). But that is a result not so much of the language in which he states his position but of the content of that position

----

[52] See e.g. Aristotle, *Nicomachean Ethics* 1109ᵇ30–1, 1126ᵇ7. The contrast between 'moral' and 'intellectual' virtues in Aristotle noted by Anscombe (26–7) is between virtues of character and those of thought. Aristotle's 'morally good person' would be required to possess both.

[53] This is not to say that the notion was alien to the Greeks. Zeus came to be seen as the most prominent of the gods, and part of his role was to punish moral transgressions. This aspect of Zeus can be found even in Homer (*c*.8 BCE) (Lloyd-Jones, *The Justice of Zeus*, 7, 77–8) (see also Hesiod, *Opera et Dies*, e.g. 9–10, 238–9). See in general Dover, *Greek Popular Morality in the Time of Plato and Aristotle*, 246–61, and in particular 255, which gives some useful examples from the orators in which certain positive laws are ascribed to divine prescription. For a particularly clear expression of a divine law conception of ethics, see Sophocles, *Antigone*, 450–7. We should remember also that for Aristotle theology is 'first philosophy', so that there is a theological grounding for ethics as for everything else.

[54] See Baier, 'Radical Virtue Ethics', 128.

[55] Dover, *Greek Popular Morality*, 152. One finds a similar contrast—between 'wickedness' and the 'frailty' of the tragic hero—in Aristotle's account of tragedy (*De Arte Poetica* 1453ᵃ8–10).

itself.[56] As is the case with, say, utilitarianism, and not the case with the 'Hebrew–Christian ethic' to which Anscombe subscribes, it is not easy to find room in Aristotle's ethics for 'agent-centred options',[57] in the sense of a sphere of life free from moral demands in which it is entirely up to the agent how she shall act, or for a clear and distinct conception of supererogation.[58] There is always something that one is required to do: to act as the virtuous person would act. Any deviation from that standard would be to 'miss the mark' and that is never permitted. And the fact that Aristotle uses *hamartanein* in the moral context, in which missing the mark is blameworthy, unless also involuntary, shows that he does—*pace* Anscombe (30–1)—have a 'blanket term . . . meaning much the same as our blanket term "wrong"'. Missing the mark, in the moral context, just is acting wrongly, according to Aristotle. And to say that someone has missed the mark is to express an 'absolute verdict' on them: they have acted wrongly, and are hence candidates for blame.[59]

In fact, *hamartanein* strikes me as not the most obvious word in Aristotle to study in search of claims about moral obligations. That word is *dei*, a standard word in Greek for 'one ought', 'one should', or 'one must'.[60] It is most plausibly seen as an impersonal form of *deō*, 'to need'. So it is quite natural to translate Aristotle's doctrine of the mean as follows:

For example, fear, confidence, appetite, anger, pity, and in general pleasure and pain can be experienced too much or too little, and in both ways not well. But to have them at the time one ought [or: it is necessary; or: one is required to; or: one is obliged to; or: one is bound to; or: it would be wrong not to; or: one

[56] There are of course Greek concepts Aristotle could have used: *exesti* ('it is permitted'), for example.

[57] See Kagan, *The Limits of Morality*, 3.

[58] Aristotle does speak of 'superhuman virtue' at *Nicomachean Ethics* 1145ᵃ19. But gods and heroes likewise cannot go beyond what is required by virtue at their level.

[59] Here it is worth noting the origin of 'right' in the Latin root 'reg-', 'to make or lead straight', and the fact that 'wrong' has for at least a thousand years had as one of its senses 'having a crooked course or direction; twisted', and has been used to mean 'marked by deviation' (which is perhaps why the OED chooses to elucidate its moral sense as 'deviating from equity, justice, or goodness'). For these and other relevant references in my text below, see *Oxford English Dictionary*, s.v.

[60] Nor should one forget *chrē* (see below in the text), or *adikia*, 'justice', especially the notion of 'universal justice' employed at the beginning of *Nicomachean Ethics*, bk. 5; see Pigden, 'Anscombe on "Ought"', 33.

should; or: one must; or: one has to; or: at the right time; or:...], about the
things one ought [or: it is necessary...]...is the mean and best.[61]

Indeed, *dei* came to be used in the fifth century, in contrast to *chrē*, for
'objective' necessities or constraints.[62]

What about the word 'ought' itself? Its history is illuminating. It is
a petrified imperfect of 'to owe', which has now taken a self-standing
present ('You ought to φ'), past ('You ought to have φ-ed'), or future
sense ('When the clock strikes, you ought to φ'). 'Owe' replaced the
Old English *sculan* (a form of 'shall', from which derives 'should' ('You
should φ')), which meant both 'to owe' and 'to have it as a duty'.[63]
Now it is almost certain that *chrē* is related to *chreos* ('need' or 'debt').[64]
This suggests a general conception of practical necessity or 'bindingness'
running from the Greeks, through Old English, into the modern day.[65]

Here, then, as far as the moral sense of *dei* and 'ought' is concerned,
we have a metaphor for morality as something that 'binds' us, a
matter of necessity whose requirements are, like a debt, to some degree
inescapable—something adherence to which can be demanded from
us. A not implausible hypothesis is that this conception of morality as
something binding emerged from the sense of morality as something
external to one's self and its largely egoistic desires, putting constraints
on one's actions, these constraints to be understood as a kind of
'law' (*nomos*). The divine law conception of ethics, then, is one early
expression of the notion of a binding morality, a notion which can
be expressed, as in Aristotle and secular modern philosophy, without
reference to divine law.

---

[61] *Nicomachean Ethics* 1106^{b}18–22. Translation adapted from that cited in Bibliography. See White, *Individual and Conflict in Greek Ethics*, 113.

[62] See Williams, *Shame and Necessity*, 184, who refers to Bernardete, 'XRH and DEI in Plato and Others'.

[63] See Mitchell, *Old English Syntax*, sects. 932–3, quoting S. Ono: 'It was towards the end of the eleventh century that the meanings [of *agan*] "to have to pay" and "to have as a duty (*to do*)" became prevalent. In the earlier period these meanings were usually expressed by *sculan*.' I am grateful to Brendan Biggs for this reference, and for pointing out to me that the connection between possession ('owe') and necessity is found today also in the word 'have'. Like *dei* (Liddell and Scott, *Greek–English Lexicon*, s.v.), 'shall' in Old English was used to express necessity of various kinds; cf. *OED*, s.v., B.II.3: I am most obliged again to Brendan Biggs for translating and placing in context the passages of Old English there cited. Note, for example, the passage from *Gregory's Past* (dating from *c*.897), according to which a bishop 'must remember himself, even if he is unwilling', which may plausibly be seen to concern an alleged moral obligation or duty.

[64] Cf. Goodell, 'XRH and DEI', 94.

[65] See Nietzsche, *On the Genealogy of Morals*, essay 2, esp. sects. 4–10.

So, far from its being the case that Aristotle's ethics provides us with an alternative to the modern conception of 'ought', we have found the same metaphor underlying both ancient and modern thought—of morality as a set of constraints, requirements, or 'debts'. As we have seen, this aspect of morality can be seen as analogous to law. Just as the law constrains or requires, and will exact its penal 'debt' from those who transgress it, so the same is true of morality. In one sense, of course, both positive morality and positive law do constrain me. If I violate either, I am likely to suffer various sanctions. But the mere fact that there are such sanctions is not sufficient to give either system normative or reason-giving content. Since 'ought' embodies the myth of bindingness, then, we should avoid it—and other moral terms—not for the reasons Anscombe offers, but for those outlined earlier in this chapter.

2

Reasons

1. NORMATIVE REASONS

In the previous chapter I suggested that there are no ultimate moral reasons. That is to say, there is no reason to do what is morally right, what one ought to do, what is kind or just, or whatever, except in so far as there is some ultimate reason that can be stated in non-moral terms. I may have a derivative reason to do what morality requires, but only because doing so will, say, promote my own well-being. Equally, of course, it may be that there are no ultimate reasons at all, to be moral or anything else. We cannot decide whether there are ultimate reasons for action, or how we should characterize the notion of a reason for action, until we have a candidate to consider. So let me suggest the agent's well-being as a source of an ultimate reason: the property some action has of furthering the agent's own well-being is a reason for that agent to perform that action, a reason which varies in strength in proportion to the degree of promotion. What I must now do is to articulate that reason and its nature further. It will turn out that much of what I have to say is in defence of the very idea of such a reason, but I hope that even while providing that defence I shall be able also to clarify the positive aspects of the claim.

The notion of 'reason' is used in many different ways, and for many different purposes, both in everyday life and in philosophy. Some believe that the term's sense is therefore so unclear that it should be avoided. But because one of the fundamental issues in practical ethics is ultimate reasons for action, avoiding the term would or should result only in the introduction of a synonym. Rather we must try to get clearer on the different kinds of reason, initially by drawing distinctions between them.

The first distinction is between *epistemic* reasons and *practical* reasons. The paradigm example of an epistemic reason is a reason for some belief. There will be certain distinctions to be drawn between different kinds of epistemic reason analogous to those distinctions I shall draw below between practical reasons, but a simple example will suffice for the present to capture the epistemic–practical distinction. I believe I am a popular person, but there is strong evidence available to the contrary. No one has called me for several months, I never receive presents on my birthday, people avoid my gaze. This evidence provides me with epistemic reasons to believe that I am unpopular, but were I to come to believe this I would become suicidally depressed.

It might be thought that there is here a conflict between epistemic and practical reasons, on the assumption that I have a practical reason to believe that I am not unpopular. In fact, however, there is no conflict. Practical reasons are reasons for *action*, and belief or believing is best understood not to be an action in the sense in which practical ethics is most interested. Exactly what belief is—a state, a disposition, an attitude—is not, for present purposes, important; what matters is that it is not an action, rather something that can be ascribed in explanation of actions.

But now imagine that I am considering the evidence concerning my popularity. What judgement should I come to? What should I decide? Judging and deciding do seem to be actions, so if we allow that evidence for *p* counts in favour of judging that *p* then it might appear that we have a case in which epistemic and practical reasons conflict. Above, however, I distinguished epistemic from practical reasons by saying that the former were for beliefs, while the latter were for actions. So the conflict in the case of judgement would be between practical reasons grounded epistemically (in the nature of evidence) and those grounded in the well-being of the agent.

Are there epistemically grounded practical reasons? Cases such as that of my judgement about my popularity indeed suggest that there are. But I wish now to claim that there are not, since such reasons are inconsistent with an independent and very plausible principle concerning normative reasons, that subclass of practical reasons concerned with reasons for action:

> *Welfarism about Reasons.* Any ultimate reason for action must be grounded in well-being.

The mere fact that the evidence favours *p*, then, cannot be in itself a reason for me to judge that *p*. Now it may be that judging on the basis of available evidence is itself a constituent of well-being; but then the normative weight would rest on well-being, not on the fact that the evidence for *p* favours *p* or my judging that *p*. The same would be true if adopting a practice of judging on the basis of evidence were itself to be grounded on the promotion of well-being. So, as far as my popularity is concerned, what should I believe? That I am not popular. And what should I judge? That I am popular.

I have already said that normative reasons—reasons *for* action—are a subclass of practical reasons.[1] In particular they are to be distinguished from reasons *why* an action is performed or *explanatory* reasons. Explanatory reasons can be further subdivided into *motivating* reasons and *non-motivating* reasons. Motivating reasons might be my desire for a beer and my belief that there is a beer in the fridge, both of which may play a significant role in explaining my going to the fridge. Often I shall be able to avow these as explanatory motivating reasons to myself (so we might then call them '*avowable* motivating reasons'),[2] but this is not always so, as for instance in the case of unconscious desires. Perhaps the explanation of my going to the fridge is an unconscious desire to be like my mother, whom I often imagine working in the kitchen. Or perhaps it is something more straightforward: a desire for relief from the tedium of the administrative paper I am reading. Some explanatory reasons, however, are only quite indirectly related to motivation, and serve to account for actions understood as mere events. My having had an especially salty lunch might be such a reason, or even the fact that God did not strike me dead as I rose from my chair.

The reasons which are a fundamental concern of practical ethics, however, are a different matter. A normative reason is a property of an action that counts,[3] for the agent,[4] in favour of its performance by that agent.[5] Consider the following case.

---

[1] Much recent literature has provided helpful resources for categorizing reasons. See e.g. Norman, *Reasons for Action*; Raz, *Practical Reason and Norms*; Smith, 'The Humean Theory of Motivation'; Parfit, 'Reasons and Motivation'; Skorupski, 'Reasons and Reason'; Dancy, *Practical Reality*, ch. 1.

[2] I may explain my going to the fridge by giving the content of my belief ('There's a beer in there'). But what really explains my action (as opposed to my having this belief) is my belief.

[3] One might say, if speaking of possible or future actions, 'would count'.

[4] The relativity to the agent in the definition is to allow for properties that may count *for some other agent* in favour of the performance of an action. If egoism is true, the property of some action of yours that it benefits me may be a property that, for me, counts in favour of your performing that action. But it does not count for you, and is not a reason. Note that I am seeking here to explicate the fundamental normative notion of *favouring*. For some property to count in favour in this sense does not mean that the agent's own well-being will be furthered, or that the agent is aware of the property or its normative significance. So the inclusion of the phrase is no concession to any kind of motivational internalism.

[5] To use a phrase of Hurley's, 'the space of reasons is the space of action' ('Animal Action in the Space of Reasons', 231; cf. Baier, *The Moral Point of View*, 95). I prefer

Two Buttons. You are faced with a choice between two buttons, marked 1 and 2. If you push button 1, you will receive a painful electric shock for several seconds. If you push button 2, you will receive a million pounds. You know of the two outcomes, but do not know which button will produce which outcome, and have no way of knowing. Your view is that it is well worth taking the risk of the shock for the chance of obtaining the money, and it is indeed the case that receiving the money would be better for you overall than receiving the shock would be bad for you.

It will seem to you that you have a strong normative reason for pushing the button that will produce the million pounds, and that is indeed how things are. That button is button 2, so it follows that you have a strong normative reason for pushing button 2. You do not know that, but the best understanding of the ascription of normative reasons to agents is that it takes place within a referentially transparent context. The property of pushing button 2 that it will result in your being a million pounds richer is a non-ultimate reason for doing so. It has this status only, or partly, because being a million pounds richer will promote your well-being. The property of pushing button 2 that it will promote your well-being overall, that is to say, is an ultimate reason for pushing it.

The distinction between reasons why an action is performed and the reasons for its performance is now fairly standard in the literature. But *Two Buttons* illustrates that there is another distinction lurking here which it is important to tease out, between the normative reasons which *ground* actions and the reasons which *justify* agents in performing them. Your normative reason for pushing button 2 is that it will promote your well-being to do so. This is what *counts* in favour of your pushing 2. But what counts in favour need not *speak* in favour: in *Two Buttons*, your reason for pushing 2 is, though not lessened in force, nevertheless 'silenced' by the fact that you have no epistemic access to it. Your justification for pushing 2 can appeal only to the fact that pushing it gives you a good chance of promoting your well-being. We may now ask whether you have any normative reason to act on norms such as

---

to couch my definition in terms of a property rather than a fact (e.g. that the action has a certain property, or has certain consequences) because I find the notion of a property more ontologically central and slightly less obscure than that of a fact. But not much hangs on this. For a recent example of the standard view of reasons as facts that favour, see Thomson, *Goodness and Advice*, 32.

this, a question analogous to the question whether we have practical reasons to adhere to epistemic norms. Whatever view we take of the autonomy or otherwise of epistemic reasons, it seems most plausible that in the case of practical reasons normative reasons for adherence to justificatory norms depend only on the consequences for well-being of acting on those norms. It may at first sight appear to you that you have a normative reason to push button 1 of the same strength as your reason to push button 2, because your justification for pushing either is equally good. But if you reflect on the very nature of justification, deliberation, and action, you may adopt an external perspective and recognize that having a justification for some action is not in fact an 'extra' normative reason for performing it. Your normative reason for pushing button 2 is that it will promote your well-being. Your having a justification for doing so cannot add anything to the weight of that reason, since justification and normativity are independent of one another. But they are of course related, in the sense that justification will be against a background of generally accepted normative reasons.

Consider another example: instrumental rationality. If you have adopted some end E, it is plausible to claim that you have a reason either to take the necessary means M to that end, or to abandon E.[6] There is a practical inconsistency in refusing to adopt M while holding to E. But now consider the case in the light of welfarism about reasons, and the question is whether either pursuing M or giving up E is, other things being equal, the strategy that will best promote your well-being. It may be that neither of them is, and that your well-being will be most effectively promoted by your continuing to be practically inconsistent. The means–end principle, then, is itself a justificatory norm, the ultimate reasons for adopting and conforming to which depend on well-being.[7]

---

[6] See Broome, 'Practical Reasoning', sects. 5–6.

[7] The distinction I have drawn between grounding and justifying reasons is structurally similar to that drawn between 'objective' and 'subjective' wrongness. In his discussion of that latter distinction (*Wise Choices, Apt Feelings*, 42–3), Gibbard claims that the objective sense is the less useful one. That seems to me an exaggeration. In the case of *Two Buttons* it would indeed be rather unhelpful for me to advise you to push the button that will give you the million pounds. What you are interested in will be the justificatory norms for situations such as these. But if we are considering which justificatory norms to adopt, then the issue of which grounding reasons we have must be resolved. What I am advocating is a 'consequentialist' theory of justificatory norms, as opposed to a 'deontological' one which gives them, or their adoption, weight independent of the 'consequences' of their adoption. (The term 'consequentialism', though now standard, is

The phenomenology of deliberation and reflection on the past perhaps brings out especially clearly the relationship between norms of
justification on the one hand and normative reasons on the other. Faced
with *Two Buttons*, as I have said, it will seem to you that there is some
independent normative reason attaching to the pushing of one of the
buttons, and you will do all you can to work out which button it is.
If you push button 1, then you will see immediately that you had no
normative reason to do that, whereas you did have a strong normative
reason for pushing 2.

In *Two Buttons*, your normative reason cannot explain your pushing
button 2 rather than button 1, though you do have that reason.[8]
Sometimes the presence of a normative reason can help to explain an
action. Imagine that a serious hurricane is forecast to hit my home
town tonight, and inhabitants of the area have been advised to leave.
My leaving town may be explained, at least in part, by my belief that I
have a reason to promote my own well-being, and one obvious way to
explain my having that belief is that there is indeed such a reason and
that I am, like many people, aware of it. In recent years, however, it has
become common to assume that normative reasons *must*, in some sense,
be potentially explanatory. The best-known statement of such a view is
that of Williams.[9] Williams outlines two different interpretations of the
sentence 'A has a reason to φ'. On the so-called 'internal' interpretation,
the sentence implies that A has some motive which will be furthered
by his φ-ing.[10] Williams understands 'motive' quite broadly, in terms
of what he calls the agent's 'subjective motivational set', which can
include 'such things as dispositions of evaluation, patterns of emotional
reaction, personal loyalties, and various projects'. On the 'external'
interpretation, however, the sentence will not be falsified by the absence
of an appropriate motive.

unfortunate, in that consequentialism as most now understand it may describe the very
performance of some action as itself a 'consequence'. See my 'Deontological Ethics'.)

   [8] Some would prefer to say that, though you do not *have* this reason, *there is*
nevertheless a reason. I have no objection to that, since it merely maps the distinction
between, in my sense, being aware and being unaware of a reason one has.

   [9] 'Internal and External Reasons'; 'Internal Reasons and the Obscurity of Blame'.
Cf. Woods, 'Reasons for Action and Desire', 189; Korsgaard, 'Skepticism about Practical
Reason', 329.

   [10] 'Internal and External Reasons', 101. Williams says this characterization is 'very
rough'. Especially important to remember is that an internalist may allow that I have
reason to φ if I have at present no motive to φ but such a motive would arise were I to
become aware of some fact or to engage in deliberation (ibid. 103–5).

Williams rejects the external interpretation, on two grounds. The first is that it cuts the normativity of reasons free from the potential to explain:

It must be a mistake simply to separate explanatory and normative reasons. If it is true that A has a reason to φ, then it must be possible that he should φ for that reason; and if he does act for that reason, then that reason will be the explanation of his acting. So the claim that he has a reason to φ—that is, the normative statement 'He has a reason to φ'—introduces the possibility of that reason being an explanation; namely, if the agent accepts that claim.[11]

In the case of *Two Buttons*, then, Williams could allow that you have a reason to push button 2, and a reason not to push button 1. If you knew the facts about the consequences of pushing each button, then you would be motivated in the appropriate way. But this relation between grounding and motivation is quite contingent. Imagine now that you have a generally ascetic motivational set. In this case, being informed about the consequences of each button may have no effect on your motivation. But most of us will want to say that you still have a strong reason to push button 2. What if Williams were to allow that it is a fact that asceticism is irrational? Again, it seems that connection with motivation is contingent. It may turn out that your ascetic dispositions are sufficiently strong that they prevent any self-interested motivation from arising, even though you believe that the origin of those dispositions rests on a mistake. But you still have the reason to push the button you believe yourself to have.

At this point someone may object to such ascriptions of reasons for action on grounds similar to those that motivate the so-called 'ought implies can' principle. According to that principle, if A ought to φ, then it must be the case that she can φ. Likewise, if A has a reason to φ, then it must be the case that, as Williams puts it, she can φ *for that reason*. But the italicized condition merely assumes what the principle itself is being used to prove. Further, even without the condition, it is not obvious that 'oughts' and 'reasons' are in the same boat. One reason that 'ought implies can' seems so plausible is the close relation between 'ought' and emotional responses such as guilt or blame. If I really cannot φ (and I have not negligently caused myself to be in

---

[11] 'Internal Reasons and the Obscurity of Blame', 38–9.

that situation), then guilt, blame, and other such emotions seem, on their internal rationale, to be out of place.[12] But the notion of a reason is comprehensible quite independently of the emotions. A normative reason is a property of an action that counts, for the agent, in favour of the performance of that action by that agent. We can speak of actions which cannot in an ordinary sense be performed, such as my flying several metres through the air to avoid a charging tiger. Why can we not say that the property of that action that it would further my well-being counts in favour of it? It is of course largely irrelevant to deliberation that this is so, but grounding and justification are, as we have seen, to be kept apart.[13]

Williams's second argument for internalism is that the point of external reason statements is unclear.[14] He imagines a man who behaves badly towards his wife, but in whose motivational set there is nothing that would lead to his being nicer to her. Williams allows that we may say various things about him, such as that he is ungrateful or brutal, but asks:

> what is the difference supposed to be between saying that the agent has a reason to act more considerately, and saying one of the many other things we can say to people whose behaviour does not accord with what we think it should be? As, for instance, that it would be better if they acted otherwise.

I suspect that many people might say that there is no great difference, because when they say that the man is ungrateful, or that it would be better if he acted otherwise, they mean just that he has a reason to be more grateful, or a reason to act otherwise because it would make things better overall. But now that we have at hand an account of normative reasons, there is anyway a simple answer to Williams's question. When we say that this man has a reason to be nicer to his wife, we are saying that there is something that counts, for him, in favour of his being nicer. And whether this is so or not is a matter quite independent of whether he can be moved by or even appreciate that reason.

---

[12] Though note that they can and do occur in situations such as that of the driver who, through no fault of his own, kills a child: see Williams, 'Moral Luck', 27–8. Their occurrence can be understood as part of a strategy in which agents are encouraged to take all steps to avoid ending up in such a situation.

[13] Against this, see Streumer, 'Reasons and Impossibility'.

[14] 'Internal Reasons and the Obscurity of Blame', 39–40.

Why has a link between normativity and motivation appeared so plausible? One reason, noted above, is that motivation often involves beliefs about normative reasons. Another is the influence of a view of instrumental rationality based on a certain common interpretation of Hume. On this interpretation Hume suggests that the only normative reasons are 'hypothetical' in the sense that they ground acting so as to satisfy some independent desire. We have no reason to desire anything in particular, but once we do have a desire, then we have reasons to act so as to satisfy that desire.[15]

As Christine Korsgaard and others have pointed out,[16] whether it is Hume's or not, this view is incoherent. It suggests that there are no reasons to act in any particular way independently of one's desire so to act; but it then postulates just such a class of reasons to act instrumentally. The Humean can be confronted with a dilemma. Either there are categorical reasons, and there seems little justification for restricting them only to instrumental action (if I can have a reason to take the means to φ, then why can I not have a reason to φ?); or there are no categorical reasons, and the theory of practical reasons turns out to be nihilist. Can you take seriously the view of someone who claims that you have no reason to do anything, and that given a choice between, say, a period of great agony and one of deep enjoyment, you have no reason to choose the latter?

In fact, the whole notion that desires ground or provide reasons is mistaken.[17] It is not especially implausible to suggest that any human action must involve a desire in some sense.[18] But welfarism about reasons suggests that it is an error to allow desire's role in motivation to lead one into giving it a role in normativity. Desire is a mere psychological state, with no value in itself or in its fulfilment or satisfaction.[19] If I desire something worth having, then in ordinary cases I shall have a reason to

---

15 See esp. *Enquiry*, app. 1; *Treatise*, 2. 3. 3, 3. 1. 1.

16 'The Normativity of Instrumental Reason'.

17 See Quinn, 'Putting Rationality in its Place'; Parfit, 'Reasons and Motivation', 128; Crisp, *Mill on Utilitarianism*, 55–7; Scanlon, *What we Owe*, 41–55; Parfit, 'Rationality and Reasons', esp. 20–5. For the opposite view, see e.g. Chang, 'Can Desires Provide Reasons for Action?'

18 Nagel, *The Possibility of Altruism*, 29; Smith, 'The Humean Theory of Motivation', 54–8.

19 This claim depends on the non-desire-based hedonist account of well-being I shall defend in Ch. 4.

act so as to satisfy that desire. But that is because I will thereby obtain the worthwhile object, not because my desire will be satisfied.

2. REALISM ABOUT NORMATIVE REASONS

According to the account sketched above, normative reasons are properties of actions that count, for the agent, in favour of their performance. These properties are 'real' in the sense that they are not to be understood entirely in terms of, say, human projection or expression; indeed they may be said to attach to the actions of any agent, including those—such as certain non-human animals—who are unable to grasp them as reasons. As Korsgaard puts it, 'Realists try to establish the normativity of ethics by arguing that values or obligations or reasons really exist.'[20]

This kind of realism has in recent years been attacked on two fronts—one Humean, the other Kantian. According to the Humean argument,[21] if normative reasons were indeed properties of actions, about which we can form beliefs, we should expect that someone might have a belief that they have some normative reason for action, and yet be quite unmoved by it, since belief is motivationally inert. In fact, however, the 'judgement' by some agent that she has a normative reason will necessarily motivate her to act, not in the sense that she will act in that way but in the sense that she will have *some* motivation to act in that way, which may of course be overridden by other desires or perhaps by irrational states such as weakness of will or depression. This suggests that the 'judgement' is better understood as some non-cognitive state such as a desire, an emotion, a commitment, or whatever. And if that is the case, then we should not assume that there is anything to 'cognize'. The alleged belief that there is a reason to φ is in fact merely some kind of non-cognitive attitude towards φ-ing.

The view that a judgement by an agent that she has a reason to act will necessarily motivate her—so-called 'motivational internalism'—is hard to grasp. The kind of motivation we are discussing is not, as we have seen, that which results successfully in action. Nor can the internalist

---

[20] *The Sources of Normativity*, 19.
[21] For a brief and especially clear account of this argument, see Smith, 'Realism'; for further analysis and criticism, see Parfit, 'Reasons and Motivation', 100–9.

mean by motivation 'felt desires', for, as Hume himself recognized, many of our desires have no introspectible 'feel'.[22] The best sense that can be given to the view involves certain counterfactual claims of the form:

> Necessarily, if P judges that she has a reason to φ, and countervailing motivations are absent, she will φ.

But commitment to such a counterfactual seems an article of faith to which the internalist is drawn by a prior acceptance of internalism. Not only can we conceive of a case in which someone makes such a judgement and is not in the relevant circumstances motivated successfully to φ, but such cases do not seem especially mysterious unless one is already a motivational internalist. Successful motivation follows most naturally on recognition of a reason grounded in the agent's well-being. But even here there is weakness of will. Other-regarding motivation may also fail. Imagine someone who believes, sincerely, that she has a reason to make a donation to some charity.[23] She is not moved by sympathy for the beneficiaries; it is just that, on her view of morality and reasons, she has a duty to assist. But she does not do so. Now imagine her to lack any possible counter-motivation to assisting—she no longer, for example, desires to keep her money for her own use. It seems possible to imagine her still not assisting, and explaining her action by saying, 'I do believe I have a reason to help. But I haven't been brought up to be the sort of person to care about people I don't know, or to care whether I do what I have reason to do. I can see that I have a reason; but I'm just not moved by it'. Often, perhaps, the belief that one has a normative reason to φ may itself engender a desire to φ, and one would indeed expect such a capacity to respond to reasons to be closely linked with motivation. But—as one might expect also of such 'distinct existences'—the relation between the belief and the desire is quite contingent.[24] Weakness of will, that is to say, is just that; it is not a failure to make a proper judgement.

---

[22] *Treatise*, 2. 1. 1. 3, 2. 3. 3. 8.

[23] Similar examples are used in defence of motivational externalism by e.g. Brink, *Moral Realism and the Foundations of Ethics*, 27, 46–8; Svavarsdóttir, 'Moral Cognitivism and Motivation', 176–8.

[24] Narrowing the scope of motivational internalism to a claim about rational persons (see e.g. Korsgaard, 'Skepticism about Practical Reason', 317; Smith, *The Moral Problem*, 61) will make it more credible, but less significant (see Svavarsdóttir, 'Moral Cognitivism and Motivation', 164–5). An externalist of the kind discussed in my text may allow that rationality is to be defined partly in terms of being motivated by reasons. In general I

It might be claimed that this person's lack of motivation shows that she must be using the phrase 'I have a reason' in an 'inverted commas' sense.[25] Perhaps what she really means is that in her society it is generally believed that people have a reason to help others, but that she herself does not accept this as a genuinely normative claim. But this view again seems to rest on a prior acceptance of motivational internalism. If we are clear on the distinction between a property's being normative on the one hand, and belief in it resulting in motivation on the other, we can allow the possibility that someone may quite sincerely believe that some property of a course of action open to her counts, for her, in favour of performing it, but not be motivated in any degree to perform that action. Human beings usually are motivated to act in accordance with what they take to be their reasons; but they may not be.[26]

Michael Smith has claimed that motivational externalists are unable satisfactorily to explain how, in the case of a 'good and strong-willed person', a change in motivation reliably follows a change in moral judgement.[27] In brief, his argument is as follows. Imagine that I am inclined to vote for the libertarian party at the next election, but you persuade me that I should vote for the social democrats. If I am a good and strong-willed person, then I shall cease being motivated to vote for the libertarians and acquire the motivation to vote for the social democrats. How is this to be explained? For the motivational internalist, there is no problem, since as a matter of conceptual necessity any sincere normative judgement brings motivation with it. The externalist, however, has to postulate some independent motivation to do the right thing, in so far as it is the right thing. That is, the good and strong-willed person's motivation is to be read *de dicto* rather than *de re*; and the problem is that this, rather than being a characteristic of a good person,

---

prefer to avoid the terms 'rational' and 'rationality', since they are usually understood in the light of practical norms, and these rest, contingently, on ultimate grounding reasons.

[25] See Hare, *The Language of Morals*, 124–5, 164–5; *Freedom and Reason*, 190; *Moral Thinking*, 24, 58.

[26] The evolutionary history of this particular aspect of human agency is an intriguing matter. On the face of it one might have expected humans to have evolved in accordance with motivational internalism. But perhaps weakness of will and so on are the costs of our capacity to act reflectively, a capacity which may be seen as a kind of freedom.

[27] Smith, *The Moral Problem*, 71–6. Smith elaborates his argument in e.g. 'The Argument for Internalism: Reply to Miller' and 'In Defense of *The Moral Problem*: A Reply to Brink, Copp, and Sayre-McCord'. Helpful discussion and criticism can be found in e.g. Miller, 'An Objection to Smith's Argument for Internalism'; Lillehammer, 'Smith on Moral Fetishism'; Svavarsdóttir, 'Moral Cognitivism and Motivation', 194–215.

is in fact a 'fetish' or moral vice: 'Good people care non-derivatively about honesty, the weal and woe of their children and friends, the well-being of their fellows, people getting what they deserve, justice, equality, and the like, not just one thing: doing what they believe to be right, where this is read *de dicto* rather than *de re*.'[28]

Smith's argument faces at least two difficulties. First, caring about what is right for its own sake is not usually thought of as a vice: it is the virtue of conscientiousness or integrity.[29] Second, there is no reason why the externalist must accept that this is the only moral motivation of the good and strong-willed person.[30] As well as caring about doing the right thing, she is likely also to care about all the things on Smith's list. What the externalist will insist upon, of course, is that any motivation that follows upon any moral judgement by the good and strong-willed person concerning honesty, her friends, or whatever, is contingent.

Smith's argument is couched in the kind of moral terms that I have urged that we avoid. But it can be restated in the terminology of reasons. The externalist, then, might be committed to the claim that what explains a change in motivation in the case of the reasonable and strong-willed person is a standing motivation or disposition to respond to reasons. In this form there seems even less reason to think that this is an unfortunate implication of externalism. For in this context the most obvious way to characterize what it is to be reasonable is to attribute to the reasonable person an overarching responsiveness to reasons.

So much for the Humean argument. Before I move on to the Kantian argument, this is an appropriate point to consider Simon Blackburn's suggestion that realists face a problem in the supervenience of the non-natural (including the normative) on the natural.[31] Essentially, the difficulty for the realist is to explain why, though natural properties do not entail normative properties, it is constitutive of competence in the use of normative language that one recognize the constraint that it is not possible that two objects differ in normative properties without any

---

[28] Smith, *The Moral Problem*, 75.

[29] See Lillehammer, 'Smith on Moral Fetishism', 191–2.

[30] Svavarsdóttir, 'Moral Cognitivism and Motivation', 198–9, 206.

[31] See Blackburn, *Spreading the Word*, 182–7; 'Moral Realism', 114–23; 'Supervenience Revisited'. Blackburn focuses on moral properties, but his argument carries over to the normative and evaluative in general. For useful discussion, see e.g. Dreier, 'The Supervenience Argument against Moral Realism'; Zangwill, 'Moral Supervenience'; Ridge, 'Moral Non-Naturalism', sect. 6; Shafer-Landau, *Moral Realism: A Defence*, 84–9.

underlying difference at the natural level.[32] The projectivist, Blackburn suggests, can explain this as a product of the purpose of normative language—to guide desire and choice among the natural features of the world. That practice requires stability across cases. But if, as the realist says, the purpose of such language 'is to describe further . . . [normative] aspects of the world', it remains entirely unexplained why obeying the supervenience constraint is constitutive of competence as a user of normative language.

What the realist must continue to insist on here is the explanatory element in the relation to normative properties of properties which are not conceptually or analytically normative. I might think, for example, that the property of some experience that it is pleasant explains why it is good for me and hence why I have a reason to pursue it, if I also accept the claims that pleasure is a constituent of well-being, and that one has a reason to promote one's own well-being. Properly grasping synthetic a priori principles such as these requires that one see them as necessary in the sense that if they are true in one possible world then they will be true in all. Acceptance of the supervenience constraint, then, is involved in a proper grasp of the concept of a reason for action. The realist, that is to say, does not have to accept in the first place that properties which are conceptually normative and those that are conceptually non-normative but underlie or explain the normative are entirely 'distinct existences' in such a way that the former could vary without variation in the latter.[33]

From the Kantian perspective, Korsgaard provides several arguments against realism. In her book *The Sources of Normativity* she focuses on what she calls 'the normative question',[34] asked of morality in particular, of what justifies the claims morality makes on us, 'whether there is really *anything* I must do, and if so whether it is *this*' (9–10, 34). In the previous chapter, I suggested that the normative question asked specifically of morality should be answered negatively. Moral requirements are not, in themselves, ultimately reason-giving. But we often do have reasons, grounded in well-being, to act as morality requires. It is clear that Korsgaard is prepared to ask the same normative question in connection with this claim about reasons (20). Take a paradigmatic case of a self-interested reason. You are given a choice between two, and only

---

[32] 'Supervenience Revisited', 137.

[33] Dreier, 'The Supervenience Argument', 18; Ridge, 'Moral Non-Naturalism', sect. 6, para. 2.

[34] *Sources*, lect. 1. References in the text in this section are to this work.

two, options: an hour of torture, or an hour listening to some enjoyable music. Nothing hinges on your choice except what happens to you in the next hour. So the normative question is: Is there really anything you have a reason to do here, and is it to choose the hour of music? And the realist answer is, of course, 'Yes'.

Korsgaard's first objection to realism we might call the *fiat argument* (33–4). If someone claims that we have a reason to act in some way or other, we can, Korsgaard notes, keep asking 'Why?' questions, apparently without end. Thus:

> You: Why do I have a reason to choose the music rather than the torture?
>
> Me: Because the music's enjoyable, while the torture will be agonizing.
>
> You: But why do I have a reason to choose what's enjoyable over what's agonizing?
>
> Me: Because enjoyment is good for you, and suffering bad for you.

This exchange is indeed somewhat bizarre, but that is primarily because we think it obvious why one has a reason to choose enjoyment over suffering. It does not seem that another 'Why?' question is appropriate. But in claiming that the 'Why?' questions have been brought to an end, I open myself to Korsgaard's objection that the realist brings this kind of 'regress to an end by fiat: he declares that some things are *intrinsically* normative ... The very nature of these intrinsically normative entities is supposed to forbid further questioning.'

The term 'entity' is not intended by Korsgaard to have any especially heavy metaphysical connotations. Later in her lectures, for example, she allows that what Kant calls a 'maxim' is an entity. So it is not the realist's metaphysics which Korsgaard finds unpalatable. One worry appears to be that the realist claim that there are ultimate normative reasons is in some way arbitrary or unreflective: 'Having discovered that he needs an unconditional answer, the realist straightaway concludes that he has found one.'

Some realists may be unreflective, but presumably so may non-realists. The charge of arbitrariness is also hard to understand. If the dialogue continues with your asking the question 'Why do I have a reason to promote what's good for me?', I confess that all I can say is 'Well, you just *do*'. But that is not because I have not already given you the best and final answer available. Nor is it that I cannot imagine someone's asking such a question. A nihilist about reasons, for example, may sensibly ask it, or a Christian who thinks that one should be concerned only for others and never for oneself. But at this point we seem to have reached philosophical bedrock.

Korsgaard goes on to compare the realist position to a version of the cosmological argument for the existence of God, according to which God must exist because the only way we can explain the existence of contingent things is by postulating a being which exists necessarily. Korsgaard notes two problems with this argument. First, the cosmologist's placing of necessity in God amounts merely to placing it where the cosmologist wanted to find it. Second, the cosmologist has to assume that the existence of contingent beings must in a sense be necessary, in the sense that there must be some explanation showing why they *must* have existed. And, she continues:

Moral realism is like that. Having discovered that obligation cannot exist unless there are actions which it is necessary to do, the realist concludes that there are such actions, and that they are the very ones we have always thought were necessary, the traditional moral duties. And the same two problems exist. The realist like the cosmologist places the necessity where he wanted to find it. And the argument cannot even get started, unless you assume that there are some actions which it is necessary to do. But when the normative question is raised, these are the exact points that are in contention—whether there is really *anything* I must do, and if so whether it is *this*. So it is a little hard to see how realism can help.

These arguments can be adapted so that they apply to realism about normative reasons. The first appears to be related to the charge of unreflectiveness, and concerns the realist's methodology. Take the example of the reason to promote one's own well-being. The objection is that the realist recognizes that there cannot be such a reason unless there are normative reasons to act in some way or other; she then concludes that there are such reasons, and indeed one of them is to promote one's own well-being.

It is clear that, if this is indeed the realist's argument, it is invalid. Korsgaard does not make reference to any particular realist here, so it may be that she believes that any realist must argue in this way. But a form of realism which begins by reflection on cases such as that of the choice between torture and music, then moves on the basis of that reflection to the view that there is a normative reason to promote one's own well-being, and thus answers the normative question in the affirmative, cannot be accused of any logical error. All that Korsgaard can say is that it is a mistake to believe—just on the basis of reflection on the case in question—that there is a reason to choose music over torture, and that one needs further (Kantian) argument to support that claim. Again we have reached bedrock, but it might be worth recording that when I have described this case to non-philosophers and asked the normative question, everyone turns out to be a realist. Anyway, this analysis of the realist position also deals with an adapted version of Korsgaard's second argument in the passage above. The realist does not begin by assuming that there are certain actions we have reason to do, but arrives at that conclusion by reflection on certain cases.

Korsgaard is not a nihilist about reasons, and I now want to suggest that, since the only alternative to the kind of realism Korsgaard criticizes is nihilism, Korsgaard is herself a realist. She admits that she is a *procedural* realist, in the sense that she believes there are correct and incorrect ways to answer moral questions (or, presumably, questions about reasons), but denies *substantive* realism, 'the view that there are answers to moral questions *because* there are moral facts or truths, which those questions ask *about*' (35). She elaborates as follows on the difference between the two views:

procedural realism does not require the existence of intrinsically normative entities, either for morality or for any other kind of normative claim. It is consistent with the view that moral conclusions are the dictates of practical reason, or the projections of human sentiments, or the results of some constructive procedure like the argument from John Rawls's original position.

Procedural realists, then, may advocate the existence of intrinsically normative entities (indeed Korsgaard says that substantive realism is a version of procedural realism), but they need not. The kind of procedural realism Korsgaard herself advocates is meant to be an alternative to both substantive realism and nihilism. But those latter two positions occupy all the available territory—there is no third alternative. Take the question 'Should I φ?' According to the substantive realist, as understood by Korsgaard, this question may in some cases be answered straightforwardly by reference to an intrinsically normative entity (INE), namely, the fact that I should φ. The non-substantive procedural realist position is more complicated. According to this position, mere reference to the fact that I should φ is an insufficient answer to the question whether I should. Rather we must work out the implications of a certain procedure—the application of the dictates of practical reason, of the projection of human sentiments, or of a construction. Then we may say that it is indeed a fact that I should φ, in the weak sense of 'fact' that follows trivially from its being the case that the deliverance of the relevant procedure is indeed that I should φ.

But at this point one is entitled to ask the following question. If we allow that I should φ only in so far as a certain procedure has as its upshot that I should, do I have reason in the first place to act on the basis of the deliverances of the relevant procedure? Do I have reason, for example, to act in accordance with norms based on the projection of human sentiments? If the answer is affirmative, then we have an INE—a different INE from that referred to by the substantive realist, but an INE nevertheless. If the answer is negative, then we have nihilism.[35] Why should I act on the deliverances of some procedure if I have no reason in the first place to do so?

If the answer is affirmative, we may now expect the debate to repeat itself at this higher level. The substantive realist, it will be said, will be insisting that we have an INE—a fact that I should abide by the deliverances of the relevant procedure. But the non-substantive realist may seek to apply the same analysis here as she did originally. She may claim, for example, that I do indeed have reason to abide by the deliverances of a projective procedure, but that this claim itself is to be understood in an expressivist way, *rather than* as a response to an independent INE.[36] But if understanding the claim in an expressivist way itself involves *denying* the proposition that it is a fact that I have reason to abide by the procedure, saying the words 'There is a reason to abide by the outcome of the procedure' is insufficient to avoid nihilism. For nihilism just is that denial, whatever one's other commitments allow one to say or to express. Essentially, an INE is nothing more than an ultimate reason, so if you deny their existence at all stages in your analysis you are committed to nihilism.

Consider now Korsgaard's own version of non-substantive procedural realism, according to which practical conclusions are the dictates of practical reason. She illustrates that view with an interpretation of Kant's account of the reason we have to take means to our ends:

Kant tells us that the means/end relation is normative because of a principle of practical reason which he calls the hypothetical imperative. The hypothetical

---

[35] Or the first step in an infinite regress, which I take to be practically equivalent to nihilism. See Rakzik, 'A Normative Regress Problem'.

[36] Compare Blackburn's claim that moral reflection can be understood as the expression of attitudes towards structures of sensibilities; see e.g. *Spreading the Word*, 189–96; 'Errors and the Phenomenology of Value', 152–8; 'How to be an Ethical Anti-Realist'.

imperative tells us that if we will an end, we have a reason to will the means to that end. This imperative, in turn, is not based on the recognition of a normative fact or truth, but simply on the nature of the will. To will an end, rather than just wishing for it or wanting it, is to set yourself to be its cause. And to set yourself to be its cause is to set yourself to take the available means to get it. So the argument goes from the nature of the rational will to a principle which describes a procedure according to which such a will must operate and from there to an application of that principle which yields a conclusion about what one has reason to do. (36)

On this view the normativity of the means–end relation is said to follow analytically from the nature of the will itself, so that there is no need to postulate the normative fact that we have a reason to take the means to our ends. But there is a prior question: Do we have a reason to do what we will? If we do, then we have here an INE—a fact about what we have reason to do. If we do not, then it is not clear how the means–end relation can inherit any normativity from the nature of the will. If I do not have reason to will some end, then how can I have reason to take means to that end?[37]

There is a difference between the kind of substantive realism Korsgaard is criticizing and her own. But it is merely a difference in where the 'Why?' questions stop. According to the version of realism I am defending, you have a reason to choose music over torture because you have an ultimate reason to promote your own well-being. According to Korsgaard's Kantian version, you may well have a reason to promote your own well-being, but it is not ultimate. Rather your ultimate reason is to perform those actions which a certain procedure—the proper application of certain principles of practical reason—would identify as required. But this raises questions about the nature, and epistemological status, of such a procedure, which have been asked since at least the time of Hegel. Does the Kantian Categorical Imperative, for example, seem plausible because it requires actions (or rather non-actions), such as not harming others, which we already take ourselves to have reason to perform? If so, what is its function? Or, if we are to apply it quite independently of any views we may have about what we have reason to do, is that Imperative likely to issue in any specific requirement at all?

---

[37] In a later work, Korsgaard suggests that willing an end is 'committing yourself to realizing the end . . . an essentially first-personal and normative act' ('Normativity of Instrumental Reason', 245). But it is normative only in the sense that one is giving oneself a norm to follow. The question remains whether one has a reason, independent of one's will, to follow the norms one gives oneself.

And what is to prevent its requiring actions we think we have strong reason not to perform? And behind all this remains the question: Do I have reason to adopt this procedure? An affirmative answer is a form of substantive realism, while a negative is a form of nihilism.

An implication of Korsgaard's turning out to be a substantive realist after all is that the questions she asks of substantive realists will be questions for her too. A central question she has concerns the relation between reasons and rationality:

According to . . . realism . . . there are facts, which exist independently of the person's mind, about what there is reason to do; rationality consists in conforming one's conduct to those reasons . . . The difficulty with this account in a way exists right on its surface, for the account invites the question why it is necessary to act in accordance with those reasons, and so seems to leave us in need of a reason to be rational . . . we must still explain why the person finds it *necessary* to act on those normative facts, or what it is about *her* that makes them normative *for her*. We must explain how these reasons get a grip on the agent.[38]

Korsgaard seems to be raising two issues here. One concerns normative reasons (the 'reason to be rational'), the other motivating reasons (how normative reasons 'get a grip' on the agent). The first issue is itself somewhat difficult to get a grip on. If I have an ultimate reason to φ, then—if rationality consists in conforming my conduct to that reason—I have no reason to be rational other than that ultimate reason itself. It may be that Korsgaard is here raising again the notion that realist stopping points in chains of 'Why?' questions are arbitrary. I have already expressed doubt that this need be so, and it is not clear anyway why the Kantian stopping point is any less arbitrary than any other.

Korsgaard's second issue calls for an explanation of why it is that a person finds it necessary to act on the normative fact that she has a reason to φ. She is correct in thinking that we should be able to offer some account of what happens when an agent's recognition of a reason motivates her to act, when it does; but what that account will be is likely to vary depending on the reason, the action, and the person in question. If we take simple self-interest, and seek an explanation of why people given the choice between music and torture will choose the former, the explanation is straightforward: they have a strong interest in avoiding suffering and pursuing enjoyment, that is, a strong interest

---

[38] Ibid. 240.

in promoting their own well-being. But why, for example, people make donations to charity to benefit distant strangers is a more complicated matter and will involve some account of the way in which their moral education has shaped those dispositions that have come to constitute their character. And the issue of why someone should be motivated to guide their action by an abstract principle such as the Categorical Imperative will likewise be complicated—and indeed fascinating—but it is not one that will be any less tractable for a Kantian than accounts of motivation are for other realists.

3. OUGHTS AND NORMATIVE REQUIREMENTS

According to my account, normative reasons are constituted by those properties of actions which count, for the agent, in favour of their performance. When any such property is instantiated in some action, then it is a fact that there is a normative reason to perform that action. And there are also normative facts about which kinds of properties constitute reasons for action. I have been suggesting that it is a fact that, if some action promotes the agent's well-being, then the agent has an ultimate normative reason to perform that action. Of course, there may be other sources of ultimate reasons and that is something I shall come to later.

Now consider the following case. You have a day off and are considering which of three options to select. Being a rather systematic kind of person you decide to allocate scores to the enjoyment you know you will gain from each of the activities in question:

Option	Score
Staying at home	0
Walking	5
Fishing	5
Visiting the cinema	7

A positive score for some activity gives you a *pro tanto* reason—one might just say 'a reason'—for engaging in that activity. These reasons have different strengths or weights, and it is clear here that other things being equal your strongest reason is to visit the cinema. Let us assume that there are no competing reasons in this case. Then you have *overall* reason, or reason *all things considered*, to visit the cinema. The *pro tanto*–overall distinction is especially useful if there are different sources of reasons for the same action. Imagine now that walking will enable you to deliver a package you had promised to take to someone and that you attach a score of 3 to the fulfilling of that promise. Then you have reason overall to walk. But note that the normative force of reasons lies solely in the substantive reasons themselves—that is, *pro tanto* reasons. That some action has the property of being that action which you have overall reason to perform cannot itself be an additional reason to perform it.

These two notions, of *pro tanto* and overall reason understood in the way I have described, are fundamental and along with the ultimate/non-ultimate distinction provide a comprehensive basis for a theory of normative reasons and hence for ethics. Recently John Broome has cast some doubt on this view and it is to his arguments that I turn in this section. First, I shall discuss Broome's own account of reasons, which uses the notions of 'ought' and 'explanation'. Second, I shall address the claim that not all normative reasons for action can be understood as *pro tanto* reasons. Third, I shall examine his suggestion that normativity extends beyond reasons, and that failure to recognize this has been a fault in recent discussions of reasons.

I have suggested that a reason to φ is some property of φ-ing that counts in its favour. This idea of 'counting in favour' seems simple and straightforward and something we use all the time in making decisions about what to do.[39] Because it is so simple, it seems to me well suited to a fundamental role in an account of normative reasons. Broome, however, takes the concepts of 'ought' and 'explain' as primitives and gives his account of normative reasons by reference to them. Take the case of your day off. Here the property 'being enjoyable' is a reason for you to engage in one or more of the outdoor activities rather than staying at home, which you will not enjoy. And if you have the time you have reason overall to walk to the river to fish. As long as we remain clear about the fact that normative weight lies only in *pro tanto* reasons,

---

[39] It might be said that it is so simple that it is unhelpful. Parfit claims that 'counts in favour of' *means* 'is a reason for' ('Rationality and Reasons', 18). This seems unlikely. The debate between Broome and advocates of the favouring analysis is a substantive one. Gert (*Brute Rationality*, 65) describes this conception of normative reasons as 'overly simple', because (among other things) it cannot account for the intuition that we are rationally permitted to donate to public radio rather than to a development charity, even though the reason for doing the latter is significantly stronger. I have already eschewed the language of permission and requirement, as well as that of rationality. The claim that we have stronger (far stronger) reason to donate to charity says all we need, and leaves no important practical question unanswered.

we could say that the ultimate reason for you to walk to the river is that you will by so doing maximally promote your well-being. Broome claims that in any such case:

X is the reason for you to φ

is to be understood as

X is the reason why you ought to φ.

In general, in providing a philosophical account of something, one should always seek to use as few philosophical concepts as possible. Sometimes, of course, dropping or avoiding some concept might damage an account's plausibility or coherence. But that is not the case here. As Broome himself says, he is treating 'ought' as 'our ordinary, workaday, normative verb',[40] and in fact any such use of 'ought' can be translated into the language of reasons without loss. In the case of a *pro tanto* reason, that would give us:

X is the reason why you have a reason to φ.

And in the case of reason overall:

X is the reason why you have overall reason to φ.

Given this equivalence, may we just choose one or the other notion—*ought* or *reason*—to play a foundational role in our normative theory? There are two reasons why *ought* is less well suited to this role than *reason*. First, *ought* is more often used to speak of overall rather than *pro tanto* reasons. In the case of your day off, it sounds somewhat odd to say that you ought to go fishing, because doing so will be enjoyable. Second, as we saw in the previous chapter, *ought* imports the myth of bindingness, with its metaphors of necessity. In the case of your day off, there is no one or nothing binding you. There are merely your different degrees of enjoyment in the various activities available, and the reasons grounded in such enjoyment to act in one way or another.

Nor should we appeal to the concept of explanation in our basic account of reasons. First, because the favouring relation is so basic and straightforward, we need no further analysis in terms of explanation. Second, though there has admittedly been much more philosophical work on the notion of explanation, and it is a notion central to many areas of philosophy, the nature of explanation is philosophically highly

---

[40] 'Reasons', 32. References in the text in this section are to this work.

contested. Third, it may be that Broome is anyway not replacing the favouring relation with something more philosophically tractable, since it may be that explanations of the form

X is the reason why you ought to φ

trade on the favouring relation. Consider, say, the enjoyableness of visiting the cinema. That does indeed explain why you have a reason to visit the cinema. But this is surely because enjoyableness favours visiting the cinema. Finally, appeal to the notion of explanation can be misleading, and here we begin to touch on the issue of whether all reasons are *pro tanto*. On the view that all reasons are *pro tanto* ('protantism'), reasons for acting in any particular case can be seen as analogous to weights in a balance, counting in favour of acting in some way or other. If we expunge the notion of *ought* from Broome's account, I would not wish to deny that the fact that walking to the river to fish will maximally promote your well-being might plausibly be said in some explanatory context to be the reason why you have a reason to do just that. But of course there may be lots of other reasons why you have that reason, such as that your boss decided to reward you for all your hard work by giving you a day off. It would be a simple mistake to think that facts such as these are themselves reasons for you to walk to the river to fish; they are merely enabling factors in your so doing. But it would equally be a mistake to think that, because these explanations do not themselves involve 'weighing', we are entitled to think that reasons are not *pro tanto*. Broome says: 'It would be a prejudice to expect normative explanations always to take a weighing form, and to consist of *pro tanto* reasons' (46). It would be more than a prejudice—it would be a simple error. But it is an error made more likely by couching one's account of reasons in terms of explanations, as well as an error that the protantist, even if she accepts Broome's explanatory account, has no need to fall into.

Note, however, that if we restrict normative explanations to those involving the favouring relation—such as the case of enjoyment and visiting the cinema—it need not be a mere prejudice to claim that one always has reason overall to act in accordance with the balance of reasons. It could be a view arrived at after reflection on the nature of reasons. Indeed it seems arguably analytic to the notion of a normative reason understood in terms of the favouring relation that one always has reason overall to act in accordance with the balance of reasons. For in any purported counter-example, such as the idea that there may be certain rights which should never be violated so as to act in accordance with the balance of reasons, those factors themselves can be said to have a certain weight in the balance.[41]

Broome claims also that normativity extends beyond reasons for action. Consider the suggestion that if I intend some end then I should intend the means to that end. Broome says:

> Intending an end clearly stands in some sort of normative relation to intending a means. So if the only normative relation you can think of is the relation of being a reason to, you are likely to think that intending an end is a reason to intend a means. Then your view implies that, if you intend an end, you have a reason to intend a means. (30)

Broome rightly goes on to object to such a view. If you have no reason to intend the end, then it cannot be the case that you have any reason to intend the means necessary to that end. So, he suggests, we need to speak of normative requirements rather than reasons.[42] When you intend an end, in other words, you are normatively required either to intend the necessary means or to drop your end.

Though Broome is correct that there is no reason to intend means to an end merely because that end is intended, his introduction of the notion of *requirement* is objectionable for the same sorts of reasons as was his use of *ought*.[43] There is no one or nothing doing any requiring in the case of means and ends. Broome believes that restricting normative talk to reasons alone is likely to cause us to miss distinctions such as the one he so clearly identifies between narrow- and wide-scope *ought*s. But since a normative requirement is itself a kind of reason, I cannot myself see how using that term will do anything more than add to any existing confusion. The narrow-/wide-scope distinction is important, but the notion of reasons does not obscure it.

Are there normative requirements? What Broome is speaking of in the means–end case is, as he has put it to me, not a reason for action so much as 'a reason to satisfy a conditional statement': either intend the necessary means or do not have the end in question. Are there such reasons? I am inclined to think that any there are will ride on

---

[41] There is also the question whether reasons may be incommensurable, perhaps because of incommensurability of values. Some forms of incommensurability would indeed cast doubt on the idea that the balance of reasons always either comes down on one side or remains level. But the favouring relation itself does not depend on the idea of the balance of reasons.

[42] See also his 'Normative Requirements' and 'Practical Reasoning'.

[43] See Piller, 'Normative Practical Reasoning', 197–8.

the back of the epistemic reasons I have already allowed for earlier in this chapter. So it may be, for example, that there is an epistemic or quasi-epistemic reason not, say, to intend both to φ and not to φ, perhaps because that implies contradictory beliefs. Such norms may well be worth seeking to follow for extraneous reasons related to well-being; but they have no normative weight in themselves. I suspect that this is true of the means–end principle Broome discusses. There is no ultimate reason to adhere to it; and any normative reason one has to seek to act in accordance with it will be based on well-being (it could be argued, for example, that seeking to live up to the norm will make one a more effective promoter of one's own well-being). For, as Broome himself allows, such norms do not in themselves provide any reasons for us to follow them; any normative reasons we have to do so must come from elsewhere.

There is a general moral to draw from this discussion of Broome. We should not assume that we need any particular apparatus for our theory of normative reasons until we have begun to spell out exactly which reasons we have and how they function. On the theory I have outlined, all that we need are the concepts of *pro tanto* and *overall* reason, to be understood in terms of the ideas of counting in favour and weighing. Introducing at the outset further concepts such as *ought, requirement, permission*, or *supererogation* is unnecessary and potentially confusing.

4. REASONS AND VALUES

I have already proposed it as a 'bedrock principle' that any individual has an ultimate normative reason to advance their own well-being, a reason that varies in strength in proportion to the degree of such advancement. There may be other ultimate normative reasons and this is a matter I shall come to later. But any such reasons, I have suggested earlier in this chapter, must be grounded only on the promotion of well-being, either the agent's or that of others. This claim depends on the thought that, if some action is of no benefit, there can be no reason to perform it. It is well-being—and only well-being—that gives point to what we do. Note that this view—welfarism about reasons—does not imply that well-being is the only *value*. The concepts of normative reason and of value should be kept clearly distinct.[44] Reasons are properties of

---

[44] See my 'Motivation, Universality and the Good', 188–9.

actions that count, for the agent, in favour of their performance; values are properties of any object—perhaps including actions—that make them good or valuable. Value has no direct, analytic, or conceptual link with normativity. The fact that something is good or has some other evaluative property, that is to say, does not in itself imply any particular actual or hypothetical reason to act or to respond in any other way.

One obvious implication of welfarism about reasons is that we can have no reason to act in cases where no well-being is promoted, and, since the promotion of well-being includes the diminution of what is bad for individuals, a reason against acting where nothing good for anyone results and something bad results for at least one individual.[45] An example of the first kind of case would be G. E. Moore's two worlds, one beautiful, the other ugly, neither of which any individual ever sees.[46] Moore himself appears to believe that we have a reason to bring about the first world: 'Would it not be well, in any case, to do what we could to produce it rather than the other?' I am willing to allow that the beautiful world may be better than the ugly, in so far as it contains more aesthetic value.[47] But I fail to see why an agent should see any reason to bring it about except in so far as some benefit might accrue to some sentient being or other—including the agent, perhaps, if the bringing about is itself enjoyable. If there is some *cost* in well-being, either to the agent or to others, in the bringing about, then there is a reason against it. And if there is neither benefit nor cost, then there is nothing to be said in favour of or against the bringing about. An example of Jonathan Glover's nicely brings out the force of the link between reasons and well-being, though, like Moore and most other writers, Glover fails to distinguish between values and reasons:

My sympathies are strongly on the side of Sidgwick here, being quite unmoved by any of the excellences of universes eternally empty of conscious life.... If, travelling in a train through the middle of a ten-mile railway tunnel, I saw a man leaning out of the window into the darkness, I might wonder what he was doing. If it turned out to be G. E. Moore spraying the walls of the tunnel with

---

[45] For helpful discussion and criticism of welfarism in general, see e.g. Temkin, *Inequality*, ch. 9; 'Egalitarianism Defended'.

[46] *Principia Ethica*, 83–5.

[47] In fact I am inclined to take seriously views that explain our experience of aesthetic value in functional or evolutionary terms: see e.g. Miller, *The Mating Mind*, chs. 5, 8 (ch. 9 concerns morality). Well-being—especially when hedonistically construed (see Ch. 4 below)—seems less subject to destabilization by reflection on views such as Miller's. So it may be that *all* value is best understood in welfarist terms.

paint, because painted walls are better than unpainted ones, even if no one ever sees them, I should not be able to prove him irrational. But I should not accept his offer of the use of a second paint spray, except possibly out of politeness.[48]

A version of the Moorean scenario in which there is a cost to at least one individual and no gain to any other illustrates the second kind of case mentioned above (imagine, plausibly enough, that in Glover's case Moore finds spraying the walls of the tunnel rather unpleasant). Another example is that of Kant's island population who decide to disperse throughout the world. Kant claims that the last murderer in prison should be executed before they leave, so as to ensure that each receives what he deserves.[49] Even if we allow that murder deserves a lesser punishment, Kant's strict injunction seems, from the perspective of welfarism about reasons, quite literally pointless. Nothing good for anyone can come from it, only harm, so that the desert island people have not only no reason to obey, but a strong reason to disobey. I mention this case partly to show how welfarism about reasons may affect our views about what is valuable. That is, having decided that there is nothing to be said in favour of pure retribution, we may start to doubt the status of desert as a value, independently of the various doubts cast on it in the previous chapter.

I have been arguing for a conceptual and substantive distinction between the ideas of value and of reason. Recently, however, an attempt to explain the concept of value *in terms of* that of reason has received a good deal of attention. This is the so-called 'buck-passing' account of value (BPA), defended by T. M. Scanlon.[50] According to Scanlon, being good 'is not a property that itself provides a reason to respond to a thing in certain ways. Rather, to be good or valuable is to have other properties that constitute such reasons' (97).

Scanlon calls this view 'the buck-passing account' since the normative 'buck' rests not with goodness but with certain lower-order properties.

---

[48] *What Sort of People should there Be?*, 110.
[49] *The Metaphysics of Morals*, 6. 333.
[50] *What we Owe*, 95–100. References in the text in this section are to this work. Dancy points out that something very close to Scanlon's account can be found in the work of A. C. Ewing, who defines the good as that which ought to be the object of a pro-attitude ('Should we Pass the Buck?', 161–3; Ewing, *The Definition of Good*, 148–9; see also Rabinowicz and Rønnow-Rasmussen, 'The Strike of the Demon: On Fitting Pro-Attitudes and Value', 394–400). Dancy notes that both Scanlon and Ewing provide accounts of goodness in terms of reasons; but it is interesting also to observe that the idea of buck-passing can be found in Ewing's version, though he does not use that phrase (Ewing, *The Definition of Good*, 157–8).

He sets BPA in opposition to the view—attributed to Moore—that when something has the relevant lower-order properties it has the further property of being good and it is this property which gives us reasons to respond in certain ways.

I have claimed that something's being good *for* me gives me a reason to pursue that thing. Moore himself, of course, attacked the very idea of 'goodness for',[51] but there is no difficulty in describing as *Moorean* the view that goodness-for is what provides reasons rather than, say, the enjoyableness of some experience or other.

As far as my substantive claims about normative reasons are concerned, not a great deal hangs on the correctness or otherwise of BPA. But accepting it would require me to restate certain of my positions and would remove any appeal that attaches to welfarism about reasons resulting from the role I have given within it to goodness-for as reason-providing. And the general question of the relation between goodness, or value, and reasons for action is of obvious independent importance. So a brief assessment of BPA is not out of order at this point.

Scanlon's main argument for BPA I have previously called the *redundancy argument*.[52] Scanlon claims that reflection on particular cases suggests that reasons are provided not by goodness but by the lower-order properties.[53] For example, the fact that a resort is pleasant provides a complete explanation of the reason to visit it, and 'It is not clear what further work could be done by special reason-providing properties of goodness and value, and even less clear how these properties could provide reasons' (97).[54]

If goodness is redundant, however, then it is not clear why Scanlon bothers with it at all. Consider the following theory of mind. There

---

[51] *Principia Ethica*, 99–102.

[52] 'Value, Reasons and the Structure of Justification: How to Avoid Passing the Buck', 81. A second argument—the *argument from pluralism*—is persuasively criticized in Stratton-Lake and Hooker, 'Scanlon versus Moore on Goodness', sect. 3.

[53] The fact that Scanlon mentions more than one case means that he cannot be accused of generalizing from the particular. His argument is inductive.

[54] It might be thought that the second clause here contains another argument in addition to the redundancy argument stated in the first clause, according to which, perhaps, there is some conceptual difficulty in allowing goodness to provide reasons. As I read Scanlon, however, both clauses are concerned with redundancy: First, even if we allow that goodness is reason-providing, what explanatory work is there left for it to do? Second, given that there is no work for it to do, how can it make sense to speak of it as reason-providing in the first place? Support for this interpretation comes from the inductive nature of the redundancy argument (see previous note). If Scanlon's argument were a priori, then he would not need to consider particular cases.

are mental properties such as that of being a belief. Beliefs are in some way constituted by lower-order properties. These properties may vary considerably, so in that sense mental properties are multiply realizable. But such mental properties and physical properties are not the whole story. There is also the higher-order property of possessing lower-order properties that realize the mental property of being a belief.

Postulating this higher-order property, however, seems unmotivated. And the same seems true of the postulation of goodness on a buck-passing view. If goodness is *just* the higher-order property of having certain lower-order reason-giving properties, then it is unclear why one should be especially interested in retaining the concept of goodness at all.[55]

So should we, on the basis of something like Scanlon's redundancy argument, eliminate the notion of goodness, or goodness-for, from our theories? One immediate problem with the redundancy argument is that it can be run by a Moorean in favour of goodness. Imagine that I am worn out and in dire need of a holiday, so I decide to take a trip to some resort because it will be good for me. A Moorean may claim that the fact that the trip will be good for me provides a complete explanation of the reason I have for taking it, and that 'it is not clear what further work could be done by special reason-providing properties' (97) at a lower level. It is not as if its being pleasant could *add* to the reason I already have to visit the resort based on the fact that it will be good for me.

But the very nature of reasons suggests that it is a mistake to think in terms of a 'buck', whether passed or kept, in the first place. The kind of reasons we are concerned with here are grounding reasons, reasons *for* agents to act or respond in certain ways. These reasons are to be distinguished from purely explanatory reasons, reasons *why* some action or event occurs. But grounding reasons can play their part in explanations.[56] In his statement of the redundancy argument Scanlon says about natural properties that they 'provide a complete explanation of the reasons we have for reacting' (97). So we can see a justification of φ-ing as the provision of an explanation of why one has a reason for φ-ing. And that explanation can be more or less complete. In the case

---

[55] Scanlon himself has claimed that he is not offering a biconditional account. That is, there may be cases in which there are reason-giving properties that do not give rise to goodness. (See my 'Value, Reasons, and the Structure of Justification', 83.) But it is then incumbent on him to say more about why only *certain* reasons give rise to goodness, and in his explanation not to appeal to any non-buck-passing conception of goodness.

[56] See Broome, 'Reasons', esp. 31–6.

of the resort, both the Moorean account and BPA seem incomplete. A full explanation (or 'account') of my reason for visiting the resort will state not only that the visit will be good for me, but in what way. And merely saying that it will be pleasant leaves out the fact, of which we can imagine someone's being unaware, that pleasantness is a good-making property.

That this is so can be seen clearly if we return to the case of the resort. In Scanlon's view, what provides a complete explanation of my reason for visiting is the resort's being pleasant. But there are many kinds of pleasure, and someone might ask what kind of pleasure I hope to obtain there. My plan is to spend the morning in the funfair and the afternoons lazing on the beach, so my holiday will consist primarily in two kinds of pleasure: exhilaration and relaxation. But if we are inclined to buck-passing, then we may now ask what normative work can be done by the property of pleasantness, once the buck has been passed to those of being exhilarating and being relaxing. Questions arise at a certain point, as in any account of explanation, about the individuation of properties. But it may be that one can individuate yet further, characterizing the kind of exhilaration as, say, thrills, or even as the release of certain endorphins within the opioid circuit of the brain.[57] It should be clear that an attempt to base a full justification of my visit on the fact that it will release endorphins will fail unless the person to whom I am offering the justification is already aware of the relation between endorphins, thrills, exhilaration, pleasure, and the good.

What, then, is the relation of goodness to 'lower-order' properties? I understand the higher–lower relation here in terms of generality and specificity. Goodness is the highest-order or most general evaluative property. Though it may have contained various species, in fact it contains only one: well-being. This species can itself be understood as a genus, which might well have included several values—accomplishment, knowledge, friendship, and so on. As it happens, this genus also contains only one species: pleasantness. This, as a genus, does contain many species, as we saw in the case of the resort above. If some property is constitutive of goodness, in the sense that its instantiation will necessarily give rise to goodness, then I would describe that property as evaluative. Pleasantness, then, is an evaluative property, but so are the properties of the brain states that correlate with pleasantness. So the idea that natural properties are non-evaluative, and to be characterized as those properties

57   See Phillips, 'The Pleasure Seekers'.

that form the subject matter of the natural sciences in particular, is mistaken. As I said above, this is not to say that we cannot draw a distinction between goodness and pleasantness at the conceptual level. It is an open question whether pleasure is good in so far as someone who denies that it is does not show that she misunderstands the concept. But I myself am inclined to the view that, since pleasure is indeed good, the question at the level of properties may be considered closed.

I suspect that few will accept completely the account I have just given. Indeed all accounts of these matters, once spelled out, tend to become the particular property of a single individual. But one lesson here does seem clear—that it would be a mistake to think that an account can be given of these issues in independence from a first-order account of what is good and what we have reason to do.

5. WELL-BEING: MOORE AND SCANLON

As I have already mentioned, Moore is critical of the very idea of goodness-for. Interestingly, Scanlon also argues that the notion of well-being should not play a significant role in ethical theory. Any kind of welfarism, including welfarism about reasons, must therefore address their challenges.[58]

First, Moore. I should begin by admitting that the notion of 'good for' does seem puzzling. Consider a world that contains only a beautiful landscape. Leave aside any doubts you might have about whether landscapes can be good in a world without viewers and accept for the sake of argument that this landscape has aesthetic value in that world. It seems intuitively plausible to claim that the value of this world is constituted solely by the aesthetic value of the landscape. But now consider a world which contains one individual living a life that is good for them. How are we to describe the relationship between the value of this world, and the value of the life lived in it for the individual? Are we to say that the world has a value at all? How can it, if the only value it contains is 'good for' as opposed to just 'good'? And yet we surely do want to say that this world is better ('more good') than some other empty world. Well, should we say that the world is good, and is so because of the good it contains 'for' the individual? This fails to capture

---

[58] Moore, *Principia Ethica*, 98–9; Scanlon, *What we Owe*, ch. 3.

the idea that there is nothing of value in this world other than what is good for the individual.

Thoughts such as these led Moore to object to the very idea of 'good for'. Moore argued that the notion of 'my own good', which he saw as equivalent to 'what is good for me', makes no sense. When I speak of, say, pleasure as what is good for me, he claimed, I can mean only either that the pleasure I get is good, or that my getting it is good. Nothing is added by saying that the pleasure constitutes my good, or is good for me.

The distinctions I drew between different categories of value above, however, show that Moore's analysis of my claim that my own good consists in pleasure is too narrow. Indeed Moore's argument rests on the very assumption that it seeks to prove: that only the notion of 'good' is necessary to make all the evaluative judgements we might wish to make. The claim that it is good that I get pleasure is analogous to the claim that the world containing the landscape is good. It is, so to speak, 'impersonal', and leaves out of account the special feature of the value of well-being: that it is good for individuals.

One way to respond both to Moore's challenge, and to the puzzles above, is to try, when appropriate, to do without the notion of 'good' and make do with 'good for', alongside the separate and non-evaluative notion of reasons for action. Thus the world containing the single individual with a life worth living might be said not to be good per se, but merely to contain a life that is good for that individual. And this fact may give us a reason to bring about such a world, given the opportunity. This position, though coherent, strikes me as potentially misleading. Preferable would be to allow us to attribute goodness to a world, making it clear that, though it is permissible to speak of a world's being made valuable by the presence of well-being within it, the goodness of that world is nothing over and above the goodness for the individual or individuals in question.[59] And a welfarist about value and reasons will want to add that it is only 'goodness for' or well-being which can make a world good or ground reasons for action.

---

[59] See Thomson, *Goodness and Advice*, 14–15. Thomson herself rejects the notion as it is understood by consequentialists on the ground that it licenses one to harm others if the loss to them is less than the gain to oneself. I consider this problem in Sect. 5.2. Thomson goes on to reject the very idea of 'goodness per se', claiming that what is good is always good 'in some way'. If that usage allows us to speak of, say, a world's being good 'as a world', then there is no difficulty here for the consequentialist. If it does not, then the consequentialist can appeal to the fact that most people do not seem to find it hard to decide whether some world is good, or to compare worlds with one another.

Moore's ultimate aim in criticizing the idea of 'goodness for' was to attack egoism. Likewise, Scanlon has an ulterior motive in objecting to the notion of well-being—to attack so-called 'teleological' or end-based theories of ethics, in particular, utilitarianism, which in its standard form requires us to maximize well-being. But in both cases the critiques can be assessed independently.

One immediately odd aspect of Scanlon's position that 'well-being' is an otiose notion in ethics is that he himself seems to have a view on what well-being is.[60] It involves, he believes, among other things, personal relations and success in one's rational aims. But Scanlon claims that his view is not a 'theory of well-being', since a theory must explain what unifies these different elements and how they are to be compared. And, he adds, no such theory is ever likely to be available, since such matters depend so much on context.

Scanlon is, however, implicitly making a claim about what unites these values: they are all constituents of well-being, as opposed to other kinds of value, such as aesthetic or moral. Nor is it clear why Scanlon's view of well-being could not be developed so as to assist in making real-life choices between different values in one's own life.

Scanlon suggests that we often make claims about what is good in our lives without referring to the notion of well-being, and indeed that it would often be odd to do so. For example, I might say, 'I listen to Alison Krauss's music because I enjoy it', and that will be sufficient. I do not need to go on to say, 'And enjoyment adds to my well-being'. But, as emerged in the discussion of buck-passing above, this latter claim sounds peculiar only because we already *know* that enjoyment makes a person's life better for them. And in some circumstances such a claim would anyway not be odd. Consider again an argument with an ascetic, or with someone who sees no value in the experience of art or music. Further, people do use the notion of well-being in practical thinking. If someone is given the opportunity to achieve something significant which will involve considerable discomfort over several years, she may consider whether from the point of view of her own well-being the project is worth pursuing.

Scanlon argues also that the notion of well-being, if it is to be philo-sophically acceptable, ought to provide a 'sphere of compensation'—a context in which it makes sense to say, for example, that I am losing one good in my life for the sake of gain over my life as a whole. And, he

---

[60] The following draws upon my 'Well-Being'.

claims, there is no such sphere. For Scanlon, giving up present comfort for the sake of future health 'feels like a sacrifice'. For his argument to go through, he must mean an uncompensated sacrifice—or at least a sacrifice understood independently of compensation. But his example does not chime with my own experience. Donating blood feels to me like a sacrifice; but when I visit the dentist, it feels to me as if I am weighing up present pains against potential future pains. Further, we can weigh up different components of well-being against one another. Consider a case in which you are offered a highly paid job, but many miles away from your friends and family.[61]

Scanlon denies that we need an account of well-being to understand benevolence, since we have not a general duty of benevolence, but merely duties to benefit others in specific ways, such as to relieve their pain. But from the philosophical perspective it may be quite useful to use the heading of 'benevolence' in order to group such duties. And again comparisons may be important. If I have several *pro tanto* duties of benevolence, not all of which can be fulfilled, I shall have to weigh up the various benefits I can provide against one another. Here the notion of well-being will again come into play.

The notion of well-being, then, remains a candidate for a significant role in an ethical theory. In this chapter, I have several times relied upon the suggestion that each of us has a reason to promote our own well-being, a reason of a strength proportionate to the degree of promotion in question. But if this is a practical truth, or if there are other practical truths, how do we, or can we, know them? The following chapter attempts to answer this question.

---

[61] A hedonist, of course, will claim that these components should be seen as different sources of pleasure.

3

Knowledge

1. INTUITIONISM AND SELF-INTEREST

In Chapter 1 I claimed that a fundamental and primary question in philosophical ethics is what ultimate reason or reasons we have to act, if any. One aspect of that question is whether morality provides such reasons and I suggested that, since morality is relevantly analogous to law (especially the criminal law) and law provides us with no ultimate reasons to act, we should assume that there are no ultimate moral reasons. So any principle attempting to capture our ultimate reason or reasons is best stated without the use of narrowly moral terminology. In the following chapter I examined the notion of a reason for action in greater depth and claimed that the reasons of central interest to practical ethics are practical and normative as opposed to epistemic, grounding as opposed to justificatory or motivational, and external as opposed to internal, in Bernard Williams's sense of that contrast. And I suggested also that self-interest is a source of such a reason.

Anyone who claims that there is some ultimate reason for action is likely to be asked two questions. First, *How* do you know? That is, what capacity gives you this special insight? And, second, What *justification* do you have? We might call the first the *epistemic* question, and the second the *justificatory* question. Further, and possibly related, questions may concern metaphysics, semantics, or other matters. My aim in this chapter is to answer both initial questions and others as they arise.

The view I shall defend is a form of *intuitionism*. During the first half of the twentieth century, ethical intuitionism was proposed by some major thinkers, including Sidgwick, Moore, and Ross. But largely because of the metaphysical and other baggage attached to intuitionism by Moore in his influential *Principia Ethica* the view fell into decline, to be eclipsed by the 'expressivist' theories of Ayer, Stevenson, and Hare.[1] Over the last decade, however, there has been increasing interest in the position, partly because foundationalism in epistemology has regained some of its former respectability, but also because of renewed interest in Ross.[2] This chapter may be seen as part of this general movement, though the position that emerges has more in common methodologically and substantively with that of Sidgwick than of Ross.

The 'standard' argument for what one might call normative intuitionism (that is, intuitionism about normative reasons for action) makes three assumptions:[3]

(1) *Foundationalism*: Epistemically justified beliefs are either justified in themselves through some kind of direct perception or apprehension or rest essentially on inferences from beliefs justified in this way.

(2) *Normative Non-Scepticism*: Beliefs as to what we have reason to do may be justified.

(3) *The Autonomy of Normativity*: No normative conclusion about what we have reason to do may be inferred from premises which do not at least implicitly include a premiss stating what we have reason to do.[4]

From these assumptions one may conclude that any justified normative belief must be either justified in itself through some kind of direct apprehension or perception or inferred from some such belief. One natural term for such apprehension is 'intuition'.

I am inclined to accept some form of the standard argument; but explicating and defending these assumptions would be a large task.

---

[1] Audi's detailed and powerful defence of a broadly Rossian form of intuitionism, *The Good in the Right*, brings out clearly how many earlier critics of intuitionist epistemology were objecting to the position on irrelevant metaphysical or other non-epistemological grounds. See also Lucas, 'Intuitionism II', 1. Modern expressivists are more careful. See e.g. Gibbard: 'Expressivism too . . . needs intuitions. Normative knowledge rests in the end on intuitions; on this, expressivists can agree with non-naturalists. To think such a thing, however, we don't have to believe in non-natural properties; non-naturalistic concepts of natural properties will do the job' ('Knowing What to Do, Seeing What to Do', 228).

[2] See e.g. Stratton-Lake (ed.), *Ethical Intuitionism*.

[3] See Frazier, 'Intuitionism', 853; Sturgeon, 'Ethical Intuitionism and Ethical Naturalism', 191. Sturgeon's n. 18 contains further useful references; see esp. those to Sidgwick, *Methods*, 98, and Ewing, *Ethics*, 119–20.

[4] The notion of inclusion may be construed quite broadly, so as to permit arguments such as: (1) What the majority believes is the case is the case; (2) The majority believes that we have a reason to φ; therefore (3) It is the case that we have a reason to φ.

Fortunately there may be a more direct—because more non-committal and specific—route to ethical intuitionism, one that would also involve me in some discussion of the three assumptions of the standard argument but need not rely upon them. This route would start from an initially plausible example of a normative proposition believed on the basis of grasp by intuition, and self-evident in being justified by that grasp, perhaps to the extent that it is entitled to be called knowledge. This would immediately provide some support for normative non-scepticism and require no commitment either to foundationalism in general or to the autonomy of normativity.

This strategy, however, faces a rather large immediate problem. Ethics is characterized by such deep and widespread disagreement that coming up with the kind of principle required is difficult indeed.[5] But I have already claimed that self-interest provides such a principle and will now state that principle in a more precise form:

> *The Self-Interest Principle* (*SI*). Any agent at time t who has (*a*) a life that can go better or worse for her and (*b*) a range of alternative actions available to her at t which will affect whether that life does go better or worse overall for her has a reason to act at t in any way that makes her life go better overall, the strength of such a reason varying directly in proportion to the degree of promotion of her well-being.

Note that SI is not equivalent to normative egoism, the view that any agent has reason only to maximize her own well-being. It concerns only one reason that an agent may have; there may well be others and they may conflict with reasons of self-interest. My suggestion is that we have the capacity to grasp SI by intuition and that, since such grasp provides some justification for believing SI, then SI is self-evident. Note that I am not denying that properly to grasp SI requires possession of certain concepts—such as that of well-being or of a reason—which may itself involve the non-inferential grasp of normative propositions by intuition. So to that extent normative intuitionism may require a certain degree of coherence between beliefs. But what the intuitionist will insist on is that justification itself depends not (only) on coherence, but on intuitive grasp itself.

---

[5] See Williams, 'What Does Ethical Intuitionism Imply?', 183; Kappel, 'Challenges to Audi's Ethical Intuitionism', 8.

SI will be disputed by some. A particularist, for example, may claim that the fact that a certain action advances my well-being may well be a reason to perform that action, but in some other case may count against performing an action, or at least not count in favour.[6] A Williams-style internalist may object that any self-interested reason must always be grounded in the right way in an agent's motivational set. Or Scanlon may dispute the usefulness of the notion of well-being lying behind SI. Particularism I shall discuss briefly below and Williams and Scanlon have been dealt with in a previous chapter. But I shall be unable to deal with every objection to SI and that may be thought to undermine my claim to knowledge.

Widespread disagreement concerning some proposition I accept, in the absence of a plausible explanation of how those who disagree with me might be in error, undermines any claim to knowledge of that proposition. But the disagreement with SI is not widespread, especially if one seeks to finesse it in various ways to answer objectors such as Williams and Scanlon, and always appears to rest on theoretical commitments which are themselves noticeably less secure than SI itself. I am anyway concerned less with knowledge than with degree of justification. Even if my claim to know SI is too strong, it appears *significantly* better justified than most other ultimate normative principles. Of course, widespread reflective acceptance of some kind of global normative scepticism would put paid to any justification of SI, but such scepticism is not common. I shall say more about disagreement and its implications in the final section of this chapter.

Let me return to the epistemic and justificatory questions. I am construing intuitionism primarily as a position in epistemology. Of course it brings with it a certain metaphysics and that raises the question whether that metaphysics is sufficiently unattractive seriously to count against the epistemology. On my construal of intuitionism nothing more is required for the position from the metaphysical point of view than the claim that there are reason-giving properties, that is, that certain properties have the normative property of giving us reasons. These normative properties need not be seen as, say, entities existing in some special realm, like Platonic forms. Allowing metaphysical space for them seems to me modest to the point that refusing to entertain them is itself a kind of extravagance, one of excessive attachment to a particular view of the world, and I have provided some defence of this

---

[6] See Dancy, *Ethics without Principles*, 7.

modest form of realism in the previous chapter. But the epistemic and the justificatory questions remain. What is this capacity for intuition, and how does it supply knowledge?

The best place to begin is with introspection, with how one's own mind appears to one to be working. When I reflect upon my own grasp and acceptance of SI, it strikes me as an implausible candidate for knowledge by experience. Once I understand SI, I may see that circumstances are such that SI recommends a particular course of action. But my grasp of the truth of SI itself is intellectual, based on an understanding of the concepts it involves and their practical significance. That grasp seems direct, in that it does not rest on, for example, any inference or the testimony of another. It may be that belief in SI can be justified also in these less direct ways,[7] though I have to confess that given SI's capture of such a basic aspect of practical reason I find it hard to see from what it might plausibly be inferred, and how an agent's belief in it could rest on testimony rather than on a form of self-understanding which would make testimony unnecessary.

This makes SI a priori rather than a posteriori.[8] It may well be that one could not even understand a proposition such as SI, let alone know it to be true, without having *had* experiences characteristic of those whose lives can go better or worse for them. But a conception of the a priori that restricted it to only those propositions that do not involve concepts not derived from experience would be far too strict. Rather we should allow that a proposition is a priori if, once it is understood, no appeal to experience is required for it to be justifiedly believed.[9]

Normative intuition, then, is a capacity that enables us to grasp the truth of certain a priori propositions as to ultimate reasons for action. Are these propositions necessary? It is debatable whether a priori propositions are necessary.[10] And not a great deal hangs on whether SI is best construed as necessarily true. But because the matter is of some independent interest let me point out that, since claims about normative reasons such as SI are universalizable, they are in fact necessary because true in all possible worlds. According to the thesis of

---

[7] See Ewing, *The Definition of Good*, 91–2, discussed by Audi, 'Prospects for a Value-Based Intuitionism', 116–18.

[8] Greco, 'Introduction: What is Epistemology?', 20.

[9] BonJour, *In Defense of Pure Reason*, 9; Boghossian and Peacocke, 'Introduction', 2; Peacocke, *Realm of Reason*, 200, 206.

[10] Boghossian and Peacocke, 'Introduction', 3–4.

universalizability as applied to the concept of 'ought', as R. M. Hare puts it, 'it is a misuse of the word "ought" to say "You ought, but I can conceive of another situation, identical in all its properties to this one, except that the corresponding person ought not" '.[11] The thesis seems to carry directly across to the notion of a normative reason. In itself, the thesis of universalizability is weak.[12] It becomes stronger as the notion of 'identical in all its properties' is replaced with 'identical in all its relevant properties', according to the arguments for the particular notion of relevance in question. In the case of SI, the relevant properties underlying the application of SI to an agent are (*a*) that agent's having a life which can go better or worse for her, and (*b*) that agent's having certain options open to her which vary in their consequences for her well-being overall. Reflection across worlds strongly suggests that whenever those properties are instantiated in any possible world then SI is true of the agent in question. Hence in that respect it is a necessary truth.

Claims such as this about normative principles have in recent decades been criticized by particularists, especially Jonathan Dancy.[13] A particularist might object to SI and the claims about necessity above on the ground that reasons and their force vary across cases. In his more recent work Dancy allows that there may be cases of what he calls 'invariance'—cases of reasons that in fact always do function in the same way across different cases.[14] That is going to be enough for most defenders of SI, though of course it would limit the claims of necessity that might be made, since Dancy wants to suggest that invariance is in a sense contingent. But it has to be said that the defender of SI who advocates necessity does then have an explanation of invariance which Dancy lacks. For him, it must remain something of a mystery why SI, or any other invariant principle, applies across all cases.

Particularist arguments usually proceed by example, and in this Dancy's strategy has not changed: 'that there will be nobody much else

---

[11] Hare, *Moral Thinking*, 10.

[12] Locke, 'The Trivializability of Universalizability'.

[13] See esp. *Moral Reasons*; *Ethics without Principles*. For detailed criticism of Dancy's position, see my 'Motivation, Universality and the Good'; 'Particularizing Particularism'; 'Ethics without Reasons?' For positions related to Dancy's, see Temkin, 'Intransitivity and the Mere Addition Paradox', 'Rethinking the Good, Moral Ideals and the Nature of Practical Reasoning', and 'Rethinking the Good, Moral Ideals and the Nature of Practical Reasoning', unpub. TS; Kagan, 'The Additive Fallacy'; Kamm, *Morality, Mortality*, ii. 51 and *passim* (the 'Principle of Contextual Interaction').

[14] See e.g. *Ethics without Principles*, 77–8.

around is sometimes a good reason for going there, and sometimes a very good reason for staying away. That one of the candidates wants the job very much indeed is sometimes a reason for giving it to her and sometimes a reason for doing the opposite.'[15]

The problem with these and other alleged examples is that they rely on non-ultimate or derivative reasons, which anyone will admit might vary from case to case. Consider Dancy's examples here. On Monday I think I shall enjoy some solitude; so the fact that there will be nobody else around on the hills on that day is a good reason for going there. But on Tuesday I have had enough and want some company. So the fact that there is nobody around counts against heading for the hills. But on both days what I am after is enjoyment, something (perhaps) I always have ultimate reason to pursue for myself. A similar story can be told about the second case. Imagine a scenario similar to that of Williams's famous story of George.[16] In the morning Georgina is interviewed for the post of primary school teacher. She wants the job very much. Her wanting the job is a reason to give it to her. In the afternoon Georgina is interviewed for the position of chief researcher in a chemical weapons plant where weapons are being developed for purposes of genocide. She wants the job very much and in this case her wanting it is a reason not to give it to her. What might be the higher-order principle here? One obvious possibility is the utilitarian principle that we should do what produces the most good; but there are many others.

Particularists have to be able not only to provide good examples of ultimate reasons that vary across cases, but—unless they are to allow invariance—to explain how any alleged ultimate reason could so vary. I cannot myself think of a case in which SI would not be true. Likewise I cannot imagine a case in which an action's causing suffering to a non-rational being would not count against that action. So the ball seems to me to remain very much in the particularist's court.

Normative intuition, then, is a capacity that enables rational beings to understand and to believe certain a priori, necessary, and universal principles asserting normative reasons for action.[17] Another common objection to the claim that human beings have such a capacity is that it assumes an implausible degree of infallibility. But this is a mistake.

---

[15] Ibid. 74.   [16] Williams, 'A Critique of Utilitarianism', 97–8.
[17] This may be only one of its roles. I do not at this stage wish to rule out the possibility of intuitive singular normative judgements about particular cases.

Consider Sidgwick: 'By cognition I always mean what some would rather call "apparent cognition"—that is, I do not mean to affirm the *validity* of the cognition, but only its existence as a psychical fact, and its claim to be valid.'[18] Intuition is not some mysterious sixth sense giving us infallible access to necessary truths. It is merely a capacity to accept a priori propositions on the basis of intellectual grasp of those very propositions, and that capacity is undoubtedly highly fallible, especially as far as practical reasons are concerned.[19]

I have spoken of intuition as a doxastic capacity and suggested that a priori normative knowledge is available through intuition. When that capacity is exercised, we might call it *intuiting*. George Bealer, however, argues that an intuition—an intuiting—is not a belief (or a believing), but an intellectual 'seeming':

> there are many mathematical theorems that I believe (because I have seen the proofs) but that do not *seem* to me to be true and that do not *seem* to me to be false; I do not have intuitions about them either way. Conversely, I have an intuition—it still *seems* to me—that the naive truth schema holds; this is so despite the fact that I do not believe that it holds (because I know of the Liar paradox).[20]

Bealer goes on to claim that intuition should be seen as a self-standing propositional attitude. But his argument is too swift. The point about mathematical theorems is by the by, since no one who thinks that intuition is a form of belief is likely to claim that all beliefs are intuitive. Bealer's alleged intuition (or intuiting) that 'p' is true if and only if p does, however, require explanation. It would not be plausible to claim that Bealer has two conflicting beliefs, one that the naive truth schema is correct and the other that it is incorrect. He clearly believes it is incorrect. Rather I suggest that, though this is indeed a case of intellectual seeming, it is not a case of intuition.

Consider the analogy with perception. In a standard case I see a rabbit in front of me, and this seeing both leads me to believe that there is a rabbit in front of me and justifies that belief. Perception here is the capacity that is exercised in my perceiving—that is, in my seeing. Now

---

[18] *Methods*, 34 n. 2; see also 2, 211. I take it that Sidgwick is not intending any real distinction here between validity and truth. See also Moore, *Principia*, pp. x, 75; Ewing, *Fundamental Questions of Philosophy*, 49; 'Reason and Intuition', 52; Audi, 'Intuitionism, Pluralism, and the Foundations of Ethics', 107–8; BonJour, *In Defense of Pure Reason*, 16, 110.

[19] Bealer, 'The A Priori', 245, 247.   [20] Ibid. 247.

take the proposition that $x = x$, as a standard object of intuition. When I reflect upon that proposition, I understand what it means and also grasp its truth. (We need the distinction here between understanding a proposition and grasping its truth; it may be that one can understand an a priori proposition perfectly well and yet fail to grasp its truth.) Unlike perhaps in the case of perception, there is no gap between the exercise of the capacity and a resulting belief. Grasping the truth that $x = x$ is partly to acquire the belief that this identity statement is true. In other words the exercise of intuition cannot consist merely in an intellectual 'seeming'. It consists partly in the acquisition of a belief in the truth of some proposition, a belief which may itself be justified by the understanding of the proposition and the grasp of a truth. Note that the two cases I have discussed are standard ones. Illusion and error are possible in both perception and intuition, and I shall say more about this shortly.

So intuition is a doxastic capacity. But still isn't there something just *weird* about the very idea of intuition? In his famous 'argument from queerness' Mackie rightly notes that asserting the existence of what he calls 'objective values', which would almost certainly include the reason-giving properties involved in SI, brings with it a certain epistemology; and it is an epistemology which he believes adds to the case against objective values: 'if we were aware of them, it would have to be by some special faculty of moral perception or intuition, utterly different from our ordinary ways of knowing everything else... These points were recognized... by the intuitionists in their talk about a "faculty of moral intuition".'[21]

In response the intuitionist may begin by confronting Mackie with Ross's claim that 'The objection that many feel to Intuitionism can hardly be an objection to the admission of intuition; for without that no theory can get going.'[22] By 'intuition' here, Ross means some non-inferential normative or moral proposition or a belief in such a proposition. If Mackie wishes to offer a first-order moral view (as the later chapters of his book suggest that he does), then he must either accept that there are some such normative propositions, allow for an infinite regress of inferential justification, or explain how coherence relations between a set of mutually entailing propositions can stop such a regress. The final task has not been successfully accomplished by anyone, and is not attempted by Mackie himself.

---

[21] Mackie, *Ethics*, 38. [22] *Foundations of Ethics*, 82.

So I suspect that he would have been inclined towards the second option, which is essentially a form of nihilism few would wish to accept.

2. ACQUISITION AND APPLICATION: PARTICULAR CASES

SI is a universal principle. In this section I want briefly to look both at the idea that knowledge of the universal arises from knowledge of particular cases and at how we should understand the application of the universal principle in particular cases.

Ross asks how it is that moral principles come to be understood, and answers using another mathematical analogy:

We find by experience that this couple of matches and that couple make four matches, that this couple of balls on a wire and that couple make four balls: and by reflection on these and similar discoveries we come to see that it is of the nature of two and two to make four. In a precisely similar way, we see the *prima facie* rightness of an act which would be the fulfilment of a promise, and when we have reached sufficient maturity to think in general terms, we apprehend *prima facie* rightness to belong to the nature of any fulfilment of promise. What comes first in time is the apprehension of the self-evident *prima facie* rightness of an individual act of a particular type.[23]

Ross later calls this process 'intuitive induction', making it clear how it differs from empirical induction: 'the general principle was later recognized . . . as being implied in the judgements already passed on particular acts'.[24] It is important to note that Ross is here making a point about the order of discovery, not the order of justification.[25] The judgements about the particular cases pre-date the universal judgement, but that universal judgement is itself self-evident and need not be seen to gain support from the judgements about particular cases.

The particular story Ross tells about promising does not carry across straightforwardly to SI. On that account, agents first see that a particular

---

[23] *The Right and the Good*, 32–3.

[24] *Foundations of Ethics*, 170. The phrase occurs in Broad, *Five Types of Ethical Theory*, 214. He attributes it to W. E. Johnson. For discussion of Ross, see Audi, 'Prospects for a Value-Based Intuitionism', 49; also Stratton-Lake, 'Introduction' to Stratton-Lake (ed.), *Ethical Intuitionism*, 6 n. 18.

[25] Frazier, 'Intuitionism', 855; Gaut, 'Justifying Moral Pluralism', 141 n. 12.

action will be in their self-interest, then another, and so on; and later recognize that they always have a reason to advance their own self-interest. But this assumes an implausibly advanced grasp of the very concept of self-interest. A three-stage process is more likely. At first the child avoids threats to her well-being on the ground that, for example, they will hurt. Then, as she matures and her decisions become more global in scope, we may often explain those decisions as the result of an inarticulate or background grasp of SI. For example, she may choose a particular school on the ground that she will know more children there from the beginning, and would probably assent if asked whether she is aware that she will be happier overall if there are more children she knows. At this stage she might perhaps be said to possess the concept of self-interest. Finally, when old enough to understand SI, she may assent to it. And it may well be that it is only in this assenting that the concept of self-interest first becomes explicitly apparent to her.

One of the reasons I chose SI as my candidate a priori normative principle is that the concept of self-interest does seem implicated in various ways in our decisions and actions from an early age. And, as I have just shown, some kind of intuitive inductive account of how we come to understand that principle is quite plausible. But I see no reason why there might not be cases without any such induction, in which an agent comes to see the truth of a normative principle which has never been implicit in any of her previous particular judgements.

The question of how the universal SI principle operates in particular cases has been largely answered by the discussion of its acquisition. But an issue still remains of the role of the principle in the particular decisions of those who are explicitly aware of it. One important point to note here—which I shall say more about in the final chapter—is that principles such as SI may recommend a decision procedure for particular cases which requires no direct reference to or application of those very principles. But there may well be cases in which someone is, not unreasonably, seeking either to apply an individual a priori normative principle, or to judge what to do in the light of two principles which state reasons that must be weighed against one another in particular cases.

Ross does not describe the capacity to make such particular judgements as a matter of intuition, preferring to speak of 'our sense of our particular duty in particular circumstances' and quoting Aristotle's dictum that 'the judgement lies in perception'.[26] I can see a case for this. In the exercise of intuition an individual understands some a priori proposition and grasps its truth. It might be said, then, that the application of any universal a priori principle or set of principles in a particular case can have nothing to do with intuition. For the belief arrived at—'that I should φ', say—could not be said to be self-evident, in the sense that it could be accepted purely on the basis of understanding that proposition itself. Rather, if we are considering a case of the application of SI, what is required is something like perception that *this* course of action rather than that is the one that will be best for me.

Nevertheless, it does seem to me that the capacity to make such particular decisions involves a capacity for judgement which is exercised also in the case of intuition. The capacity, when exercised in the normative sphere, is a matter of apprehending the normative significance of certain properties of certain actions. Whether those actions are classes or kinds, as in the case of intuition, or particular actions, the capacity is the same. It is possible that someone might have better or worse judgement at the universal level than in particular cases. For example, she may be prone to becoming flustered or panicky in everyday decision-making, though particularly insightful during periods of calm and abstract reflection. But, though it is easier for her to use a capacity for normative judgement in one kind of situation than another, the capacity exercised in each is the same. Because I prefer to restrict the objects of intuition to a priori normative principles, however, I shall like Ross speak of decisions in particular cases as the concern of *judgement* rather than intuition, and the role of judgement and its deliverances when working correctly will be discussed further in Chapter 5 below.

3. THE MATHEMATICAL ANALOGY

To return to Mackie. He holds an 'error theory' of ethics, so might well admit that it *seems* to us as if we have normative intuition. But, he will claim, that capacity and the metaphysics it brings with it are just too 'queer' for us to accept either. My strategy earlier in

---

[26] *The Right and the Good*, 41–2; Aristotle, *Nicomachean Ethics* 2. 9, 1109^{b}23; 4. 5, 1126^{b}4. For discussion, see Audi, 'Intuitionism, Pluralism, and the Foundations of Ethics', 130 n. 9.

this and the previous chapter has been to claim that intuitionism is metaphysically and epistemologically more modest than Mackie seems to think. But it is also helpful for the normative intuitionist, as Mackie recognized,[27] if she can make plausible the notion that we have an intuitive grasp of the truth of a priori propositions of other kinds, so that if one is to take seriously the kinds of objection Mackie develops then the epistemological upshot may be more significant than one might initially have thought. So it is unsurprising to find that normative or ethical intuitionists in the rationalist tradition have often sought to draw illuminating analogies between normative intuition and the quasi-perceptual, intellectual understanding found in our grasp of certain axioms in mathematics. To use Aristotle's example, as one sees for oneself that a triangle is the final geometrical object in an analysis (since there is none with fewer sides), so one sees that one has an ultimate reason to φ.[28] Consider this from Sidgwick: 'the propositions, "I ought not to prefer a present lesser good to a future greater good," and "I ought not to prefer my own lesser good to the greater good of another," do present themselves as self-evident; as much (*e.g.*) as the mathematical axiom that "if equals be added to equals the wholes are equal" '.[29] Or what Ross says of the proposition that an act fulfilling a promise is prima facie right: 'when we have reached sufficient mental maturity and have given sufficient attention to the proposition it is evident without any need of proof, or of evidence beyond itself. It is self-evident just as a mathematical axiom, or the validity of a form of inference, is evident.'[30]

When I consider my own grasp of the truth of SI, it does seem strongly analogous to the grasp I have of the truth of Sidgwick's additive axiom. Both are a priori, necessary, and universal, and they are self-evident in that my knowledge of them is justified sufficiently by my understanding. It has to be admitted that not everyone's view of the phenomenology is the same. John Skorupski, for example, while allowing that we may have normative knowledge, claims that this knowledge rests not on 'receptive awareness', but only on

the non-receptive cognitive capacity of rationality, a capacity which involves spontaneity and regulation by the universality of reasons, not receptivity. And here 'receptivity' covers *any* capacity of receptive awareness—be it the uncontroversial ones based in the human senses, the more controversial ones

[27] *Ethics*, 39.   [28] *Nicomachean Ethics* 6. 8, 1142ª23–30.
[29] *Methods*, 383; see also 229, 338, 507.
[30] *The Right and the Good*, 29. See also Gaut, 'Justifying Moral Pluralism', 140.

involved in self-awareness of one's own state of mind, or some other ones such as Platonic intuition or Martian telepathy or whatever.[31]

My inclination is to think that Skorupski—like many others who claim not to have experienced the operation within themselves of a capacity for 'receptive' intuition—has been directed into a particular interpretation of his own experience by unjustified worries about the metaphysical and epistemological implications of intuitionism. In the previous section I suggested that these implications may be more modest than has often been thought. Are they still immodest? At this point we reach bedrock and I can only report that in my judgement these implications do not count against taking the phenomenology at face value. Nevertheless, the mathematical analogy in particular has been found problematic in various ways, so let me now provide some defence.

The most common objection I have already mentioned—that it is difficult to find the self-evident normative propositions required to make the analogy worth drawing. Here I would appeal to the self-evidence of SI, and the fact that it is so widely accepted, though I shall suggest below that there are fewer such propositions than intuitionists have traditionally tended to claim.

A second objection is made by Audi against Ross: 'it takes more reflection and maturity to see the truth of the proposition that promises generate prima facie duties than to see the validity of a logical principle like the syllogistic "If all As are Bs and all Bs are Cs, then all As are Cs" '.[32]

Even if this claim were correct, it is not clear that it is pointing to a disanalogy between mathematics and ethics of great significance in the present context. But it strikes me anyway as a dubious empirical hypothesis. Some people seem able to grasp certain basic normative truths before they are able to understand even quite simple mathematical or logical principles. Indeed some people—who certainly seem to understand certain reasons they have to act—are never able to cope with the level of abstraction required to articulate a mathematical principle. In general it does seem correct that understanding and grasping normative and mathematical truths comes later than understanding particular examples or instantiations of those truths. For example, a child may know that if she puts two bricks alongside two other bricks, she will

---

[31] 'Irrealist Cognitivism', 456.
[32] Audi, 'Intuitionism, Pluralism, and the Foundations of Ethics', 114. See Aristotle, *Nicomachean Ethics* 6. 8, 1142ᵃ11–20.

have four bricks, without any understanding of principles of calculation. Likewise she may see that she has stronger reason given her preferences to choose the chocolate ice-cream over the pistachio. That is, she can see that she has reason to do something the grounding of which is captured in SI, well before she could understand or articulate SI itself.

A third and related point has to do with conditions for understanding. Brentano says, of the allegedly a priori claim that knowledge is good:

'Knowledge is good' is not like the law of contradiction; the concepts, just by themselves, do not enable us to see that it is a true proposition. In this way it differs from the principles of mathematics; one *can* see, from the concepts alone, that two plus one is equal to three, for 'two plus one' is the analytic definition of 'three' . . . another experience is needed. The concept of knowledge must give rise to an act of love, and this love, just because it does arise in this way, is experienced as being correct. For a purely intellectual being, the thought that 'two plus one is not equal to three' would be sufficient to give rise to its apodictic rejection; but (supposing, for the moment, that the concept of the good is given *a priori*) the thought that 'Knowledge is not good' would not give rise to apodictic rejection.[33]

If one of Brentano's claims here is that mathematical propositions are analytic, that may of course be doubted; nevertheless, he may well seem to be pointing to a significant disanalogy between mathematical and normative truths. The former can be grasped by a purely intellectual being, solely on the basis of understanding the concepts involved; but could a purely intellectual being grasp the truth of SI? I do not see why not, if the being has some grip on the notions of 'good for' and of a normative reason for action. The claim that understanding these notions itself requires certain non-intellectual capacities, such as the capacity for well-being itself or for feeling *concern* for one's own well-being, is, however, not implausible. If it is correct, then only those beings who meet those conditions would be able to grasp the truth of SI. Again, however, this particular disanalogy between mathematics and normativity is not in the present context especially significant. Both sets of propositions would remain a priori, and both would be available to intelligent human beings.

A fourth worry about the mathematical analogy arises out of a general concern with the mathematical epistemology implied by intuitionism. Take the alleged knowledge by intuition that $7 + 5 = 12$. This knowledge, like all knowledge, has an object. But what are the objects of

---

[33] *The Origin of our Knowledge of Right and Wrong*, 112–13.

mathematical knowledge? A natural view is that they are of a rather special kind: abstract, non-physical and so beyond space and time, independent of our minds. This view is Platonism, and it has both a good and a bad aspect. The good aspect is that it captures the most immediately plausible conception we have of mathematical objects: that there *are* a number 7, a number 5, and a fact that when combined their product is another number, 12. The bad aspect is what has become known as 'Benacerraf's problem'.[34] If the Platonic mathematical realm is beyond space and time and independent of our minds, then it is quite unclear how there could be any explanation of exactly *how* it is that we gain epistemic access to it. In particular, as Hartry Field puts the challenge, the difficulty is to account for the *reliability* of our mathematical knowledge, on the assumption that we cannot say it is a mere coincidence that we get things right in mathematics when we do.[35] It is hard to exaggerate the philosophical seriousness of this problem for any account of a priori knowledge,[36] so let me sketch a few initial lines of response on behalf of normative intuitionism.

An immediate rejoinder would be to claim that this ongoing debate in the philosophy of mathematics is in a sense a meta-debate about mathematical knowledge, since few in the debate are questioning the authoritative status or even correctness of mathematical judgements in general. So if we allow that 'intuition' refers to the capacity for acquiring mathematical knowledge *whatever it turns out to be*, then we can allow the debate to continue and return to our first-order ethical concerns.

This response, however, seems less than satisfactory, since many of those in the debate—fictionalists such as Field, for example, or those such as Boghossian or Peacocke who offer accounts of a priori knowledge grounded in meaning—are explicitly seeking to avoid having to appeal to a rationalist conception of intuition.[37] So it might be wiser for the normative intuitionist who wishes to appeal to the mathematical analogy to point out, first, that the debate in philosophy of mathematics is very much ongoing, and, second, that the intuitionist position is still a major player within that debate.[38]

---

[34] Benacerraf, 'Mathematical Truth'.

[35] Field, *Realism, Mathematics and Modality*, 25–6.

[36] Boghossian, 'Inference and Insight', 635.

[37] Field, *Realism, Mathematics and Modality*; 'Recent Debates about the A Priori'; Boghossian, 'Knowledge of Logic'; Peacocke, 'Explaining the A Priori: The Programme of Moderate Rationalism'; *Realm of Reason*.

[38] See BonJour, *In Defense of Pure Reason*; Maddy, *Realism in Mathematics*.

Nevertheless, it may be asked, is there not something mysterious about this capacity? How is it supposed to work? Here the intuitionist may point out that the fact that we have no consensus on how our capacity for a priori knowledge operates is not a good reason for assuming that there is no such capacity.[39] We would not think that an argument of unavailability of explanation could plausibly be used to demonstrate the unreality of consciousness, or indeed perception, on the nature of both of which there is no agreement.

The above are hedging responses.[40] Let me finally outline one possible positive line of reply a defender of normative intuitionism might offer to a version of the Benacerraf challenge directed against alleged normative knowledge. The first component of this response involves the intuitionist distancing herself once again from heavily Platonist metaphysics. According to normative intuitionism, we have knowledge of certain normative *propositions*. It is an interesting philosophical question what kind of object, if any, a proposition is or is not, but that question does seem clearly to address a meta-issue as far as normative intuitionism is concerned. Second, the intuitionist can point out that there is some kind of causal story to be told about why and how human beings have acquired the capacity to grasp such propositions, and why and how that capacity functions not entirely unreliably. Consider our capacity for grasping mathematical truths.[41] Imagine a being stalked by three tigers which enter the cave where she lives. If that being can see that only two of the tigers have emerged and disappeared, it is in that respect more likely to survive than an innumerate creature. And once a general capacity for grasping basic a priori truths has developed, it would seem that we might then be on the 'escalator of reason',[42] able by pure reflection to enlarge our understanding. Field objects to this line of argument in the case of mathematics that the amount of

[39] BonJour, 'Replies', 674.

[40] Also worth noting is the response to Benacerraf that causal theories of knowledge and reference are irrelevant to mathematics, since they concern a posteriori knowledge of contingent truths. See Maddy, *Realism*, 36–41, with references to Wright, *Frege's Conception of Numbers as Objects*, sect. 11; Hale, *Abstract Objects*, 86–90.

[41] Cf. Maddy's psychological and neurological explanation of how we acquire knowledge of sets in Maddy, *Realism*, ch. 2. If Maddy's general line is congenial to naturalizing epistemologists, it may be that the same would be true of an account such as that outlined here, if adequately developed. That is, if our understanding of the natural is generous enough, and our understanding of the non-natural parsimonious enough, certain disputes may vanish.

[42] Singer, *How are we to Live?*, 225.

mathematics so explained would be quite small, and it is not plausible to claim that all of mathematical knowledge can rest on such meagre foundations.[43] But what the intuitionist in mathematics or ethics should claim is not that further a priori knowledge can be *inferred* from that supplied by evolutionary pressure. Rather the idea is that evolutionary pressure provides a general capacity which can then be put to use with ever greater sophistication through reflection and cultural development. In the case of normative reasons, we can sometimes be quite certain that the exercise of our capacity to grasp a priori normative truths has indeed enabled us to grasp one: SI is an example. But how common are such cases? In the final section, let me address the issue of ethical disagreement.

4. CERTAINTY, DISAGREEMENT, AND DOGMATISM

My claim has been that SI provides a good example of a normative principle stating an ultimate reason for action, of which we can claim to have intuitive knowledge in the sense of a true belief justified by intuition—an intellectual understanding and grasp of the truth of SI on the basis of reflection upon the proposition itself. Justification here consists first, then, in an appeal to the initial strong credibility of SI.

This justification, however, is not indefeasible. That is to say, if I intuitively accept some normative principle, I may be justified in accepting this principle and if it is true then I may know it. But it may not be true. So such principles are not entirely certain, and I cannot be entirely certain about them. And now the question arises what might be—to quote Sidgwick—the 'conditions, the complete fulfilment of which would establish a significant proposition, apparently self-evident, in the highest degree of certainty attainable'.[44] Sidgwick himself suggests four conditions.[45]

1. *Clarity*. 'The terms of the proposition must be clear and precise.'[46] That is, they must be clear to and clearly understood by the subject.

43 *Realism, Mathematics and Modality*, 29.
44 Sidgwick, *Methods*, 338. The arguments here have developed out of my 'Sidgwick and the Boundaries of Intuitionism'.
45 Sidgwick, *Methods*, 338–42. Cf. Audi, *Good in the Right*, 33–6.
46 Sidgwick refers to Bacon's requirement that we avoid 'notiones vagae, nec bene terminatae', *Novum Organum*, 2. 19.

We might add that, since the normative principles and other a priori philosophical propositions found self-evident by a subject are often plural, the relevant relationships among these propositions should also be clear to the subject. This is an issue that goes beyond the mere establishment of consistency (condition 3 below), since less formal entailments and indeed the overall coherence—in a broad sense—of the believer's world-view are relevant. For example, if I hold a certain view of personal identity and also accept SI, I should strive to be clear about the relation between these views. If I believe, for instance, that what matters is not in fact identity but the degree to which some future self is related to my present self, and I also think that these relations weaken over time, this may give me a reason to prioritize the interests of nearer 'selves' in decision-making.[47] Indeed in general in the case of normative principles such as SI, the subject should try to be as clear as possible about the practical implications of that proposition.[48]

2. *Reflection.* 'The self-evidence of the proposition must be ascertained by careful reflection.'[49] This condition is of course related to the first, since clarity can be increased only by reflection. An intuition, if it is to be well justified, should be neither a gut reaction nor an instinct nor something accepted purely on the basis of external authority, but a belief which to 'careful observation' presents itself as a dictate of reason. Reflection itself, then, should be such as to be as far as possible guided by reason, and in particular as impartial as possible (I shall say more below about what impartiality requires). Note that, in so far as it is based on intuition, it must not be a conclusion based on rational argument, whether deductive, inductive, or of any other kind, since self-evident beliefs, by definition, stand on their own, providing if required the ultimate premises for such arguments. I take it that much of the reflection in question will concern the origin of the intuition: Is it a product of my upbringing? Am I adopting it merely on the basis of societal or other authority? Does it rest on my subjective likes and dislikes? Much of course also will concern the content of the proposition itself. But it might concern as well the implications of the proposition and whether they can be accepted (as, for example, in Sidgwick's own dialectical testing against common-sense morality of

---

[47] Parfit, *Reasons and Persons*, 313–14.   [48] See e.g. *Methods*, 215.
[49] See Audi, 'Good in the Right', Ch. 2. By 'self-evidence', Sidgwick means 'genuine self-evidence', and by that he means 'certainty', or perhaps rather 'the entitlement of the believer to claim certainty for the proposition'.

apparently self-evident principles). Ultimately I am seeking to vindicate my beliefs, to reassure myself that I believe that *p* because it is indeed the case that *p*.[50] In general we can see here Sidgwick's attempt to avoid Bentham's and Mill's criticism of intuitions as mere prejudices.[51]

3. *Consistency.* 'The propositions accepted as self-evident must be mutually consistent.'[52] It may be that someone can accept two inconsistent propositions if they have failed to notice the inconsistency. But Sidgwick's condition requires me to check any belief I have in a normative principle against other relevant beliefs of mine. Again this condition is related to the first two. Part of my gaining a clear understanding of any normative principle with initial credibility requires reflecting upon its relation to other beliefs I hold, and internal inconsistency is of such significance that it rules out any claim to certainty of either of two inconsistent beliefs that remain stable after reflection. It is unclear whether Sidgwick himself is speaking only of logical or also of practical consistency. The first would rule out as self-evident, for example, the two logically contradictory propositions 'One should always be spontaneous' and 'One should not always be spontaneous', if held in that form by a single person. Practical inconsistency would rule out not only such sets of propositions, but also, for instance, 'One should always be kind' and 'One should always be just', if a case can be imagined in which the demands of justice conflict with those of kindness. The conclusion of the *Methods*, in which Sidgwick discusses attempts to make egoism and utilitarianism practically consistent, suggests he had the practicality test in mind. Sometimes, as I shall suggest in Chapter 5 below, the result of reflection upon practical inconsistencies of this kind will—or rather should—result in a restatement of the normative principle in question as *pro tanto*. In this case, for example, it may be claimed that kindness is one property that counts in favour of an action and justice another. If there is a practical conflict, these different considerations will require weighing against one another to determine what one has reason overall to do.

4. *Consensus.* 'Since it is implied in the very notion of Truth that it is essentially the same for all minds, the denial by another of a proposition that I have affirmed has a tendency to impair my confidence

---

[50] See Wiggins, *Needs, Values, Truth*, 152–5, 199–202, 346–9.
[51] See Schneewind, *Sidgwick's Ethics and Victorian Moral Philosophy*, 134, 179.
[52] Broad, *Five Types*, 159; Frankena, 'Sidgwick and the History of Ethical Dualism', 457–8.

in its validity.' Sidgwick does not go as far with Aristotle as to say that what seems so to all is so.[53] Indeed he claims that if I accept some proposition as true on the sole ground of its being otherwise universally accepted, this proposition has neither 'self-evidence nor demonstrative evidence for the mind that so accepts it'. But it is a mark of truth that it commands convergence,[54] and that there is a tendency at least among believers to such convergence. So—on the assumption that there is no reason for postulating universal error—the fact that everyone believes *p* does seem *some* evidence for the truth of *p*. Sidgwick allows that beliefs on scientific matters, even those of experts, rest on consensus, and goes on to say that consensus is 'an indispensable negative condition of the certainty of our beliefs'. If others disagree (rationally) with a belief of mine, it can no longer be said to be certain, even if it meets the other tests for self-evidence. This is so, however, only 'if I have no more reason to suspect error in the other mind than in my own'.

The consensus condition strikes me as by some margin the most problematic for normative intuitionism, because of the prevalence of serious disagreement between reflective participants in first-order debate.[55] I may non-inferentially and firmly accept normative proposition *n*. I have carefully reflected upon it, and now fully understand it, its implications, and its relations to my other beliefs, and there is no internal inconsistency. Unfortunately, you are equally convinced of not-*n*. Once I am aware of this, and I have no good reason to suspect your understanding of not-*n* to be less clear or precise than mine of *n*, your reflection to have been less careful or impartial than mine, or your beliefs overall to be internally inconsistent, Sidgwick suggests:

reflective comparison between the two judgments necessarily reduces me temporarily to a state of neutrality. And though the total result in my mind is not exactly suspense of judgment, but an alternation and conflict between positive affirmation by one act of thought and the neutrality that is the result of another, it is obviously something very different from scientific certitude.[56]

All of Sidgwick's conditions are, in a sense, matters of degree. A belief can be more or less clear, more or less reflective, and assessed to a greater or lesser extent for inconsistency. The same goes for the consensus condition. A belief accepted by all, both past and present, meets the

[53] *Nicomachean Ethics* 10. 2, 1172[b]36–1173[a]1.
[54] See Wiggins, *Needs, Values, Truth*, 147, 149–51.
[55] See Sinnott-Armstrong, 'Moral Relativity and Intuitionism', 314.
[56] *Methods*, 342.

condition well. If one person and only one disagrees with some belief of mine, and everyone else agrees, and yet I have no reasonable explanation of that person's disagreement, that does of course damage the claim to certainty of that belief. But certainty itself is a matter of degree. We cannot aim in ethics to ground our normative theories on principles that are entirely indubitable—the ethical analogues of the Cartesian *cogito*. That is not only because of doubts about the viability of the Cartesian project, but because we will not find in ethics any principle on which there is *complete* consensus among those who are considering the matter with sufficient impartiality for their views to deserve consideration. As I pointed out above, some thinkers will deny even SI. But here I suggest that they are small enough in number and their positions driven by theories of sufficient epistemic insecurity that we are entitled to claim *enough* certainty for SI for it to serve as a foundation in constructing an ethical theory.

But where do we go next? Our account of self-regarding or prudential reasons seems safely enough grounded on SI. But once we move beyond self-interest to consider how we should act in relation to others, the mathematical analogy is in trouble. In the case of $7 + 5 = 12$ we may indeed quite plausibly claim that there is nothing else to think. There is almost complete consensus and the views of at least the majority of those who disagree will be either explicable (they are pretty bad at mathematics, perhaps, or they hold some clearly mistaken view of the nature of mathematical judgement) or incomprehensible. There do seem to be some normative judgements on which there is something like this degree of convergence, and I have suggested that SI is one of them. But once we move beyond what we might call the 'normative core' of our beliefs,[57] there is such disagreement on what other normative principles there are and how they are to be weighted, it may be objected, that any claim to certainty can be little more than an individual psychological report. It is true that there is sufficient convergence on a few substantive first-order claims, such as: 'There is always a reason for a parent not to torture her own baby solely for her own enjoyment'. But these claims are too specific and few in number to provide any sort of systematic account of ethics, and once we ascend to the more abstract level at which some kind of justification for the more specific claims is provided, consensus disappears entirely.

---

57 See Griffin's discussion of 'beliefs of high reliability' in *Value Judgement*, index, s.v.

This objection is an overstatement, since some degree of consensus tends to give some degree of justification. And there is some consensus at the level of ethical theory. A person who believes that our strongest reasons are to act in accordance with the virtues will find herself in the company of many others who think alike; and to that extent at least her views are better justified than those of someone who thinks our strongest reason is to contemplate the number three. But any claim to knowledge of the truth of her own theory and the falsity of others on the part of the virtue ethicist, or any other normative theorist, is bluster. Normative ethics is divided into many camps and they are of sufficient number to make it clear that no comprehensive normative theory can yet meet the consensus condition to a significantly greater degree than any other.[58]

To return to the case of *n* and not-*n*. Assume that *n* is some widely accepted normative theory, and that this theory is also widely rejected by reasonable people. At this point, according to Sidgwick, I should give up my adherence to *n* and adopt a position of neutrality between *n* and not-*n*. Sidgwick says that 'this is not exactly suspense of judgment', since I may continue to affirm *n* 'by one act of thought' while remaining neutral in another. But this sounds like a description of a kind of epistemological schizophrenia, in which the contradictory affirmations are somehow kept apart. What should emerge on a proper understanding of the consensus condition is indeed suspension of judgement, alongside an affirmation of a mere appearance. That is to say, if I am asked about my judgements regarding *n* and not-*n*, I will if I understand the consensus condition be neutral between them, but admit that it still *seems* to me that *n* is true.[59] If two people who believe themselves to be in roughly the same epistemic circumstances are confronted by what one of them takes to be a redwing, the other a song thrush, they should suspend judgement on which of the two the bird is. But the bird's appearance to each as one or the other may not change.

On this account, whether I am justified in my basic normative beliefs depends to some extent on the views of others, and how well grounded those views turn out to be. Here someone hostile even to this degree of

[58] See Gaut, 'Justifying Moral Pluralism', 144.

[59] See Sextus Empiricus, *Outlines of Scepticism* 1. 15, 31, 151, 196, etc.; also Striker, 'Historical Reflections on Classical Pyrrhonism and Neo-Pyrrhonism', 16. It is worth noting that since the consensus condition itself is controversial its advocates may have to suspend judgement on it. But, as I shall explain below, this does not prevent their continuing to advocate it.

contextualism in justification might raise the issue of epistemic closure and object that epistemic entitlement cannot be so contingent. In fact I do not need to find out whether others also accept p. Rather I have merely to ask myself whether it is possible that another person, in as epistemically good a state as I am, might reasonably hold not-p. If it is, then I should suspend judgement on p.

This objection rests on a dim view of human epistemic capacities. A philosophical intuitionist is likely to put some faith in the notion that our intuitive faculty is to some extent truth-tracking. This claim might be supported by reference either to consensus on certain non-ethical truths such as those of basic arithmetic or logic or to consensus on normative truths such as SI. If there is in fact near-universal consensus on some normative principle among those who have considered the matter aright, and such dissensus as there is rests either on apparent misunderstanding of that principle or commitment to doubtful theory, we may be justified in believing that any dissenting thinker we can imagine must fall into one or other of these categories.

So contingent consensus on some normative principle provides, in the appropriate circumstances, some justification for a high degree of certainty about such principles, although this is not of course to claim indefeasibility. Likewise, widespread dissensus among epistemically similarly situated thinkers not only precludes certainty, but requires suspension of judgement.

It might be said that usually, when confronted by someone with a different ethical viewpoint from ourselves, we are inclined to think that they have failed to see something that we have appreciated. But here we should remember that they will think the same about us, and the question is whether either of us is justified in thinking that the other is in a worse epistemic position. I suggest that such justification in ethics is really quite rare, and that to this extent philosophical ethics is characterized by an unjustified dogmatism or over-confidence. Nor should it be thought that the consensus condition does not apply to dogmatists who hold without justification that they are in a better epistemic position than others. Sidgwick may state it in the form of autobiographical description: 'if I have no more reason to suspect error in the other mind than in my own, reflective comparison between the two judgments necessarily reduces me temporarily to a state of neutrality'. But he clearly means his claim to imply that someone who is not so reduced is in error.

What are the implications of the consensus condition for philosophical ethics, given a context of widespread disagreement? There are at least three strategies worth considering: resignation, impartiality, and debate. The first would involve one's refraining from any kind of philosophical debate about normative theory. This strategy, however, is likely to seem to most intuitionists excessively pessimistic about the prospects for convergence on the truth in ethics and resulting ethical progress. The case of SI suggests that truth is available, and there are many standard examples of apparent ethical progress, such as the recognition of racism, sexism, and speciesism.

So, on the assumption that progress in ethics is possible, one might seek to engage in impartial consideration of and debate concerning the various current normative theories. There is more to be said for this strategy than for resignation, and it is certainly likely to be part of the best overall philosophical package. But the fact remains that one will usually persist in one's attachment to the normative principles that strike one as plausible, and one is thus in an especially good position to spell out those principles and display their advantages to others.

So this leaves us with the final strategy, in which debate between the advocates of the different normative theories continues. But carried out between intuitionists or indeed others who have suspended judgement as to the correctness or otherwise of the view which they themselves find attractive, such debate would be less adversarial and more constructive than much in philosophy at present.[60] This would have several significant advantages. First, each participant would be more likely to see the faults in her own position and the advantages in those of others. Second, philosophers would see that there is often greater epistemic benefit in discussing issues with those of radically different views than with some clique of one's own. Third, the aim of debate would be not the victory of one's own position but convergence on some truth, which might well be a conglomeration of various elements from several existing ethical theories. Ethical enquiry must be informed by a spirit of impartiality, in which those who propose normative principles are prepared both to hold up those principles to the light of rational reflection and the arguments of

---

[60] The tendency of human beings to avoid so-called 'cognitive dissonance' probably goes a long way to explaining why most normative ethical theorists are inclined to ignore the implications of disagreement and to stick so firmly to their own position as clearly correct.

others, actual or imagined, and to look enthusiastically at the views of others, in search of enlightenment rather than dialectical victory. Critical argument, of course, would continue to be the mainstay of moral philosophical discussion, but if it were freed of its unjustified dogmatism there would be a greater likelihood of convergence on the truth.

Finally, how should suspension of judgement change the way I live my life as a whole? The implications may be significant. I may have started with a belief in certain apparently self-evident comprehensive ethical principles, the force of which I allowed to guide my practical decisions. Once I realize that these principles fail to meet the consensus condition, it will become clear to me that they have no claim to self-evidence, to being objects of knowledge, or to any directly justified role in my deliberation. Because I accept SI, however, and am no sceptic, I cannot aim for the *ataraxia*, or tranquillity, of the Pyrrhonist sceptic.[61] At the end of *The Methods of Ethics*, Sidgwick—who himself fails to face up to the implications of his own consensus condition—runs into the problem that he himself cannot decide between egoism and utilitarianism, and says: '[In] the...cases of a recognised conflict between self-interest and duty, practical reason, being divided against itself, would cease to be a motive on either side; the conflict would have to be decided by the comparative preponderance of one or other of two groups of non-rational impulses.'[62]

In many cases there is a good deal of first-order or substantive agreement among ethical theorists. But when there is a conflict, should I merely consult my own tastes and preferences? If we accept SI as certain, then the answer to this question is that I should pursue my own tastes only if doing so most promotes my own good. And here two issues are likely to be salient. First, going against my own ethical view may impose costs in terms of guilt, shame, regret, depression, lack of self-esteem, and so on. But, second, going with my own view as opposed to that of others may damage my well-being in other ways, especially if that view is an especially demanding one (as that I shall outline in my penultimate chapter indeed appears to be).

That ethical intuitionism should lead to a scenario in which each of us might be left deciding which ethical theory to follow on the

---

[61] See Sextus, *Outlines* 1. 10, 12, 18, 25–31, etc.   [62] *Methods*, 508.

basis of how much each will advance our own self-interest is somewhat odd. But if normative philosophical ethics can progress to the point of widespread convergence on a comprehensive view, it would provide a decisive practical role in our lives for ethical theory to which such theory has not yet earned any entitlement.

4

Well-Being

1. HEDONISM'S DECLINE

In the previous chapter I claimed knowledge of SI, according to which
each of us has a reason to promote her own well-being. SI leaves open the
question of what well-being consists in. Should we understand it in terms
of the satisfaction of desires or preferences? Or of some 'objective list'
of goods, such as knowledge, accomplishment, friendship?[1] Desire or
preference theories and objective list theories have become the dominant
views in recent philosophy.[2] In this chapter I wish to outline and defend
an alternative to both: hedonism.[3]

Hedonism has a distinguished philosophical history. It was central in
ancient philosophy. One interpretation of Plato's *Protagoras* has Socrates
defending the view, and it is taken seriously in many other dialogues,
including the *Philebus* and the *Republic*. Aristotle analyses it closely in
his *Ethics*. It was defended vigorously by the Epicureans and Cyrenaics,
and attacked equally vigorously by the Stoics. More recently, hedonism
was the standard view of the British empiricists from Hobbes to J. S.
Mill.[4]

---

[1] See Parfit, *Reasons and Persons*, app. 1; Hooker, *Ideal Code, Real World*, 37–43.

[2] For the purposes of this chapter, I draw no distinction between preference and
desire, though of course various such distinctions may be drawn.

[3] This chapter is based on my 'Hedonism Reconsidered'.

[4] See esp. or e.g. Plato, *Protagoras* 353c1–355a5 (for discussion, see Plato, *Protagoras*,
tr. and annot. Taylor, 174–9; Irwin, *Plato's Ethics*, 81–3); Aristotle, *Nicomachean Ethics*
7. 11–14, 10. 1–5; on Epicurus, Cicero, *De Finibus* 1. 30–54; on Aristippus, the
founder of the Cyrenaic school, Xenophon, *Memoirs of Socrates* 2. 1, 3. 8; on the Stoics,
Diogenes Laertius, *Lives of Eminent Philosophers*, 7. 85–6; Hobbes, *Human Nature: or
The Fundamental Elements of Policy*, 7. 3; Locke, *Essay concerning Human Understanding*,
2. 20. 3; Hume, *Enquiry concerning the Principles of Morals*, app. 2.10; *Treatise of Human
Nature*, 2. 3. 9. 8; Bentham, *Introduction to the Principles of Morals and Legislation*, 1. 1;
Mill, *Utilitarianism*, 2. 2.

In the twentieth century, however, hedonism became significantly less popular.[5] There are at least three reasons for this. First, Mill's attempt to deal with the objection that hedonism was the 'philosophy of swine', using his distinction between higher and lower pleasures, was thought to be either an abandonment of hedonism or incoherent.[6] Second, G. E. Moore provided several vigorously stated arguments against hedonism in chapter 3 of his influential *Principia Ethica*. Finally, while hedonism was down, Robert Nozick dealt it a near-fatal blow with his famous example of the experience machine.[7] The result has been that these days hedonism receives little philosophical attention,[8] and students are warned off it early on in their studies, often with a reference to Nozick. This is what happens, for example, in James Griffin's influential *Well-Being*.[9] The reference to Nozick comes three pages into the main text, and that is the end of hedonism.

My hunch is that people no longer take Moore's criticisms all that seriously, especially since the publication of the preface to the revised edition of *Principia* in which Moore admits that the book 'is full of mistakes and confusions'.[10] The two major concerns are versions of the philosophy of swine and the experience machine objections.

Philosophers of religion used to aim at persuading their audience to accept the truth of theism. These days it is quite common to find them trying merely to show that theism is not unreasonable.[11] In this chapter I want primarily to do the same sort of thing for hedonism, though of course I shall not be unhappy if I manage to persuade anyone to see well-being as I do. I shall try to articulate the most plausible version of hedonism, before showing how hedonists might deal with the

---

[5] Most of the attacks were on hedonism as a theory of the good as a whole, not merely as a theory of well-being. See Sect. 2 of this chapter.

[6] See Mill, *Utilitarianism*, 2. 3–8; and for an example of the objection to the distinction, see Green, *Prolegomena to Ethics*, 168–78.

[7] *Anarchy, State, and Utopia*, 42–3.

[8] In fact the same general complaint was well made in 1926 by Blake in the first paragraph of his 'Why Not Hedonism? A Protest'. There are of course modern exceptions: see e.g. Sprigge, *The Rational Foundations of Ethics*, chs. 5, 7; Tännsjö, *Hedonistic Utilitarianism*, ch. 5. These two writers are best understood as offering theories of the good rather than of well-being in particular (see main text below). Fred Feldman, in e.g. his *Pleasure and the Good Life*, offers only what I shall call below an 'enumerative' hedonistic theory, not an 'explanatory' one. That is, he allows '*good-for*-making' properties other than pleasantness or enjoyableness into his account of well-being.

[9] See also e.g. Kymlicka, *Contemporary Political Philosophy*, 12–14.

[10] *Principia Ethica*, rev. edn., 2.

[11] See e.g. Plantinga, 'Reformed Epistemology'.

philosophy of swine and experience machine objections. My conclusion will be that the 'unkindness' of recent ethics towards hedonism is not justified.[12]

2. HEDONISM

First, then, let me try to specify more precisely the kind of hedonism I want to discuss. It is not psychological hedonism, the view that human action—or perhaps rational and deliberate human action—is motivated by a concern for some balance, perhaps the greatest expected balance, of pleasure over pain. Nor is it a view about morality, such as hedonistic utilitarianism, according to which the right thing to do is maximize impartially the balance of pleasure over pain.[13] Nor is it a view about the good, since the kind of hedonism I have in mind is consistent with the view that there are non-hedonist values, such as aesthetic values.[14] Nor is it a view about what makes for a good life, or a good human life.[15] Nor, even, is it a view about happiness, which may well be understood most plausibly in a non-hedonistic way.[16] Rather I wish to discuss hedonism as a theory of well-being, that is, of what is ultimately good for any individual.[17]

---

[12] See Sumner, *Welfare, Happiness, and Ethics*, 83.

[13] This enables the hedonist about well-being to sidestep the objection that hedonists must ascribe weight to 'evil pleasures'. There is nothing to prevent a hedonist about well-being from claiming that such pleasures contribute to well-being, but should be given no weight in moral decisions, or indeed prudential ones (since hedonists need not believe that well-being always grounds self-interested reasons, regardless of its nature or source).

[14] The distinction between hedonism as a theory of well-being and as a theory of the goodness of outcomes is clearly made in Temkin, *Inequality*, ch. 9, esp. 262–4. See also e.g. his 'Egalitarianism Defended'. Temkin also brings out well the implications for welfarism of the distinction. Temkin's view of the good is importantly non-welfarist, and that view, like my own, rests ultimately on claims based on reflection on certain examples. This is a case in which, though each of us is required to suspend judgement (see Sect. 3.4), debate is far from concluded.

[15] For the distinction, and use of it in criticism of Aristotle, see Glassen, 'A Fallacy in Aristotle's Argument about the Good'.

[16] See Haybron, 'Happiness and Pleasure'.

[17] Often I shall speak merely of what is good for an individual, meaning 'what is good (overall) for' and therefore including also what is bad for an individual. Hurka ('"Good" and "Good For"') suggests banishing the phrase 'good for' from philosophical ethics, because of its ambiguity. But the distinction between what is good 'impersonally', in

A question arises for any ethical theory about what its *focus* might be. Does it concern actions, say, or states of affairs, or character, or virtue? Or does it concern several or all of these, perhaps with primacy attached to one notion in particular? The same question arises for theories of well-being. Which question should they begin with? Perhaps: What is it most rational to do, from the self-interested point of view? Or: Which actions will most further well-being? Which question to begin with is to some extent a matter of other theoretical commitments one has. But I believe a strong independent case can be made for the focus of a theory of well-being on the goodness of the *lives* of individuals for the individuals living those lives. So our question is: What makes a life good for an individual?

Over the last few decades in particular, several useful distinctions have been drawn between different types of theory of well-being. One is between those that claim well-being to consist only in some kind of (conscious) mental state, and those that allow well-being ultimately to be affected or even constituted by states of the world, understood independently of mental states.[18] Hedonism must surely be a mental state theory. We should try to avoid, then, that use of 'pleasure' in which it can refer to an *activity*, as in 'Golfing is one of my pleasures'.[19]

Indeed we should try as far as possible to avoid talk of 'pleasure', for a reason noted by Aristotle and many writers since: 'the bodily pleasures have taken possession of the name because it is those that people steer for most often, and all share in them'.[20] This, of course, is why a version of

the sense of making a world or universe good, and what is good for an individual, in the sense of making her life better for her than it would otherwise have been, seems to me fundamental. The closest Hurka comes to describing this sense of 'good for' is as 'good from the point of view of', but this notion itself seems to cut across the distinction between 'good' and 'good for'. It may be that, from my point of view, Moore's beautiful world, never seen by anyone, is good, and that, from my point of view, my headache's coming to an end is good for me. See Moore, *Principia Ethica*, 83–4.

[18] See e.g. Griffin, *Well-Being*, ch. 1. The contrast here is not as stark as it might appear, since on some views the content of mental states is tied to states of the world, and most of the goods listed by non-mental-state theorists as constituents of well-being involve mental states in some sense or other (consider, say, accomplishment, or knowledge).

[19] For a classic discussion of this notion in the context of Aristotelian ethics, see Owen, 'Aristotelian Pleasures'. Failure to attend to the distinction between this usage and the use of 'pleasure' to refer to a mental state vitiates Brink's attempt to interpret Mill's theory of well-being as objectivist, in 'Mill's Deliberative Utilitarianism'.

[20] Aristotle, *Nicomachean Ethics* 7. 13, 1153^{b}33–5. Recently a similar and similarly narrow conception of pleasure has come to the fore in some so-called 'positive psychology',

the philosophy of swine objection against hedonism—that the hedonist is advocating the life of sensualism—arises so readily. To avoid such difficulties, let me use 'enjoyment' instead of 'pleasure', and 'suffering' instead of 'pain'.[21]

So with these points in mind we might define hedonism as the view that what is good for any individual is the enjoyable experience in her life, what is bad is the suffering in that life, and the life best for an individual is that with the greatest balance of enjoyment over suffering.[22]

This seems to me correct as far as it goes. But before moving on we should note another important distinction between two questions one might ask about well-being, and hence two levels of theory providing answers to those questions.[23] The first—and prior—question is something like: 'Which things make someone's life go better for them?' Answers here might mention substantive goods such as enjoyable experiences, accomplishment, or knowledge, or something more abstract, such as the fulfilment of informed desires. These answers we might call *enumerative* theories of well-being. The second question is: 'But what is it about these things that *make* them good for people?' Take accomplishment. Someone might claim that what makes accomplishment good for someone is its perfecting her human nature. That view might be called perfectionist. Someone else might claim that something's being an accomplishment is itself what makes it good—'being an accomplishment' is itself a '*good-for*-making' property. This position

in which pleasure is understood in terms of positive emotion, to be distinguished from 'gratification', such as that found in, say, a good conversation, and 'meaning', which consists in serving some goal 'larger than ourselves . . . such as knowledge' and 'satisfies a longing for purpose in life' (Seligman *et al.*, 'A Balanced Psychology and Full Life', 278; see 276–9; Seligman, *Authentic Happiness*).

21 See Nowell-Smith, *Ethics*, 138; Goldstein, 'Hedonic Pluralism', 53; Sumner, *Welfare, Happiness, and Ethics*, 108. Note that I am using enjoyment in a broad sense to include the pleasantness of, say, certain moods to which the subject need not be attending. Rachels ('Six Theses about Pleasure', 247–8) suggests 'unpleasure' as the antonym of 'pleasure', but I prefer 'suffering' as it is in common use. It is worth noting a further possible reason for hedonism's decline at this point: the concentration in philosophy on the 'good' aspects of well-being as opposed to the bad. To many people, the hedonistic account of what is bad for people seems on the face of it more plausible than the hedonistic account of what is good.

22 Since it is not necessarily a conscious mental state, I believe that 'propositional' pleasure (being pleased *that* e.g. one has won some prize) should be excluded from hedonism, except in so far as it constitutes enjoyable experience (as one might enjoy contemplating the fact that one has won the prize). Feldman (*Pleasure and the Good Life*), however, offers an account of pleasure which is entirely propositional.

23 See Frankena, *Ethics*, 84; Moore and Crisp, 'Welfarism in Moral Theory', 599.

might be called an objective list theory. And all answers to the second question we might call *explanatory* theories.

This distinction is somewhat rough. Often someone will offer an enumeration which is also intended to be explanatory, and an explanatory theory might well be expressed as an enumeration (a perfectionist, for example, might in her enumeration list only 'perfection of human nature'). But it is surely important that any theorist of well-being be prepared to answer both kinds of question, and this brings us back to hedonism. Since I have not stipulated that enumerations be restricted to 'intrinsic', non-instrumental, or 'final' goods, a hedonist may list, say, accomplishment as a constituent of a person's well-being. Or she may—perhaps more informatively—list only enjoyable experiences. But even this last position is consistent with an answer to the second, explanatory question with reference to, say, perfection of human nature: enjoyable experiences are good because it is human nature to experience them, and well-being consists in the perfection of human nature. This kind of view—combining a restriction to enjoyable experiences or enjoyment at the level of enumeration with explanatory perfectionism—seems to me not to capture the spirit of the hedonist tradition (though admittedly the enumerative–explanatory distinction has not been recognized in that tradition as clearly as it might have been). Rather the hedonist, as I shall understand her, will say that what makes accomplishment, enjoyable experiences, or whatever good for people is *their being enjoyable*, and that this is the only '*good-for-making*' property there is. This brings us to the question of what it is for an experience to be enjoyable, and that is the topic of my next section.

3. ENJOYMENT

Wayne Sumner helpfully distinguishes between internalist and externalist conceptions of enjoyment or pleasure.[24] On the internalist view, found in Hume and Bentham, what enjoyable experiences have in common 'is their positive feeling tone: an intrinsic, unanalysable quality of pleasantness which is present to a greater or lesser degree in all of them'. The standard objection to the internalist view is that introspection and reflection make it clear that there is no such common quality

---

[24] Sumner, *Welfare, Happiness, and Ethics*, 87–91.

of enjoyableness to all of the things we in fact enjoy: 'eating, reading, working, creating, helping'.[25]

So perhaps, then, we should adopt an externalist model of enjoyment, according to which 'what all pleasures share is not a homogeneous feeling tone, but the fact that they are . . . objects of some positive attitude on our part'.[26] Which attitude? The obvious one, as noted by Shelly Kagan in a nice exegesis of the dialectic, is desire.[27] Kagan himself, however, suggests that the move to an externalist account may be too swift.[28] We might admit that enjoyment is not a single common 'component' of enjoyable experiences, but allow enjoyment to serve as a single 'dimension' along which experiences can vary. Kagan uses an analogy with the volume of sounds. Volume, he suggests, is not a 'component' of auditory experiences, but 'an aspect of sounds, with regard to which they can be ranked'. If enjoyableness is like volume, then arguing that it is not a single property common to enjoyable experiences, because of the qualitative differences between them, would be like arguing that, because sounds are so different from one another, there is no single quality of volume.

How is the distinction between components of experiences and dimensions of variation meant to work? Take the sound of a tinkling bell, and the sound of a honking horn. The components of each are, respectively, tinkling and honking. Volume, Kagan suggests, is not a 'kind' of sound. So a loud tinkling is the same sound as a soft tinkling, whereas a loud honk is a different sound from a loud tinkling.

It is questionable, however, whether this distinction captures anything of great metaphysical significance. We would indeed be inclined to say that the soft tinkling is the same sound as the loud tinkling. But that is because we usually focus on aspects of how things sound other than how loud they are. In fact loud sounds do form a kind.[29] I might ask you to group sounds together according to their volume, and you would then

[25] Griffin, *Well-Being*, 8. For the same line of objection to internalism, see Gosling, *Pleasure and Desire*, 37–40; Sprigge, *The Rational Foundations of Ethics*, 130; Sumner, *Welfare, Happiness, and Ethics*, 92–3; Feldman, *Utilitarianism, Hedonism, and Desert*, 8, 132; Bernstein, *On Moral Considerability*, 25; Carson, *Value and the Good Life*, 13–14; Sobel, 'Varieties of Hedonism', 241.

[26] Sumner, *Welfare, Happiness, and Ethics*, 90.

[27] Kagan, 'The Limits of Well-Being', 170.

[28] Ibid. 172–5. Kagan cites the influence of unpublished work by Leonard Katz.

[29] In his *Values and Intentions*, 177, Findlay speaks of loudness and sweetness as examples of 'peculiar qualities of what comes before us in sense-experience'; see Goldstein, 'Why People Prefer Pleasure to Pain', 350.

categorize the loud tinkling with the loud honk, and the soft tinkling with the soft honk. As Kagan himself goes on to say, 'it seems... that there is a sense in which a specific volume is indeed an ingredient of a given sound'. Drawing distinctions between components, dimensions of variation, and ingredients of experiences does not seem a profitable direction in which to move.[30]

So must we then adopt an externalist model, perhaps using the notion of desire or preference? In response to the apparent lack of homogeneity in different enjoyable experiences, this is what Sidgwick did: 'the only common quality that I can find in... feelings [of enjoyment] seems to be that relation to desire and volition expressed by the general term "desirable"... I propose therefore to define Pleasure... as a feeling which, when experienced by intelligent beings, is at least implicitly apprehended as desirable.'[31]

Sidgwick's use of the notion of desirability, rather than that of being desired, is problematic. One problem arises if we read him as restricting his definition to 'intelligent beings'.[32] To view some experience as desirable, even 'implicitly', might be said to require a level of cognitive capacity above that possessed by many of the non-intelligent beings we believe capable of enjoyment. But perhaps lower animals can be said in a sense to evaluate certain things as desirable, or perhaps the definition is to be read in a non-restrictive way. The more serious problem with Sidgwick's definition is that it detaches enjoyment from actual desire. It seems possible that I should apprehend a feeling as desirable, and yet not desire it, and it is hard to understand how this could be a case of enjoyment. It is the conative state of desiring, that is to say, rather than

[30] Further criticism of Kagan and Katz can be found in Sobel, 'Pleasure as a Mental State'. Sobel, however, appears (232) to run together Kagan's internalist 'dimension' view with his externalist suggestion that pleasure is experience desired in a particular way (Kagan, 'The Limits of Well-Being', 173). Daniel Haybron has suggested to me that Kagan might base something like his distinction on the fact that components of experience can be isolated, while dimensions cannot. So if you hear a tinkling and a honking at once, you can attend to either the tinkling or the honking, but you cannot attend simply to the volume of the experience, perhaps because the volume is a property of the tinkling or honking. But again I see the properties here as analogous. Just as a tinkling can be said to have the property of being loud, so an instantiation of loudness can be said to have the property of being a tinkling. This is not how we commonly speak, of course, but that is a matter of contingency. Further, there seems nothing to prevent my attending to volume in particular in some array of sounds.

[31] Sidgwick, *Methods*, 127.

[32] One might read him as allowing that this feeling could in fact be experienced by beings who cannot apprehend it as desirable. But this would seem to allow for a common quality between the feeling as experienced by the intelligent and as by the non-intelligent.

the cognitive state of apprehending some feeling as desirable which is a candidate for a major role in a theory of enjoyment.

One suggestion along these lines has been that the desire in question be for an experience to continue, for its own sake.[33] This is a version of so-called 'preference hedonism'.

Sumner objects to this view as follows: 'Whatever its object, a desire can only represent (or result from) an *ex ante* expectation that the continuation of some state or activity will be experienced as gratifying; the satisfaction of the desire cannot guarantee the *ex post* gratification.'[34] Sumner's objection here seems to be the following. Take some experience *e* at time *t*, which I desire to continue. According to the preference hedonist, what would make *e* enjoyable would be the satisfaction, at t^1, of my desire. But, Sumner objects, *e* might continue, thus satisfying my desire, and turn out not to be enjoyable.

Sumner goes on to suggest that one can think of many valuable experiences—such as the birth of a baby or a romantic moment—which are not improved by prolongation: 'where many pleasures are concerned, more is not necessarily better'. Justin Gosling earlier provided the examples of a person 'enjoying a subtle whiff of scent, where the pleasure is in the ephemeral quality of the experience, and the person would be nauseated at the thought of lingering over it', and of someone who is enjoying breaking some good news to someone else but who must realize that they cannot go on doing so.[35]

This seems a good line of objection to preference hedonism so understood. To avoid Sumner's point about *ex post* gratification, the preference hedonist should insist that the desire and its satisfaction are contemporaneous. Imagine that I am enjoying the experience of teeing off in a game of golf. According to preference hedonism, my enjoyment consists in my having that experience, and my desiring to have it (the satisfaction of my desire, of course, follows from this combination).

A version of preference hedonism which makes the desire in question contemporaneous with its satisfaction seems able to make sense of the alleged problem cases. Take the whiff of perfume. Gosling's objection is that the enjoyment of smelling it cannot consist in the subject's desire that the experience continue, both because part of the enjoyment lies in the ephemerality, and because the subject would find the prospect of its continuation nauseating. But the object of the subject's desire is best

---

[33] See e.g. Brandt, 'The Concept of Welfare', 268–9.
[34] 'The Evolution of Utility', 111.   [35] Gosling, *Pleasure and Desire*, 65.

not seen as for the continuation of the experience. That introduces the gap between desire and satisfaction that led to Sumner's first problem. Rather the experience I desire when I am enjoying the whiff of perfume is that very experience. I may be quite aware that its continuing would make me sick, and hence not desire that (though I may well desire its continuing in the absence of nausea). And there seems no difficulty in accounting for the enjoyment I find in ephemerality as an experience that I desire as it is, rather than an experience that I desire to continue.

But enjoyment cannot merely be an experience desired by its subject. A creative artist who finds creativity acutely stressful might desire that stress for itself, perhaps because she believes it to be valuable in itself as a necessary part of the creative process.[36] Here the preference hedonist might try to specify further the kind of desire in enjoyment. The subject must desire the experience, in some sense, for *how it feels*, and not for some property or believed property independent of feeling.[37] But now imagine that I have never experienced serious pain. I might, during my first experience of it, desire it for its novelty, at least for a short time—and there is no need to think that I must somehow be enjoying the novelty. I desire the pain for how it feels, but there is no enjoyment here.[38] Well, might we say that the experience must be desired because it feels *good*? But this brings us back to an internalist model: enjoyable experiences are those, and only those, that feel good.[39]

---

[36] For further examples, see Rachels, 'Is Unpleasantness Intrinsic to Unpleasant Experiences?', 193.

[37] As Kagan puts it, the desire must be 'an immediate response to [the experience's] occurrent phenomenal qualities (i.e., its qualia)' ('The Limits of Well-Being', 173).

[38] It seems to me that there can also be enjoyment without desire. Imagine an ascetic who very strongly wishes that the enjoyment he is experiencing from being near to someone sexually attractive to him would stop. I fail to see why this must be construed as a case of conflict of desires.

[39] I am rejecting preference hedonism as an account of pleasure. But I would also wish to reject it as a theory of the good, primarily for the sort of reason given at the end of Sect. 2.1. Desires as mere psychological states are not plausible sources of reasons or values, independently of some other good-making property such as intrinsic enjoyableness. It might be said in favour of preference hedonism and against hedonism that the former gives more weight to the view of the subject. So a preference hedonist may allow that some enjoyable experience which the subject denies is part of her well-being is indeed not such a part, whereas the hedonist cannot. But it seems to me that whether this is seen as an advantage of a theory of well-being is likely to depend on one's prior view of well-being itself, and so cannot offer much in the way of argument for any particular position. The hedonist, in other words, will say that it is a *disadvantage* of preference hedonism that it gives excessive weight to the view of the subject.

On the face of it, this might not seem such a bad place to end up. For on the internalist model we can easily distinguish between the cases of the artist and my novel pain on the one hand, and those of, say, basking in the sun or enjoying listening to Brahms, on the other. The latter two experiences are desired because they feel good, the former for other reasons. But what about the 'heterogeneity argument' against internalism that caused all the trouble in the first place? According to this argument, when we introspect we can find nothing common to the experiences we enjoy that might be characterized as 'enjoyment'.

Internalism as I have characterized it is the view that enjoyment is a single 'feeling tone' common to all enjoyable experiences. One might attempt to make room for heterogeneity in a pluralistic version of internalism, claiming that while enjoyableness is indeed to be understood internally, there is a plurality of feeling tones. This raises the question of why these, and only these, experiences are to be described as enjoyments. Stuart Rachels offers such a view, and suggests three ways in which one might attempt to explain the unity of enjoyment:[40]

(1) Enjoyments are just those experiences that are intrinsically good due to how they feel.

(2) Enjoyments are just those experiences that are good, for the people who have those experiences, because of how they feel.

(3) Enjoyments are just those experiences that one ought to like merely as feeling; liking is an appropriate response to enjoyments alone considered merely as feeling.

Position 3 is perhaps better understood as a form of externalism, since the unity of enjoyable experience is characterized by reference to the attitude of liking.[41] The other two positions are quite similar, so given my focus on well-being let me consider the second. There clearly could be a difference between monistic and pluralistic versions of internalism about well-being, as opposed to enjoyment. Consider for the sake of argument on the one hand the view that well-being consists only in feeling warm, i.e. that this is the only experience that is good for people because of how it feels, and on the other the view that well-being consists only in feeling warm and in hearing the sound of a buzzing bee, i.e. that

---

[40] Rachels, 'Is Unpleasantness Intrinsic?', 197–8. Rachels's points are in fact about suffering, but they apply as well to enjoyment.

[41] So it is unclear why Rachels allows this to be a form of the view that (un)pleasantness consists in features intrinsic to experiences (ibid. 187).

these are the only experiences good for people because of how they feel. No reference is made in either of these views to enjoyment, and there is little doubt that the two experiences in question feel quite different. Rachels and I, however, are discussing not well-being broadly understood, but enjoyment. And if the two theories just mentioned are amended to claim that what is good for people about these experiences is that they *feel good*, then we appear to be back with a monistic form of internalism about enjoyment.

If the advocate of heterogeneity is seeking in enjoyable experiences something like a special sensation, such as sweetness, or a tingle or feeling located in a certain part of the body, such as an itch or pins and needles, or indeed something like a perceptual quality such as redness, she will fail. But there *is* a way that enjoyable experiences feel: they feel enjoyable. That is, there is something that it is *like* to be experiencing enjoyment, in the same way that there is something that it is like to be having an experience of colour. Likewise, there is something that it is like to be experiencing a particular kind of enjoyment (bodily enjoyment, perhaps, or the enjoyment of reading a novel), in the same way that there is something that it is like to be having an experience of a particular colour. Enjoyment, then, is best understood using the determinable–determinate distinction, and the mistake in the heterogeneity argument is that it considers only determinates. Enjoyable experiences do differ from one another, and are often gratifying, welcomed by their subject, favoured, and indeed desired. But there is a certain common quality—feeling good—which any externalist account must ignore.[42] The determinable–determinate distinction also helps us to be clear about the role of 'feeling' in this analysis: feeling good as a determinable is not any particular kind of determinate feeling.

There is a further feature of enjoyment which may cause confusion here. Enjoyment, though it is a 'quale' in the sense that there is something it feels like to experience it, is ordinarily in a sense second-order or intentional: enjoyment is usually taken *in* some 'first-order' property of one's experiences.[43] One enjoys experiencing the warmth of the fire, the taste of the mango, the wit of Jane Austen. As Aristotle puts

---

[42] See Duncker, 'On Pleasure, Emotion, and Striving', 399–400; Davis, 'Pleasure and Happiness', 312; Goldstein, 'Hedonic Pluralism', 52; Bengtsson, 'Pleasure and the Phenomenology of Value'; and further references in Rachels, 'Is Unpleasantness Intrinsic?', nn. 29, 30.

[43] There are also purely enjoyable states such as euphoria.

it, it is 'a sort of supervenient end, like the bloom on the faces of young men'.[44] For this reason it may be tempting to offer a purely 'intentional' account of enjoyment. But while there is indeed nothing amiss in saying, for example, 'I enjoy ballooning', this statement can be elucidated as 'I am a person who is disposed to gain enjoyment from ballooning'; and, for the hedonist, it is the enjoyment alone that matters.

Because introspection may well lead one in the direction of looking for something analogous to a sensation, I think the internalist would be well advised to refer to our ordinary understanding of enjoyment. First, enjoyableness is usually taken to be a single property of a variety of experiences. Eating, reading, and working—to use three of Griffin's examples—are very different from one another. But if you experience each, I may ask you: 'Did you enjoy those activities? Did you enjoy the experience of those activities? Did your experiences in each case have the *same felt property*—that of being enjoyable?' Of course, they are all enjoyable in different ways and for different reasons; but they are all enjoyable. Second, I can ask you to *rank* those experiences in terms of how enjoyable they are. Note that this is not asking you which you prefer, since you may have preferences which are not based on enjoyment. Nor is it asking which is better. It is asking you to rank the experiences according to the degree to which you enjoyed each.

The internalist model of enjoyment is perhaps the default one, and has been dropped by philosophers largely because of the heterogeneity argument. But that argument is spurious. Enjoyable experiences do indeed differ in all sorts of ways; but they all feel enjoyable. So among many others Locke was right: '[Pain and pleasure] like other simple ideas cannot be described, nor their names defined; the way of knowing them is, as of the simple ideas of the senses, only by experience.'[45]

William Alston objects to internalist accounts such as these that they lack what he calls 'external support':

In the case of sensory qualities . . . we can tie down the quality to a certain kind of stimulation; people ordinarily get red visual sensations when and only when their optic nerves are stimulated by stimuli of a certain physical description. Moreover, certain kinds of variations in the physical properties of the stimulus can be correlated with judgments of degrees of properties of the sensation, such as hue, saturation, and shade. These correlations support our confidence in

[44] Aristotle, *Nicomachean Ethics* 10. 4, 1174^{b}32–3.
[45] Locke, Essay, 2. 20. 1. See also the helpful discussion in Sumner, *Welfare, Happiness, and Ethics*, 87–9.

purely introspective discriminations between visual qualities. Nothing of the sort is possible with pleasantness. This quality, if such there be, does not vary with variations in physical stimuli in any discernible fashion. Nor can anything much better be found on the response side.[46]

This claim of Alston's was published in 1967. Since that time quite a lot of research has been done on enjoyment 'on the response side'. Brain-imaging studies have shown that the 'dopamine system' is involved in every kind of enjoyment, whether physical or mental. It used to be thought that this system was the basis of enjoyment, but on the basis of research by Kent Berridge and others it is now thought that the dopamine system underlies desire rather than enjoyment.[47] So where is the correlate of enjoyment in the brain? One answer is the 'opioid circuit', which involves the chemical release of endorphins and encephalins. It has been shown that opioids are involved not only in the enjoyments of appetite, but also in social enjoyments such as the feeling of security engendered by social bonding. Further, it has been suggested that one of the most important centres in the brain for enjoyment, as opposed to desire, is the ventral pallidum, a region deep in the brain; and that cell structures nearer the surface, in the orbitofrontal cortex, are involved in enjoyment, each form of enjoyment being linked with a particular subset of neurons. And there are other ideas. Research here is in its early stages, but it now seems beyond doubt that some physical correlates for some forms of enjoyment have already been discovered.[48]

4. THE PHILOSOPHY OF SWINE?

An objection to hedonism almost as old as the view itself is that it is committed to the idea that all enjoyable experiences are on the same level. Listening to a late Beethoven sonata is valuable for the same reason as purely recreational sex—because it is enjoyable. It may be

---

[46] 'Pleasure', 341.

[47] I do not wish to claim that neuroscientists have uniform or clearly worked-out conceptions of desire and enjoyment. But they probably begin with our common-sense understanding of the two, and it is at least interesting that they see no problem in drawing a distinction between them. For further helpful discussion, see Schroeder, *Three Faces of Desire*, 76–83, 103–5. I am more sanguine than Schroeder that internalism can answer various questions he asks concerning the relation between pleasure and motivation (86–8).

[48] See Phillips, 'The Pleasure Seekers', 36–40.

more enjoyable perhaps; but there is no important qualitative distinction between the two according to hedonism, whereas many would want to say that such experiences are really on entirely different evaluative levels.

Consider the following example to illustrate the point:[49]

> *Haydn and the Oyster.* You are a soul in heaven waiting to be allocated a life on Earth. It is late Friday afternoon, and you watch anxiously as the supply of available lives dwindles. When your turn comes, the angel in charge offers you a choice between two lives, that of the composer Joseph Haydn and that of an oyster. Besides composing some wonderful music and influencing the evolution of the symphony, Haydn will meet with success and honour in his own lifetime, be cheerful and popular, travel, and gain much enjoyment from field sports. The oyster's life is far less exciting. Though this is rather a sophisticated oyster, its life will consist only of mild sensual pleasure, rather like that experienced by humans when floating very drunk in a warm bath. When you request the life of Haydn, the angel sighs, 'I'll never get rid of this oyster life. It's been hanging around for ages. Look, I'll offer you a special deal. Haydn will die at the age of seventy-seven. But I'll make the oyster life as long as you like'.[50]

If all that matters to my well-being is enjoyable experience, must there not come a point at which the value of the oyster life outweighs that of the life of Haydn? And if so, is that not a strong objection to the reductionist view that only enjoyment matters? And is it not especially strong against a hedonism based on the monistic, internalist conception of enjoyment I defended in the previous section, since the same 'stuff' is what makes each life valuable and there is no way of distinguishing between them on the basis of external attitudes?

As is well known, J. S. Mill, developing some lines of argument from Plato's *Republic*, sought to answer this kind of objection by distinguishing between 'higher' and 'lower' pleasures, on the basis of a distinction between quantity of pleasure (understood in terms of intensity and duration) and quality:

It is quite compatible with the principle of utility to recognise the fact, that some kinds of pleasure are more desirable and more valuable than others. It would be absurd that while, in estimating all other things, quality is considered

---

[49] See Plato, *Philebus* 21c; McTaggart, *The Nature of Existence*, ii. 452–3. For an excellent modern discussion of the question of aggregation within lives, see Temkin, 'Rethinking the Good, Moral Ideals and the Nature of Practical Reasoning', unpub. TS, ch. 4.

[50] Crisp, *Mill on Utilitarianism*, 24.

as well as quantity, the estimation of pleasures should be supposed to depend on quantity alone.

If I am asked, what I mean by difference of quality in pleasures, or what makes one pleasure more valuable than another, merely as a pleasure, except its being greater in amount, there is but one possible answer. Of two pleasures, if there be one to which all or almost all who have experience of both give a decided preference, irrespective of any feeling of moral obligation to prefer it, that is the more desirable pleasure. If one of the two is, by those who are competently acquainted with both, placed so far above the other that they prefer it, even though knowing it to be attended with a greater amount of discontent, and would not resign it for any quantity of the other pleasure which their nature is capable of, we are justified in ascribing to the preferred enjoyment a superiority in quality, so far outweighing quantity as to render it, in comparison, of small account.[51]

Mill's argument has come under a great deal of scrutiny and it is commonly thought that he faces a dilemma.[52] Either the higher pleasures are higher because they are more pleasurable or enjoyable, in which case no special distinction between higher and lower pleasures can be drawn on the basis of anything except intensity and duration; or they are higher for some other reason, such as their being more 'noble', in which case Mill has abandoned hedonism by allowing non-hedonistic values into his formal theory.

In earlier work I suggested a way in which Mill might avoid the dilemma.[53] Logically Mill is not prevented from claiming that properties such as nobility do in fact increase the enjoyableness of experiences, thus adding a dimension along which value can increase in addition to intensity and duration. But this solution fails to get Mill entirely off the hook, since it is not clear why, if nobility can increase enjoyableness and hence value, it cannot be a good-making property in its own right, nor why an experience could not be noble without being in the slightest enjoyable.[54]

I now want to suggest that Mill was on the right track, but that to bring out his main point requires us to change the structure of his position a little. Essentially, the context of Mill's argument was as follows. Earlier empiricists had seen pleasure as something like a sensation such as an itch, the value of which depended on two factors only: intensity and

---

[51] Mill, *Utilitarianism*, 2. 4–5.   [52] See Sect. 1 above, and n. 2.
[53] *Mill on Utilitarianism*, 33–5.
[54] *Utilitarianism* 2. 9 may be read as claiming that it is absurd to deny that 'a noble character is always the happier for its nobleness'.

duration. Mill was inclined to accept this view as far as it went, merely seeking to add a third determining factor: quality. If we are reluctant to allow that enjoyment is such a sensation, however, we are likely to want to deny any special role to intensity. We may well account for one experience's being more enjoyable than another on the ground of its greater intensity, but 'intensity' here seems just another property of the enjoyed experience. Nor is intensity so understood restricted to bodily enjoyments. I might judge one massage as more enjoyable than another because of its intensity; but I might make the same sort of judgement between the enjoyment I take in listening to the opening of Brahms's Piano Concerto No. 1 and that in a Debussy étude. It might be suggested that an internalist conception of enjoyment, according to which enjoyment is a special kind of feeling, is committed to the idea that increases in the intensity of that feeling must increase the level of enjoyment. But this is to assume that internalism must involve the sensation model of enjoyment, the view that enjoyment is a determinate rather than a determinable. Enjoyment itself is not something that can be more or less intense. Enjoyed experiences can be so, and this, as we just saw, can affect enjoyableness. But one not very intense experience (listening to the Debussy, say) may well be found far more enjoyable than some quite intense experience (such as the rush from the first coffee of the day). It may be claimed, of course, that what Mill meant by intensity was not intensity of sensation, but intensity of enjoyment.[55] But enjoyment is more or less intense, as enjoyment, only in the sense that the experience in question is more or less enjoyable. Intensity so understood does not provide an independent criterion of assessment.

Duration can also be seen as yet another property or quality on which the degree of enjoyableness of some experience depends. I may judge one massage to have been more enjoyable than another because of its having been longer; and again the same point applies to mental pleasures. If I have a day to spare and am offered a choice between reading Shakespeare's sonnet 'Let me not to the marriage of true minds' and *Hamlet*, one of the reasons I might anticipate more enjoyment from the latter is simply its greater length.

So I am rejecting Mill's quantity–quality distinction as he construes it. If one experience is more enjoyable than another, it must be because the qualities of the two experiences differ in some way. But those qualities may well be intensity or duration. Nevertheless, what is at the

---

[55] See Sidgwick, *Methods*, 94.

heart of Mill's position on evaluating enjoyments seems correct, and provides us with a way of avoiding the Haydn–oyster problem.

It may have been the dream of some hedonists—Bentham perhaps—that one could invent some kind of objective scale for measuring the enjoyableness and hence the value of certain experiences, independently of the views of the subject. But that—as Plato and Mill saw—is merely a dream. In most cases, the final arbiter on how enjoyable some experience is, and how it compares to some other, is the subject herself. It is true that even a subject's own view is not guaranteed correct: she may suffer from some kind of cultural bias or self-deception, for example, leading her to play down how enjoyable some kind of experience actually was for her, or her memory may be unreliable.[56] But what those who experience enjoyment say must be given proper attention in a satisfactory account of the value of enjoyment.

So imagine someone who has just drunk a cool glass of lemonade and has also completed her first reading of Jane Austen's *Pride and Prejudice*. If we ask her to rank on a scale of enjoyableness the experience of drinking the lemonade against that of reading the novel, she may well rank the novel higher than the lemonade. Why? There is much more to this judgement than mere duration. There is nothing to prevent our judge's claiming that it would not matter how long the experience of enjoyable drinking could be prolonged: she would never enjoy it as much as she enjoyed the novel. For what she enjoyed in the novel was its wit, its beautiful syntax, and its exquisite delineation of character. The loss of such enjoyments (that is, enjoyable experiences)—in the context of her own life—could never be compensated for, in terms of enjoyment alone, by *any* amount of lemonade enjoyment.[57]

So a hedonist, once she takes sufficient note of the fact that we refer to many more qualities than that of duration in explaining what we find enjoyable in our experiences, has the resources to explain the vastly greater value we put on certain enjoyable experiences without introducing non-hedonist elements into the account of well-being. To insist that the internalist hedonist must allow that the life of the oyster at some point becomes more valuable than that of Haydn is just to rule out the Millian solution of the problem at the outset.

---

[56] Many of these sources of error in self-reporting are well discussed in the 'positive psychology' literature. Kahneman, for example, notes that bad weather affects self-reports: 'Objective Happiness', 21.

[57] This would, then, be a case of what Griffin calls 'discontinuity' (*Well-Being*, 85–9).

There is nothing in the kind of internalism I have described using the determinable–determinate distinction that is inconsistent with allowing that the assessment of the enjoyableness and hence the value of an experience might depend partly on the phenomenological quality of that experience, that is, on what the subject is taking enjoyment *in*. Yes, the oyster's life becomes increasingly more enjoyable and valuable as it is extended; but it never, perhaps, becomes as enjoyable as the life of Haydn.

At this point a hedonist about well-being may wish to admit the existence of certain non-hedonistic aesthetic values, the appreciation of which can be enjoyed to such an extent that such enjoyments become discontinuously more valuable than certain bodily enjoyments. But it is still enjoyment alone that matters to well-being. Nobility on its own, for example, does not make an experience better for its subject. But if enjoyed it may justify a preference for one kind of experience over another, of whatever duration.

But, the anti-hedonist may insist, if we are to ascribe such value, or at least significance in appraisal of value, to the enjoyment of appreciating the beauty of Jane Austen's syntax, should we not admit that such appreciation on its own, without enjoyment, can increase a person's well-being? Or at the very least that what is adding value in such cases is an 'organic whole' composed of appreciation (which may well be valueless without enjoyment) and enjoyment?[58] Here the hedonist must first claim that, on reflection, we should conclude that appreciation without enjoyment is without value for the individual herself, though of course she may allow that it makes for, say, a better human life, or adds to the aesthetic value instantiated in the history of the universe in some way.[59] What about organic wholes? The hedonist will have no objection to allowing in reference to aesthetic appreciation at the level of enumerative theory. That is, enjoyable appreciation of aesthetic value may feature on the list of goods constituting well-being. But at the level of explanatory theory, she will insist that what makes such appreciation good for the subject is its being enjoyed, and that alone. Reference may be made to aesthetic value, as we have seen, in explaining what makes the experience enjoyable and what is being enjoyed. But allowing any contribution to welfare in such cases to come from the appreciation itself leaves unanswered the following question: If, as the

---

[58] See Moore, *Principia Ethica*, 82–3; Parfit. *Reasons and Persons*, app. i.
[59] See Edwards, *Pleasures and Pains*, 102–5; and Sect. 5 (D) below.

organic whole theorist suggests, appreciation can contribute to welfare alongside enjoyment, why can it not contribute on its own?

The hedonist, then, appears to have a response to the philosophy of swine objection, as stated in terms of the Haydn–oyster case. But now consider a new version of that problem, in which the angel in charge offers to manipulate my desires in the case of the oyster, so that even were I fully acquainted with the kind of enjoyments in each life, I would now desire the oyster life much more strongly, and would during my life as an oyster have very strong desires for the experience I was having. (If I express doubt concerning whether an oyster *could* have very strong desires for anything, the angel will respond by saying that this particular oyster will really be just like a human being who happens to have very strong desires for oyster enjoyments.) Is the hedonist not committed to the view that the oyster life will be better for me?

If the effect of altering my present desires, and the desires of the oyster, is to affect my judgement, then all that the angel has done is to create a scenario in which I am not in a position properly to judge my levels of enjoyment. But it may well be that my judgement is not affected. I may be a compulsive hand-washer, but know perfectly well that were I to listen to some music rather than stand at the sink for the next few hours, I would have a much more enjoyable time.

5. THE EXPERIENCE MACHINE AND THE VALUE OF ACCOMPLISHMENT

Hedonism is a form of mental state theory according to which what matters to well-being is experiences alone. That leaves it open to objections based around the following notorious case described by Robert Nozick:

> *The Experience Machine.* Suppose there were an experience machine that would give you any experience you desired. Superduper neuropsychologists could stimulate your brain so that you would think and feel you were writing a great novel, or making a friend, or reading an interesting book. All the time you would be floating in a tank, with electrodes attached to your brain . . . Would you plug in? *What else can matter to us, other than how our lives feel from the inside?*[60]

---

[60] Nozick, *Anarchy, State, and Utopia*, 42–3. See also Nozick, *The Examined Life*, 104–8.

Nozick believes that the experience machine example shows that various things do matter to us in addition to our experiences: (1) we want to do certain things; (2) we want to be a certain kind of person; (3) we want to be able to make contact with a reality deeper than one that is entirely man-made. We might call these the values of accomplishment, personhood, and authentic understanding.

Let me avoid the question whether we as individuals would plug into such a machine, since it raises a variety of unnecessary technical and empirical issues, and also is likely to elicit answers influenced by contingent and differing attitudes each of us might have to risk. Rather let me restate the example in terms of the well-being inherent in various parallel lives. First consider P. P writes a great novel, is courageous, kind, intelligent, witty, and loving, and makes significant scientific discoveries. In other words, her life includes all three of the things Nozick suggests we value in addition to mere experience. Let me add, in the light of some further doubts Nozick has about such machines in general, that P makes her major life choices quite autonomously.[61] And let me stipulate also that P enjoys all these aspects of her life.

Now consider Q. Q is connected to an experience machine from birth, and has experiences which are introspectively indiscernible from P's (imagine that the superduper neuropsychologists have somehow copied P's experiences, which are then 'replayed' to Q). According to hedonism, P and Q have exactly the same level of well-being. And that is surely a claim from which most of us will recoil.

What can the hedonist reply? It might be worth noting first that the hedonist is not able to appeal to the notion of broad or wide content to argue that the experience of genuine accomplishment, with all its attendant intentional attitudes, is entirely different from the experience of quasi-accomplishment on the machine.[62] That might help a mental state theorist willing to allow good-making properties other than those of enjoyment. But the fact remains that P and Q—just because their lives are introspectibly indistinguishable—enjoy their lives equally. One might indeed argue that, in terms of broad content, enjoying really completing a typescript of a novel is different from enjoying the mere

---

[61] Nozick, *Anarchy, State, and Utopia*, 44–5.
[62] For this distinction, see e.g. Putnam, 'The Meaning of "Meaning"'; Burge, 'Individualism and the Mental'. For its use in an attempt to defend hedonism, see Donner, *The Liberal Self*.

appearance of completion. But the two experiences are nevertheless equally enjoyable.

In the previous chapter we saw that intuitions appropriately reflected upon are unavoidable in ethical theory. But one problem with the experience machine example, as it is often employed in lectures to first-year undergraduates as well as in the literature, is that it is used too swiftly, as a way of dispatching hedonism quickly and hygienically before moving on to some other view. It is true that the intuitions of many of those who are inclined to reject hedonism when faced with the experience machine example will stand up to their own calm reflection. But what I shall suggest in the remainder of this chapter is that there are considerations often not taken fully into account in such reflection that once given appropriate weight show that wholesale rejection of hedonism as unreasonable and implausible is not justified. Several of these lines of argument have their analogues in the debates between consequentialists and their critics, and the general moral of the story is that hedonism deserves at least the run for its money that consequentialism gets—and that it certainly used to get in ancient times.[63] For ease of exposition I shall concentrate on the value of accomplishment. All of the arguments below apply to accomplishment, though it is important to note that versions of most of them apply also to the alleged values of personhood, authentic understanding, and autonomy.

A. Inherent Enjoyment

Accomplishment involves many experiences, and they are often experiences people tend to enjoy.[64] In writing a novel, the planning of the plot, the exercise of the imagination in developing the characters, the engagement with writing itself, and the contemplation of one's achievements throughout and at the conclusion of the process may all be hugely enjoyable. This is not a knock-down point against a non-hedonistic account of the value of accomplishment. But it does draw attention to the fact that those goods cited by non-hedonists are goods we often, indeed usually, enjoy. Much more problematic than accomplishment

---

[63] Robert Wardy acutely described hedonism to me as 'the consequentialism of the ancient world'.

[64] See Sidgwick, *Methods*, 401. Sidgwick claims that such goods 'seem to obtain the commendation of Common Sense . . . in proportion to the degree of [their] productiveness [of pleasure]'. That seems to me a plausible hypothesis.

for a hedonist would be a case of a good which is both widely accepted as a contributor to well-being and never enjoyed.

B. The Paradox of Hedonism and Secondary Principles

Let us assume that the non-hedonist remains unpersuaded. On reflection, she thinks, the enjoyment of accomplishment is only part of the story about what makes it valuable for people; accomplishment has its own value, independent of the enjoyment inherent in and consequent on it. The hedonist may now try to draw inspiration from some of the things consequentialists say about non-consequentialist moral principles, such as those forbidding killing or requiring loyalty. According to one standard line of consequentialist argument, accepting and acting on such 'secondary' principles are justified by consequentialism, since the results of doing so will be better—in consequentialist terms—than those of any attempt consistently to live by the consequentialist principle alone.[65] Killing people is usually bad overall, from the consequentialist point of view, and loyalty, as part of a personal relationship, good.

If we allow that in the usual case someone will enjoy accomplishing more than accomplishing less, then there are good reasons to think that motivation by non-hedonist beliefs may be more successful, by hedonist lights, than motivation by hedonist beliefs.[66] One version of the paradox of hedonism is that one will gain more enjoyment by trying to do something other than to enjoy oneself. The tennis player who forgets about enjoyment and focuses on winning will enjoy the game more than were she to aim explicitly at enjoyment. What the hedonist has to note in addition is that the player who thinks that winning really matters is going to find it easier to focus on that as a goal, and to be more strongly motivated to achieve it. Thus, over time, human beings have developed dispositions and understandings of goods that, though apparently non-hedonistic, are in fact securely based on their capacity for the promotion of enjoyment.[67]

---

[65] The term 'secondary' is from Mill, *Utilitarianism*; see 2. 24. For a well-known recent version of the argument, see Railton, 'Alienation, Consequentialism, and the Demands of Morality'. Interestingly, Railton makes his case for consequentialism via the paradox of hedonism and distinctions between different forms of hedonism.

[66] See Sidgwick, *Methods*, 403, 405–6.

[67] See Railton, 'Naturalism and Prescriptivity', 167–9; Kawall, 'The Experience Machine and Mental States of Well-Being', 384.

Also worth mentioning here is Mill's associationist suggestion in *Utilitarianism* that human beings often slide from valuing something as a means to enjoyment to valuing that thing as an end in itself.[68] Mill's example is money; but a structurally similar argument could be made for accomplishment.

C. The Evolution of Values

The previous argument seeks to explain the internal evaluative view on accomplishment: why it is that creatures like us may rationally have developed non-hedonistic dispositions and beliefs. We are goal-seeking beings, and enjoy the process of achieving goals and their completion. Belief in the independent value of those goals can itself increase that enjoyment. But there is a further, external, perspective to take on our non-hedonistic evaluative beliefs, and this involves considering their historical origin. Accomplishment provides a good example of how this kind of argument might proceed. It goes almost without saying that the values each of us holds are at the very least heavily shaped by the cultural and social practices in which we found ourselves from a very young age. The attitudes of others, especially attitudes of our parents involving praise and blame, have a huge influence on what we end up valuing.

At this point, we can pull back the focus to consider the development of human values as a whole from their origins in groups or societies very different from our own. It would be surprising if human values had not been affected to some extent by the attitudes of our hunter-gatherer ancestors in the Stone Age, which in Europe, Asia, and Africa began about 2 million years ago and ended as recently as about 4000 BCE. Those who achieved more in the field—who brought back more meat, fungi or fruit—would have been rewarded by their fellows, partly with a larger share of the available goods, but also with esteem and status within the group. Now this story is of course not on its own sufficient to debunk the claim of accomplishment to independent non-hedonic value for individuals. But it does, I suggest, throw that claim into some doubt. Could it not be that our valuing of accomplishment is an example of a

---

[68] Mill, *Utilitarianism*, 4. 5–7. For a nicely stated modern version of this argument, making reference to Brandt and Railton, see Silverstein, 'In Defense of Happiness: A Response to the Experience Machine', 293–6.

kind of collective bad faith, with its roots in the spontaneous and largely unreflective social practices of our distant ancestors?

This and the previous argument apply not only to accomplishment, but also to authenticity, which is one of the values often alleged to be violated on the experience machine. Valuing honesty, transparency, genuineness, and so on has a clear pay-off: it fends off deception, and thereby assists understanding of the world, which itself issues in a clear evolutionary advantage.

D. The Anhedonic Life

Here is another kind of argument the hedonist may carry across from the debate over consequentialism, in particular the debate over the welfarism at the heart of central consequentialist views such as utilitarianism. When it is claimed that there are non-welfarist goods, such as desert or equality, which might add value to an action or a state of affairs independently of any contribution to well-being, a standard welfarist response consists in isolating those alleged goods in cases where nothing beneficial to individuals comes of them, and then questioning their status. Do we really think that there is anything to be said for punishing a criminal, even if it does no one any good and harms the criminal? Do we really think that there is anything to be said for equality, even in cases in which its promotion harms all concerned?

Consider now the life of R. R's life is as far as is possible like P's, with all the enjoyment—and the suffering—stripped out. So R writes a great novel, but finds no enjoyment in what she is doing or in what she achieves. She is not especially gloomy or depressed, and is motivated by the thought that accomplishment will advance her own well-being and that she has a moral duty to use her talents. Is it plausible to think that R's life is of any value *for her*? We might well think that R's accomplishment is admirable, as part of a good human life. Or we might think it makes her life more meaningful in some sense. But is it plausible to think that it could make her life better for her if she herself does not enjoy what she does or reflection on it, and in that sense does not care about these things?

This case, however, might be said at most to suggest only that enjoyment is a necessary condition for well-being, not its only constituent. Perhaps well-being consists wholly or partly in an 'organic whole', comprising genuine accomplishment on the one hand, and enjoyment of that accomplishment on the other.[69] It would indeed be a mistake, as G. E. Moore pointed out, to think that because accomplishment on its own does not contribute to well-being, it cannot therefore be a real contributor in the company of other goods. Indeed it may even be the case that enjoyment alone of something which is no accomplishment, but is believed to be so by the enjoyer, is without value.

Now I have to accept that this is a logically available view. But, as I have already suggested, the idea of an organic whole involves a mystery. Accomplishing something, and the enjoyment of accomplishment, seem conceptually quite distinct, and the case of R shows that they can come apart in cases that may at least be imagined without too much difficulty. The question that remains to be answered by an advocate of this kind of organic whole view is this: If accomplishment can make a contribution to well-being when it is enjoyed, why do we find that it cannot do the same in the absence of enjoyment? After all, its intrinsic good-making features appear to be present in both kinds of case. Until that question is answered, the case of the anhedonic life remains problematic for a non-hedonist theory of well-being.

E. Perspectives

Accomplishment as a constituent of well-being is tied in various significant ways to values other than well-being. When someone writes a great novel, the greatness of the novel itself—its aesthetic value, or its historical significance, say—is essential to understanding why it is that we count such activities as potentially part of well-being. But because of this link to values beyond well-being, the significance of accomplishment may be thrown into doubt. It is of course true that, viewed from the inside, what I accomplish may matter a good deal to me. I may plan my life around what I might accomplish, and make many sacrifices to achieve my goals. But the internal viewpoint is not the only one available. As Thomas Nagel puts it, 'In seeing ourselves from outside we find it difficult to take our lives seriously.'[70] We might imagine P's comparing her novel-writing to the work of God, for example. What is writing even a novel as fine as *Middlemarch* or *War and Peace* compared to creating the universe? Or imagine that we could all write as well as Eliot and Tolstoy.[71] Would we then

---

[69] See Sect. 4 above.   [70] Nagel, *The View from Nowhere*, 214.
[71] See Nozick, *Anarchy, State, and Utopia*, 241, 245.

think so highly of the achievements of those who write such books? Further, if the idea is that the value of accomplishment lies in achieving our potential, why do we think Mozart's achievements so much more significant than those of a mouse who, by murine standards, excelled as much? And in the end the products of all human activities will turn to dust. From the point of view of eternity, why does anything I do matter?

I am not saying that these questions about perspective cannot be answered. But answered they must be by anyone claiming that accomplishment makes an independent contribution to well-being. Enjoyment, because it has no intrinsic link with non-welfarist values, is not so prone to perspectival doubt. It may be true that part of my enjoyment in what I accomplish depends on beliefs I have about the significance of that accomplishment. So the external viewpoint may in fact lead to a decrease in my enjoyment. But enjoyment itself does not seem to demand justification from the outside in the same way as accomplishment, since it makes no grand claims for significance. Enjoyment seems just obviously part of well-being.

F. Agency

Accomplishment involves doing. We ascribe value to this doing independently of its outcome.[72] Imagine that Michelangelo had had a pupil more brilliant even than himself, and that he had allowed this pupil to paint the ceiling of the Sistine Chapel. The credit for the painting would have gone not to Michelangelo himself, but to the pupil. This kind of credit or admiration mirrors the blame that is directed at the captain and Pedro his henchman in Bernard Williams's famous case of *Jim and the Indians*, in the scenario in which Jim refuses to take part himself in the killing.[73] Consequentialists, of course, have long doubted the huge significance ascribed to agency in our common-sense evaluations. But the intuitions of those less sympathetic to consequentialism may also be weakened by consideration of, for example, the so-called 'paradox of deontology': does a rule against killing to prevent more killings not involve a self-indulgent or fetishistic focus on agency?[74] Perhaps

---

[72] See my 'Utilitarianism and Accomplishment'.
[73] Williams, 'A Critique of Utilitarianism', 98–100.
[74] See Scheffler, *The Rejection of Consequentialism*, ch. 4.

accomplishment involves the same sort of overvaluing of what people do over what happens.

G. Free Will

Enjoyment as a value does not seem to depend on freedom of the will. Q, whose experiences are the result of a 'playing back' of the recorded experiences of P, enjoys her life as much as P. Again, accomplishment is in a different category. If accomplishment is to merit the various attitudes of admiration we take towards it and earn a place as a constituent of well-being in our world, it must be the case that either libertarianism or compatibilism is true. Both of these views are notoriously problematic. Many argue that libertarianism is incoherent, and equally many that compatibilism, as a form of determinism, does not allow sufficient room for the kinds of evaluation and assessment of action inherent in our ordinary practices. If accomplishment is merely the 'occurrence' in my life of some productive process leading to some state of independent value, it is unclear why any special contribution should be made to my well-being in particular, as opposed, say, to the well-being of some spectator. Again, the onus of proof here is on the proponent of the view that accomplishment makes an independent non-hedonistic contribution to well-being to provide an adequate theory of free will to back this claim up. Appeals to our intuitions about specific cases of accomplishment are not enough.

To conclude. My primary aim in this chapter was not to prove hedonism about well-being beyond reasonable doubt, but to suggest that such hedonism is at least not an unreasonable position. My hope is that my positive formulation of the view itself, and my suggestions of ways in which it might be defended against two especially problematic objections, have achieved this modest goal. Maybe the time will come for us to bury hedonism for good; but that time is not now.

5

Practical Reason

1. TEMPORAL NEUTRALITY AND THE SELF

In Chapter 3 I claimed that it is self-evident that if some action of mine promotes my well-being I have a reason to do it proportional in strength to the degree of promotion. Some philosophers, however, have suggested that the strength of self-interested reasons is affected also by the temporal location of the relevant goods. Imagine that at time t I have the option of performing two actions. Action a will provide me with good g tomorrow; action b will provide me with good g many years hence. Everything else is equal. Does the fact that good g is nearer in time give me a stronger reason to perform action a than to perform action b?

It is natural to think that it does not.[1] If the good to be secured by action b were less certain than that to be secured by a, matters would be different. But the mere temporal location of some good or bad in my life is in itself irrelevant to my reasons. Now a further question. Call a person now *individual-t*, and that person in the future *individual-t¹*, *individual-t²*, and so on. What is it about the relation of *individual-t* to these future individuals that gives *individual-t* reason to promote the well-being of *individuals-t¹*, $-t^2$, and so on? Again there is an obvious common-sense answer: it is the fact that *individual-t* is the same person as *individuals-t¹*, $-t^2$, and so on, that terminology being merely a way of referring to the same person at different times. I have reason now to promote my own future well-being since I am identical to the temporally located individuals who will experience that well-being.

This common-sense view, however, has been thrown into doubt by Derek Parfit. Especially important is Parfit's case of

> *My Division.* My body is fatally injured, as are the brains of my two brothers. My brain is divided, and each half is successfully transplanted

[1] See Sidgwick, *Methods*, 119.

into the body of one of my brothers. Each of the resulting people believes that he is me, seems to remember living my life, has my character, and is in every other way psychologically continuous with me. And he has a body that is very like mine.[2]

Now imagine a case of division in which I know in advance what is going to happen. Should I believe that I have any reason to promote the well-being of either or both of the people who will result from the operation? Consider again the location of goods. If I can act either so as to bring about *g* in my life before the operation, or so as to bring about *g* in the life of one of the individuals resulting from the operation, there seems little justification for thinking that there is anything to choose between these actions. This shows that, as Parfit puts it, it is not identity that matters, but in this case 'double survival'.[3] But what does 'survival' consist in? Again we must ask what it is about my relation to these future individuals that grounds my reason to promote their good. The answer Parfit gives to this question seems attractive: it is the relations of psychological continuity and/or connectedness, with the right kind of cause.[4]

But what is 'the right kind of cause'? As Jeff McMahan brings out in a strikingly clear discussion of these issues, if the view that it is these psychological relations that matter is too liberal with what can count as the right kind of cause, this will have implications in cases of 'replication' that seem unacceptable.[5] Consider another famous example from Parfit:

> *Teletransportation.* I enter the Teletransporter. I have been to Mars before, but only by the old method, a space-ship journey taking several weeks. This machine will send me at the speed of light. I merely have to press the green button. Like others, I am nervous. Will it work? I remind myself what I have been told to expect. When I press the button, I shall lose consciousness, and then wake up at what seems a moment later. In fact, I shall have been unconscious for about an hour. The Scanner here on Earth will destroy my brain and body, while recording the exact states of all of my cells. It will then transmit this information by radio. Travelling at the speed of light, the message will take three minutes to reach the Replicator on Mars. This will then create, out of new matter, a brain and a body exactly like mine.[6]

---

[2] *Reasons and Persons*, 254–5.   [3] Ibid. 262.   [4] Ibid.
[5] *The Ethics of Killing*, 56–9.
[6] Parfit, *Reasons and Persons*, 199.

The question here is whether before I enter the teletransporter I have any egoistic reason to act to further the well-being of the individual who results from teletransportation. According to those who hold that what matter are relations of psychological continuity and connectedness and that teletransportation constitutes the right kind of cause, my reasons in relation to that individual are as strong in a case of teletransportation as they would be in a case in which I travelled by spaceship. But the individual resulting from teletransportation appears to be an entirely different person from the one who entered the teletransporter. The one who entered has been destroyed, and a new one, a replica of the original, has been created. So the only concern that I can have for that future person is not egoistic but the concern one might have for someone very like oneself.

In fact, I suggest, we need not detain ourselves in working out which kinds of cause are the right ones. According to the view that what grounds egoistic reasons are psychological continuity and connectedness, I can have no egoistic reason to promote the well-being of some future individual psychologically discontinuous and unconnected with my present self. But this seems to me—as again to McMahan—to be mistaken. Consider the following case:[7]

> *Alzheimer's.* You are diagnosed as suffering from Alzheimer's disease, and told that within ten years you will exist as an 'isolated subject', conscious only of the present moment, with no memories or expectations. You are told also that soon after you become such a subject you will, unless you take action now, suffer from a condition which will cause you extreme agony for twenty-four hours.

According to the psychological relations view, your reason to take action now is of the same kind as a reason you might now have to save some stranger, with whom you are quite unconnected, from suffering similar extreme agony. But it seems to me that your reason to take action to avoid this suffering is as strong as it would be were the suffering to be about to occur immediately, or were you in future not to be a victim of Alzheimer's and now to be strongly psychologically continuous and connected with the individual who will suffer.

McMahan's response to these problems with the psychological relations view is to adopt what he calls the 'Embodied Mind Account of

---

[7] See McMahan, *Ethics of Killing*, 65–6. The term 'isolated subject' is his.

Egoistic Concern', according to which 'the basis for an individual's egoistic concern about the future—that which is both necessary and sufficient for rational egoistic concern—is the physical and functional continuity of enough of those areas of the individual's brain in which consciousness is realized to preserve the capacity to support consciousness or mental activity'.[8] This view strikes me as largely correct, although there seems no good reason to restrict the basis of consciousness to the brain. If one's capacity for consciousness is realized in some experience machine, for example, and one is capable of performing 'virtual actions', there seems to be as strong a basis for egoistic concern as in the case in which one's capacity for consciousness is realized within a brain.

What grounds egoistic reasons, then, is continuity of capacity for consciousness.[9] I have egoistic reason to promote the well-being of some future individual to the extent that the capacity for consciousness of that individual can be seen as a continuation of my capacity now. Because of the possibility of division, we must allow that a capacity can split, but in such a way that each of the resulting capacities can be seen as continuations of that earlier capacity. Further, we must accept a certain amount of vagueness as to whether some capacity at t^1 is continuous with a capacity at t or not.[10] If we imagine a case in which all the cells in my brain are replaced all at once, there is clear discontinuity; whereas if all the cells in my brain are replaced serially over a long period, there is clear continuity. At some point on the spectrum between these two types of case, there will be no answer to the question whether there is continuity or not. But in all cases now likely to occur, the answer will not be vague in this way.

It might be thought that in serial replacement the person's egoistic reasons at t vary in strength in proportion to the degree to which the physical grounding of their capacity for consciousness at t is continuous or discontinuous with that capacity at $t^1 \ldots t^n$.[11] This, however, seems to confuse what matters—continuity of consciousness—with what grounds that continuity. In an Alzheimer's case in which all my brain cells are replaced before the suffering occurs, the replacement over time seems irrelevant to my concern for the contents of the consciousness

8 Ibid. 67–8.
9 I wish to allow that continuity of capacity is consistent with a failure or even an inability to exercise the capacity in question over some significant period, as in cases in which people fall into comas and then 'wake up' many years later.
10 Ibid. 70–2.   11 Ibid. 72.

that result from the exercise in future of this current capacity for consciousness I now have.

A hedonistic conception of well-being sits especially well with what we might call the *continuing capacity for consciousness view* of self-interested reasons (let me call it *view C*). According to hedonism, all that matters for my well-being is how much enjoyment and suffering I experience. On the view that, say, accomplishment is the primary constituent of well-being, relations of psychological continuity and connectedness may be thought of greater significance, in that they make possible that very good itself. Further, egoistic reasons may extend beyond consciousness, even to the time after a person's death, given that what I accomplish may depend on posthumous events.[12] But in fact the holder of any view that includes the so-called 'experience requirement' on well-being can plausibly adopt view C. For if what matters to me from the egoistic perspective is what affects my consciousness in future, then experiencing accomplishment may be held to be as important as experiencing enjoyment or not experiencing suffering.

I am contending that egoistic reasons concern only the quality of the experiences resulting from the exercise of the capacity for consciousness that I now possess. McMahan, though he accepts that what he calls *functional continuity*—'the retention of the brain's basic psychological *capacities*'—is sufficient for minimal egoistic concern, suggests that *organizational continuity* also matters, this consisting in 'the preservation of those configurations of tissue that underlie the connections and continuities among the *contents* of an individual's mental life over time'.[13]

McMahan asks us to imagine a sentient creature who lives pleasantly enough but entirely in the specious present (that is, an isolated subject) and claims that the reason to care *for this creature's own sake* whether it continues to live or not is 'absolutely minimal...Lacking any *unity* apart from their common grounding in the same brain, they fail to form a *unit* in any but the most minimal sense'.[14] Psychological unity, however, McMahan suggests, 'gives our lives as wholes a moral and prudential significance that the mere sum of our experiences lacks'.

---

[12] For brief discussions, see e.g. Aristotle, *Nicomachean Ethics* 1. 10–11; Parfit, *Reasons and Persons*, 495.
[13] *Ethics of Killing*, 68, 74–82.   [14] Ibid. 75–6.

Here I suspect that McMahan may be moving from an intuition about whether it matters 'from the point of view of the universe' whether this creature continues to live to a claim about whether such continuation is *good for* that creature. It may not matter much in itself whether this creature continues to live, and indeed it may not matter at all if the creature is replaced by one exactly like it. But the death of this creature seems to be one of the worst things that can happen to it. Further, if we imagine another being with full organizational continuity, but whose well-being will be overall equal to that of the isolated subject, it seems that we should have no more reason to care for this being's own sake whether it continues to live than we do in the case of the isolated subject. And note that, from the point of view of the universe, it is equally unimportant whether this individual dies and is replaced as is the case with the isolated subject. In other words, though organizational continuity will almost certainly have indirect effects on an individual's well-being, in itself it does not matter.

It may be, however, that McMahan is not making this shift in perspective but arguing that the very notion of something's being good *for* an isolated subject makes no sense. But he allows that we may speak of the 'sum' of such a subject's experiences, and this is enough for us to speak of that sum as constituting the well-being of that subject. That may leave the subject as a unit only in the 'most minimal sense', but it is, I suggest, a sense sufficient to ground the notion of well-being.

2. THE DUALISM OF PRACTICAL REASON

Each of us has a reason to promote her own future well-being, the strongest such reason being to promote it maximally across the rest of one's conscious life, on the assumption that the capacity for consciousness one now has continues to exist without division until the end of that life. Is that the only reason each of us has? This view—egoism about reasons—is a perennially attractive position. As Sidgwick says:

it is hardly going too far to say that common sense assumes that 'interested' actions, tending to promote the agent's happiness, are *prima facie* reasonable: and that the *onus probandi* lies with those who maintain that disinterested conduct, as such, is reasonable.[15]

15 *Methods*, 120.

Consider the following case:

> *Two Doors 1.* You are confronted by two doors. If you do not pass
> through one or other of them, you will suffer an extremely painful
> electric shock. If you pass through door A, nothing further will
> happen. If you pass through door B, some other person, a stranger
> and out of sight, will suffer an extremely painful electric shock.
> Once you have passed through either door, you will entirely forget
> what has happened.[16]

Some people claim that there is no reason for you to pass through door
A rather than door B. These people are in the grip of an egoistic theory
to the point where they cannot appreciate what to most of us is obvious.
Egoism is mistaken, since what I shall call the *dual-source view* is correct:
the well-being of others can provide one with reasons to act in addition
to those provided by one's own well-being, in the sense that from the
impartial point of view the well-being of all, including oneself, should
be considered. But should we think that the well-being of others can
serve only as a tie-breaker, giving us a reason to choose one action over
another of equal benefit to us? Now consider:

> *Two Doors 2.* You are confronted by two doors. If you do not pass
> through one or other of them, you will suffer an extremely painful
> electric shock. If you pass through door A, you will experience a
> minor twinge in your leg, but nothing further will happen. If you
> pass through door B, you will not experience the twinge, but some
> other person, a stranger and out of sight, will suffer an extremely
> painful electric shock.

To claim that you have stronger reason to pass through door B than
through door A is almost as implausible as the claim that in *Two Doors 1*
there is nothing to choose between the doors. The well-being of others,
in other words, can ground reasons to act which override the reason we
have to promote our own well-being.

It might now be thought that what is doing all the work here is merely
the well-being at stake, and that we should accept that we are heading in
the direction of pure impartiality. In his discussion of egoism, Hastings
Rashdall says:

It is no doubt quite intelligible that one thing should appear reasonably to be
desired from a man's own point of view, and another thing when he takes the

---

[16] I shall assume memory loss in each of the elaborations of this case below.

point of view of a larger whole. But can both of these points of view be equally reasonable? How can it be reasonable to take the point of view of the part once the man knows the existence of the whole and admits that the whole is more important than the part? Must not the point of view of the whole be the one and only reasonable point of view?[17]

Consider:

> *Two Doors 3.* You are confronted by two doors. If you do not pass through one or other of them, you will suffer an extremely painful electric shock. If you pass through door A, you will experience a less painful but significant shock. If you pass through door B, you will not experience this shock, but some other person, a stranger and out of sight, will suffer a shock of the same intensity.

Clearly, you have a reason to pass through one of these doors. If Rashdall is right, then which door you choose is irrelevant, since 'from the point of view of the whole' the outcome is the same. But this is very hard to believe. Surely you have a reason—a strong reason—to choose door B over door A grounded in the fact that it is that door which will significantly promote your well-being?[18] Rashdall may of course deny this, and we are close to intuitional bedrock at this point. But let me ask you really to imagine yourself in *Two Doors 3*. Could you accept in that situation that you have as strong a reason to choose door A as to choose door B? If not, then you will probably find Rashdall's language of part and wholes misleading. One's own well-being is indeed part of the whole, in the sense that it is one of the components of the sum total of well-beings at stake. But that whole is not the whole story. What also determines your reasons is the fundamental fact that your own well-being is yours.

An objection to my interpretation of *Two Doors 3* is that it can make sacrifice for others irrational. Imagine that in *Two Doors 3*, you choose door A, because you prefer to take the burden of suffering upon yourself rather than inflict it on someone else. We can imagine a slight variation of the case, in which the suffering of the other person will be slightly worse than yours, but not such as to outweigh (on the model I am outlining) the reason to promote your own good.

---

[17] Rashdall, *The Theory of Good and Evil*, i. 56.
[18] See Sprigge, *Rational Foundations*, 189–90.

This is a powerful objection, but some responses are available. First, most people accept that sacrifice can be irrational, even to the point where it is no longer admirable but just crazy. Consider:

> *Two Doors 4.* You are confronted by two doors. If you do not pass through one or other of them, you will suffer an extremely painful electric shock. If you pass through door A, you will experience a less painful but significant shock. If you pass through door B, you will not experience this shock, but some other person, a stranger and out of sight, will suffer a minor twinge in their leg.

Entering door A would be self-sacrificial, but it would also be widely accepted as irrational. Second, note that the terms 'rational' and 'irrational' anyway have emotive and potentially moral connotations. To describe someone as irrational often constitutes a form of blame. For that reason, and for the sake of parsimony, we should avoid these terms. So what is true of *Two Doors 3* is that your reason to enter door A is weaker than your reason to enter door B. To deny that—as no doubt many will—is likely to involve use of the moral concepts we have seen reason to avoid in trying to understand ultimate reasons. Finally, since morality as a practice is something of great value, those who believe that the kind of sacrifice that is ordinarily thought admirable is sometimes performed for less than the strongest reason may nevertheless have an egoistic or impartial reason to express admiration for such sacrifice, and not to seek to expunge any disposition they have to feel such admiration.

A further objection to my interpretation of *Two Doors 3* is that, since I suggested in Chapter 1 that there seems to be no good reason for accepting any significant ultimate difference between what one does and what one allows, the view licenses harming others to further one's own interests, even when the harm inflicted is greater than the benefit to one.[19] Consider:

> *Two Doors 5.* You are confronted by two doors. If you do not pass through one or other of them, you will suffer an extremely painful electric shock. If you pass directly through either door, you will experience a less painful but significant shock. If you push a red button in front of door B and then pass through it, you will not experience this shock. But your pushing this button will cause

[19] For a similar objection, see Kagan, *Limits of Morality*, 22; see also Scheffler, 'Prerogatives without Restrictions', and the references cited in his n. 4; and Mulgan, *The Demands of Consequentialism*, 153–4, 161–5.

some other person, a stranger and out of sight, to experience an extremely painful electric shock of the same magnitude as the one you will suffer if you stay where you are.

Unless the reason to promote your own good can never conflict with an other-regarding reason, some such scenario as the above must be possible. On some versions of the view I am describing, the reason to promote one's own well-being may be especially strong, which may allow an agent to inflict serious harm on another person to promote her own good (perhaps killing someone in the prime of their life so as to benefit from their will).

This objection rests on the notion that doing harm may be fundamentally more significant than allowing it, a notion I suggested in Chapter 1 may be flawed. What matters in one's actions is the effects on well-being, one's own and that of others, and not whether those effects arise from doing or allowing. Nor should it be thought that the dual-source view has as a practical implication that we should change the moral education of our children, teaching them that they may harm others in pursuit of their own interests. Since we have been brought up with common-sense morality, and since we live in a culture based on common-sense morality, harming others is likely to be far more psychologically and socially costly than letting harm occur.[20] Nor should it be considered a direct implication of the dual-source view that, collectively, we should seek to erase the significance of the doing—allowing distinction entirely. Human beings are not creatures of pure reason. We have an evolutionary background and an emotional make-up which cannot be ignored in ethics. In particular, we show special concern for those visibly near us, and for what we *do* to them.[21] It is likely that removing such partiality entirely, if it were possible, would have consequences far worse than seeking gradually to ameliorate its effects on those far away to whom we allow harm to occur.

The dual-source view may be understood as a version of what Sidgwick called 'the dualism of practical reason'.[22] But my version is in a significant way different from, and hence less pessimistic than, Sidgwick's. Sidgwick saw the intuitive appeal of both egoism and impartial utilitarianism as ethical first principles and could not make a

---

[20] See Scheffler, 'Prerogatives without Restrictions', 381–2.
[21] See ibid. 383–4.
[22] See e.g. *Methods*, pp. xii, 404 n. 1. On the breadth of Sidgwick's understanding of the dualism, see Frankena, 'Sidgwick and the History', 178–9.

judgement between them. Further, he could not be persuaded of the truth of any theistic position that would guarantee that these two first principles always coincide in practice. The first edition of *The Methods of Ethics* concludes with the following, now well-known, words: 'the Cosmos of Duty is thus really reduced to a Chaos: and the prolonged effort of the human intellect to frame a perfect ideal of rational conduct is seen to have been foredoomed to inevitable failure'.

Sidgwick did not believe that we possess two rational 'faculties' for assessing ultimate reasons.[23] We have a single capacity for judgement. So it is strange that he appears not to have considered an account of our ultimate reasons according to which in particular cases the force of partial, self-interested reasons and impartial reasons conflict directly with, and may outweigh, one another. Let me try briefly to diagnose the origin of Sidgwick's pessimism. Recall two of the conditions which Sidgwick requires a self-evident judgement to meet if it is to be a 'higher certainty': clarity and consistency.[24] I suggest that Sidgwick runs together clarity of sense with precision of practical implication, and this caused him both to misunderstand those of his opponents who allowed a central place to judgement in particular cases, and to miss the possibility of resolving the dualism of practical reason that leads him to despair. We may agree that we ought to be as clear as possible about the meanings of terms we employ in our ethical discourse. And we may even agree—as does Aristotle[25]—that we should make our moral principles as precise as possible. But we should not go to excess in drawing analogies between ethics and science. Science's aim is to be comprehensive in explanation. If some event occurs which is not covered by the explanatory principles of some particular science, then, to that extent, that science has failed. One cannot leave it up to the individual observer to make up his or her own story about what has happened. Sidgwick sees ethics as aiming to be comprehensive in justification, to provide in advance a mechanism for deciding what to do in any situation that may arise.

In science, *post hoc* and therefore *ad hoc* explanations are unacceptable. But in ethics *post hoc* justification may well be something not only acceptable but unavoidable. As Williams puts it, 'judgement is constantly required'.[26] It is here that Sidgwick most clearly distances himself from

---

[23] Frankena, 'Sidgwick and the History', 194.
[24] *Methods*, 338–41.
[25] *Nicomachean Ethics* 9. 2, 1165^{a}34–5.
[26] Williams, 'What Does Ethical Intuitionism Imply?', 189.

Aristotle and identifies himself with nineteenth-century proponents of the scientific method in ethics. But, as Aristotle said, in any area we should seek principles which are only as precise as they need to be. A carpenter needs only to be able to draw a right angle, not to understand its geometry.[27]

Sidgwick fails to see the implications of the unavoidability of ethical judgement. His aim is a monistic principle, with clear prescriptions in every case. Even in the case of utilitarianism alone, however, he will face problems. First, as Ross noticed, utilitarianism is not a monistic view.[28] It consists of two principles—maximize pleasure and minimize suffering—and these must be weighed one against the other. Further, even the assessment of pleasure itself is pluralistic, requiring (at the very least) the weighing of degree of enjoyment-at-a-time against duration. Again, applying any such principle, even if it stands on its own, will in each case require a sensitivity to the salient features of human well-being that could not be captured in any set of principles, however long. What Sidgwick disparages as 'aesthetic intuitionism', then, is unavoidable.[29] Nor is it clear why Sidgwick is so against the use of judgement in particular cases when it is clearly required in the application of his philosophical intuitionism.

In the following section I shall say a little more about judgement and its limits in relation to the dual-source view itself. First, however, let me note that the dual-source view as I have described it is not open to a line of objection developed by Shelly Kagan in his book *The Limits of Morality* against the view that agents have what he calls 'options' not to maximize the overall good.[30] Kagan plausibly suggests that such options are best justified by the 'appeal to cost'—the negative effect on the agent's well-being of maximizing the overall good.[31] Such an appeal, he goes on to claim, is most plausibly grounded in recognition of what he calls 'the personal point of view':

From this point of view persons assess the world, weighing the relative benefits and disadvantages of various actual or potential changes. The evaluation is

27 *Nicomachean Ethics* 1. 7, 1098ª29–32.
28 Ross, *Foundations of Ethics*, 89.
29 *Methods*, 228. Sidgwick almost certainly saw Aristotle as an aesthetic intuitionist; see T. H. Irwin, 'Eminent Victorians and Greek Ethics', 293.
30 In fact I believe that impartial reasons are not to be understood in terms of simple maximization (see Sect. 4), but this is not important at this point in the argument. The argument here is based on material in my 'The Dualism of Practical Reason'.
31 *Limits of Morality*, 21.

relative to the particular person, for it is relative to his particular personal perspective; it is a judgement of what is good from his point of view. Typically it will differ from the agent-neutral evaluation of the impartial perspective, i.e., an evaluation of what is good objectively.[32]

Kagan then considers two strategies for defending options on the basis of the personal point of view. The first—the *negative argument* (271–330)—involves the taking of a pessimistic, or negative, view of the nature of persons: morality might well require us to promote the good without limit if it could, but it cannot because we cannot be motivated to do so.

Kagan spends a lot of time arguing that we could be so motivated. But his argument seems to me unnecessary, since, first, we can be said to have certain reasons even if they could not motivate us, and, second, proponents of the view that we should maximize the good may anyway allow that we are required to do so only as far as we can be motivated to do so.

According to the *positive argument*,[33] it is *desirable* for a moral system to allow agents to pursue their own interests at the expense of the overall good.[34] Kagan puts the argument as follows:

from the subjective [personal] standpoint an agent is inclined to give greater weight to his own interests than those interests might merit from the objective point of view. But if the fact that persons are engaged in their subjective standpoints possesses a kind of moral value in its own right, then there are reasons for the agent to act in keeping with his subjective point of view. That is, there are reasons for the given agent to promote his interests . . . beyond the level indicated solely by the objective importance of those interests.[35]

Kagan considers various claims that might be made in support of the view that the objective standpoint misses certain values that might ground subjective or agent-relative reasons.[36] He argues plausibly against each of these claims and suggests, again plausibly, that there is no other such claim worth considering.

The dual-source view I have been developing—though it avoids the language of options—could be described as based on something like the appeal to cost and the personal point of view. But it avoids both of Kagan's objections, in that it involves no especially negative view about the motivational capacities of agents nor any positive view

---

[32] *Limits of Morality*, 258.   [33] Ibid. 331–85.   [34] Ibid. 333.
[35] Ibid. 333–4.   [36] Ibid. 358–69.

of action performed in keeping with the agent's personal point of view. Values are to be carefully distinguished from reasons.[37] A reason, as I suggested in Chapter 2, is a property of an action that counts in favour of or against it. A value, however, is a property of something that constitutes its goodness. What grounds self-interested reasons is the value to the agent in terms of her own well-being (a value which could be understood as assessed from 'the objective point of view') *and* the fact that this value is instantiated in the life of the agent. That non-evaluative fact is part of the ground of the self-interested reason, and so not vulnerable to Kagan's critique of the positive argument.[38]

3. WEIGHING WELL-BEING

Sometimes, as in *Two Doors 2*, you have a reason to sacrifice your own well-being for the sake of another's. *Two Doors 2* is a case in which the cost to you is small, but the benefit to another is very large. So should we accept the following principle?

---

[37] See Sect. 2.4.

[38] It may be worth pointing out the differences between the account being developed here and Scheffler's in *The Rejection of Consequentialism*. First, on my view agents have a reason to promote their own well-being independently of any other-regarding reason or any reason to promote the good overall. Scheffler's 'agent-centred prerogative' is based on (i) recognition of the fact that agents characteristically do care more about their own concerns and projects out of proportion to the place of these concerns and projects within the overall good and (ii) the claim that moral theories should reflect human nature (see Scheffler, *Rejection of Consequentialism*, 56–8). This difference in approach explains why I would be less willing than Scheffler (ibid. 58–67) to allow that a 'sophisticated consequentialism' might capture the intuitions underlying my position. He allows this because such a form of consequentialism might represent itself as taking account of the independence of the personal point of view. On my view, that independence is not just a fact about human nature. It is the basis for grounding a kind of reason which a consequentialist cannot accept. In other words, when Scheffler suggests that '[the] independence [of a person's personal point of view] is typically evidenced by the fact that *he* cares differentially about his projects just because they are *his* projects' (ibid. 57), I would want to take the 'because' as a grounding or justificatory one. Second, on my view the reason to promote one's own well-being is grounded partly on the value of that well-being, not on any kind of valuation by the agent. As Kamm points out, anything like options are best not seen as resting on appeals to possibly idiosyncratic desires ('Non-Consequentialism, the Person as an End-in-Itself, and the Significance of Status', 358). Finally, in Ch. 1 I rejected the very language of demands, requirements, and prerogatives.

The Small Cost Principle. Whenever you can greatly promote the well-being of another at small cost to yourself, then you have reason to do so.

The small cost principle seems quite plausible, and something like it often lies behind arguments to the conclusion that we are required to surrender more of our material resources to certain charities than we now do. If I refrain from buying a CD, for example, I can provide enough money to save someone with cataracts from blindness.[39] But the small cost principle appears less plausible when the requirement for sacrifice is iterated, and especially when the well-being of the individual making the sacrifice is low.[40] Consider this example:

> *Two Doors 6.* You are confronted by two doors. If you do not pass through one or other of them, you will suffer an extremely painful electric shock. If you pass through door A, you will experience a minor twinge in your leg. If you pass through door B, you will not experience the twinge, but some other person, a stranger and out of sight, will suffer an extremely painful electric shock. Once you have passed through either door, you will entirely forget what has happened, but will be confronted by two further doors. If you pass through door C, you will experience a slightly worse twinge in your leg. If you pass through door D, you will not experience the twinge, but some other person, a stranger and out of sight, will suffer an extremely painful electric shock. And so on.

Let us now imagine that you have reached doors M and N, and the voltages are very high indeed. I suggest that at this point—or at *some* point—there is a limit to the sacrifice that can be called for by reason from one individual for the sake of others. In this case, the sacrifice or cost is 'at a time', but the same threshold seems plausible in global assessments of well-being. Consider:

> *Two Doors 7.* You are currently living a reasonably good life. You are now confronted by two doors. If you pass through door A, your global well-being will drop dramatically, so that the rest of your life will be worth living but of a very low quality. If you

---

[39] Vision 2020 Eye Disease Information: Cataract.

[40] On 'moral mathematics', see the seminal discussion in Parfit, *Reasons and Persons*, ch. 3. For a good recent discussion of demandingness, see Cullity, *The Moral Demands of Affluence.*

pass through door B, nothing will happen to you, but the future well-being of some other person, a stranger and out of sight, also living a reasonably good life, will drop even further, so that her life is barely worth living.

This case involves a limit on the sacrifice that reason calls for from an individual for the sake of promoting to a greater extent the well-being of some other person. The same limit seems plausible in cases in which the well-being at stake is the same, but more people are involved:

> *Two Doors 8.* You are currently living a reasonably good life. You are now confronted by two doors. If you pass through door A, your global well-being will drop dramatically, so that the rest of your life will be worth living but of a very low quality. If you pass through door B, nothing will happen to you, but the future well-being of several other people, strangers and out of sight, also living reasonably good lives, will drop to the same extent as yours would have done.

What I am suggesting, then, is that there is a limit on an agent's reason to sacrifice herself for others that operates when the agent is already below some threshold level of well-being, or the sacrifice called for will take the agent below that, assessed either at-a-time or globally. We have here a form of what Griffin has called 'discontinuity': once the threshold is reached, it does not matter how much the well-being of others can be promoted by a sacrifice, or how many those others are.[41] Exactly where the threshold lies is difficult to say. My own view is that, given the present state of the world, it lies far below the level of well-being at which most of us would live if we were to sacrifice vastly more to promote the well-being of others than we do at present. That is to say, the lives of most of us are unjustifiable in the light of reason.

The dual-source view is grounded on two significant facts. First, the separateness of persons, the fact that each of us has a separate capacity for consciousness, and a special reason for promoting the enjoyment and minimizing the suffering arising through that capacity's being exercised. And, second, the fact that, since others also have such capacities, the value for others of the well-being experienced by them provides each agent with some reason for action, which can conflict with her own, thus requiring balancing. This latter reason is to be understood as impartial,

---

[41] Griffin, *Well-Being*, 85–9.

so that from one's perspective one's own well-being counts equally with that of others, and is given no special weight.

I must now confront the objection that the dualism as I have described it between pure self-interested partiality and pure impartiality ignores the fact that we have reasons to prioritize the well-being of those close to us—especially relatives and friends—over those of strangers.[42] Consider the following case:

> *Two Doors 9.* You are confronted by two doors. If you do not pass through one or other of them voluntarily, your beloved mother and some other person, a stranger and out of sight, will each suffer an extremely painful shock. If you pass through door A voluntarily, your mother will not experience this shock but the stranger will. If you pass through door B, the stranger will not experience this shock, but your mother will.

If the weight of the well-being of others is to be understood impartially, then it appears that you have no special reason, apart from any distress that might be caused to you, to pass voluntarily through door B and spare your mother. The dual-source view as I have outlined it, however, leaves no room for the reason-giving force of the special relationships we have with certain other people.

It is tempting to argue for reasons grounded on special relations through an analogy with one's relation to oneself.[43] Just as I now have a special relation to my capacity for consciousness in the future, and have a special reason to promote the well-being arising through the exercise of that capacity because it is *mine*, so I have a special relation to certain other people, such as my beloved mother, and have a special reason to promote her well-being because she is *my* mother.

This analogy, however, fails to take sufficient note of the ethical significance of the separateness of persons. As Sidgwick puts it:

> It would be contrary to Common Sense to deny that the distinction between any one individual and any other is real and fundamental, and that consequently 'I' am concerned with the quality of my existence as an individual in a sense, fundamentally important, in which I am not concerned with the quality of the existence of other individuals.[44]

---

[42] For excellent discussion, see Hooker, *Ideal Code, Real World*, 136–41.
[43] Cf. Aristotle, *Nicomachean Ethics* 9. 4.
[44] *Methods*, 498.

The difference between one person and another is, as Sidgwick says, real. However close I am to some other person, she will always be another person. And it is this difference which provides a source of self-interested reasons. My relations to others close to me are also, in a sense, 'real'. I stand in certain biological relations to my parents, siblings, and so on, and it might be claimed that these relations provide a source of reasons. This claim, however, seems on a par with the suggestion that because some other person has a skin pigmentation similar to mine that gives me reason to prioritize their well-being over that of someone of a different colour. On their own, biological facts are ethically inert. But often, of course, I stand in social relations to these individuals, and also to others to whom I am not biologically related. These social relations—grounded in facts such as that others have cared for me, that I like or love them, that we have a common history of shared activities, and so on—are also not imaginary. Again, however, these social relations appear on reflection to provide unstable grounds for reasons. First, they are not, as we have seen, in themselves constituents of well-being, though of course they may be important as sources of enjoyment. Second, they do have a biological basis in kin-relationships, the evolutionary benefit of which is obvious. We are naturally inclined to favour our relations and those close to us in our group. That is not enough to debunk the rational force of these social relations, but it does throw them into doubt.[45] Because of this evolutionary significance, and the importance of these relations as sources of well-being, we should not be surprised to find that we are biased towards those close to us. What we must do is hold that bias up to the light of impartial reason, where we shall find it unsupportable in itself.

It is also worth mentioning that the implications of the dual-source view for the weight to be attached to special relations in practice are not as radical as might be thought. Because of their source in deep and unavoidable aspects of human nature, they may often be sources of

---

[45] Admittedly, the same could be said concerning other-regarding reasons in general. But the impartial point of view seems to me, as presumably it did to Sidgwick, stable under reflection in a way that partiality to others does not. There are two 'pure' perspectives: self-interested partiality, grounded on the separateness of persons, and impartiality, grounded on the notion that everyone's well-being matters equally in some sense or other. If a deviation from pure impartiality is allowed on the basis of social relations, then it is hard to see why deviation on the ground of race or sex is not also allowed. Imagine a racist, for example, who feels for those of her race what most of us feel for our mothers. Why should her feelings not ground a reason for partialism if such feelings can justify partiality in the case of mothers and children?

instrumental reasons. It is true, nevertheless, that just as the weight each of us gives to her own well-being, in the world as it is, is unjustifiable, so the weight attached to special relations by most people is equally unjustifiable.

Reasons provided by the well-being of others, then, should be understood impartially. But now we must ask whether the well-being of others that matters is that of those individuals who do or will exist, or whether we should take *possible* future individuals into account. In philosophical jargon, this is the question whether other-regarding reasons are person-affecting or not, if we understand 'person' to cover any conscious being.[46]

It is hard to accept that other-regarding reasons are person-affecting. Consider the following case.[47]

> *Resources.* We have a choice of two sources of energy. One will cause the overall level of well-being of the population in two centuries' time to be much higher than at present. The other will cause it to be much lower than at present, though lives will still be worth living. Our own well-being will not be affected whichever choice we make, but the choice we make will, because of the different effects on the way we live of each choice, affect the identities of those who are born in future. Everything else is equal.

According to the person-affecting view, it makes no difference which choice we make in this case, since there will be no effect on people now existing or people who will exist regardless of our choice. Most think, however, that we should choose the resource that increases the level of well-being in the population, even though this increase in well-being is not in itself 'good for' any existing or future individual. It is true that the well-being of an individual in the well-off population is good for

---

[46] See e.g. Narveson, 'Moral Problems of Population', 73; Parfit, *Reasons and Persons*, ch. 18. A recent formulation which I find to be especially direct and clear is by Temkin (who goes on to criticize the view expressed): 'One situation *cannot* be worse (or better) than another if there is *no one* for whom it *is* worse (or better)' ('Harmful Goods, Harmless Bads', 290). This is a 'narrow' person-affecting view, according to which identity matters. A wide person-affecting view is equivalent to welfarism, a form of which I espouse in this book (see Parfit, *Reasons and Persons*, 394–7). Temkin's definition, of course, concerns outcomes rather than actions, but could easily be adapted to cover reasons for action.

[47] Adapted from Parfit, *Reasons and Persons*, 362–3. Parfit calls the difficulty for person-affecting views 'the non-identity problem'.

that individual; but that is true also of the members of the worse-off population.

Other-regarding reasons, then, are non-person-affecting.[48] But now the following question for the dual-source view arises. Egoism is—obviously—a person-affecting principle, since I can have reason to promote my own good only if I am a person, or sentient being, for whom certain things are good or bad. The account of self-regarding reasons offered in the dual-source view is structurally the same as egoism in this respect. Should we not expect symmetry across self-regarding and other-regarding reasons, so that other-regarding reasons should be expected to be person-affecting?

To expect symmetry here is again a failure to take note of the ethical significance of the separateness of persons and the source of self-regarding reasons it provides. The reason I have to prioritize my own good over that of others arises out of the fact that it is *mine*, and that is of course a person-affecting consideration. In the case of other-regarding reasons, the source lies entirely in the value for the individuals concerned and, as we have seen, this is a person-affecting consideration only in the wide, or welfarist, sense.

---

[48] It might be claimed that the argument above shows at most that possible people matter for non-person-affecting reasons, not that the reasons why existing or future people matter are not person-affecting. This view, however, would require further motivation if it is not to be rejected on grounds of parsimony.

6

Equality

1. EQUALITY

Each of us has a reason to promote the well-being of others.[1] I have argued that the way to understand other-regarding reasons is in terms of pure impartiality, in which the value of one's own well-being is counted equally alongside that of others and no weight is attached to special relations. So, given that I have also committed myself to a form of welfarism about reasons according to which our reasons to act can be based on nothing other than the promotion of well-being, it might be thought that the impartial principle to which I shall be led is a simple well-being-maximizing principle—that is, a form of act-utilitarianism. What I shall suggest in this chapter is that there is a distributive, as opposed to aggregative, element in the perspective of impartiality, just as there is in the case of self-interested partiality. The reason I have to promote my own well-being has two aspects. The first is evaluative. My own well-being is valuable. Hence, other things being equal, I have strongest reason to perform that action which maximizes my own well-being. The second consists in the separateness of persons—the fact that this well-being is *mine* as opposed to anyone else's. Likewise, in the case of the well-being of others, the fact that individuals affected by my actions are distinct from one another is also relevant, as well as by *how much* their well-being is affected. Further, just as there is a threshold of sufficiency in the case of conflicts between my own well-being and that of others such that there comes a point where I might be said to be 'doing enough' and do not have further reason to sacrifice myself for others, so there is a threshold of sufficiency in assessing well-being from

---

[1] This chapter is based on my 'Equality, Priority, and Compassion'. That article was illuminatingly criticized by Temkin in 'Egalitarianism Defended', my response to Temkin being 'Egalitarianism and Compassion'.

the impartial point of view below which some special weight is to be attached to the promotion of well-being.

It is indeed natural to think that well-being is to be maximized impartially. How can it be rational to bring out less than the best state of affairs?[2] But it has seemed to many on reflection that an impartial maximizing principle is in tension with certain other principles or values that should be respected in any plausible account of impartial distribution. One such principle is that of equality.[3] Consider the following pair of distributions, called *Equality* and *Inequality*:

	Group 1	Group 2
Equality	50	50
Inequality	10	90

Assume that each group contains the same number of people (say, 1,000), and that there are no questions of desert at issue. The numbers represent the well-being of each individual in each group: the individuals in *Equality* have equally good lives, while those in *Inequality* have lives either much better or much worse than the lives in *Equality*.[4]

According to traditional utilitarianism, given the opportunity of bringing about either outcome, there is no reason to choose one over the other. But many think that there is a strong case for *Equality* over *Inequality*. Why is this? One obvious answer is that equality is valuable in itself—or perhaps rather that inequality is bad in itself. This position may be described as

> *Egalitarianism.* One outcome is to be preferred to another in so far as (undeserved) inequality is minimized.[5]

Egalitarianism has long faced a problem which Derek Parfit has called 'the levelling down objection'.[6] Consider the following outcomes:

---

[2] See Foot, 'Utilitarianism and the Virtues', 227, in addition to the passage from Rashdall cited in Sect. 5.2 above.

[3] For important discussions of equality, see e.g. Nagel, 'Equality'; McKerlie, 'Egalitarianism'; Raz, *The Morality of Freedom*; Broome, *Weighing Goods*; Temkin, *Inequality*; Parfit, 'Equality and Priority'.

[4] No commitment to precise measures, or to any particular view of well-being itself, is intended by the use of numbers. Throughout the chapter they may always be understood in terms similar to those used in this sentence in the text.

[5] See Temkin, *Inequality*, 7. The reference to desert is bracketed since I wish to bracket the issue of desert itself. Egalitarians may or may not accept the notion of desert (see ibid. 12).

[6] Parfit, 'Equality and Priority', 10. See also e.g. Nozick, *Anarchy, State, and Utopia*, 229; Flew, *The Politics of Procrustes*, 25–6; McKerlie, 'Egalitarianism', 230–7; Raz,

	Group 1	Group 2
LD Equality	9	9
Inequality 2	99	100

According to egalitarianism, *LD Equality*—in so far as the distribution within it is perfectly equal—is preferable to *Inequality 2*. This seems highly counter-intuitive. It is indeed true that egalitarianism may be combined with other principles, so that an egalitarian may hold that *Inequality 2* is better overall or all things considered, perhaps because of its higher level of well-being overall. But the problem for egalitarianism is that its claiming *any* reason for preferring *LD Equality* appears to count heavily against it.

Before rejecting egalitarianism, however, we should try to understand what lies behind the levelling down objection. Larry Temkin has argued that much of the force of the objection rests on

> *The Slogan.* One situation *cannot* be worse (or better) than another *in any respect* if there is *no one* for whom it *is* worse (or better) *in any respect.*[7]

As Temkin interprets the slogan, 'if there is no one' may be taken as equivalent to 'if no one exists or will exist', and 'is worse' as 'is or will be worse'. In other words, the slogan is essentially a narrow person-affecting principle and, as we saw in the previous chapter, such principles run into the non-identity problem.[8] Since the slogan cannot explain why we have a reason to conserve resources, it should be rejected.[9] But I myself do not believe that it is the slogan that underlies most people's dissatisfaction with the implications of egalitarianism in levelling down cases. The slogan involves narrow person-affectingness—the notion that what matters morally can be only what affects those who do or will exist. But what is worrying about egalitarianism is independent of person-affectingness in this sense. Rather the worry arises from the idea that what matters could be something that was independent of the well-being of individuals. I have already described this as welfarism

Morality of Freedom, 235; Temkin, *Inequality*, 247–8; Hooker, *Ideal Code, Real World*, 44–5.

[7] *Inequality*, 256. See Parfit, 'Equality and Priority', 18; and the discussion of person-affectingness in Sect. 5.3 above.

[8] Sect. 5.3; Temkin, *Inequality*, 255–6; Parfit, *Reasons and Persons*, 357–9, 362–3.

[9] For a radical revision of the slogan, which I see as in the spirit of my own proposal, see Holtug, 'In Defence of the Slogan', 73–5.

about reasons. Here we might capture the force of the view in the following distributive principle:

> *The Welfarist Restriction.* In choices affecting neither the number nor the identities of future people,[10] any feature of an outcome O that favours O over some alternative outcome P must be grounded in some individual or individuals in O being better off, and any feature that disfavours O must be grounded in some individual or individuals in that outcome being worse off, than in P.[11]

The welfarist restriction differs from the slogan in that it does not involve narrow person-affectingness, merely the notion that features that speak in favour of or against outcomes must be grounded respectively on benefits or harms to individuals. In the case of *LD Equality* versus *Inequality 2*, the point is that a property of *LD Equality* resulting in benefit to no one and harm to someone cannot speak in its favour. It is acceptance of something like this restriction, I suggest, that leads many to think egalitarianism peculiarly destructive.

The levelling down objection, then, appears to rest on an intuitively secure foundation. But before rejecting egalitarianism once and for all we must consider whether it rests on some value to which the plausibility of the welfarist restriction is blinding us.[12] If we can find such a value, we may want to reject the welfarist restriction and the levelling down objection.

What is the appeal of equality? Some kinds of equality clearly have no value in themselves—mere equality in height, for example. But here we are concerned with something that does matter in distribution: how well people's lives go for them. Why should it matter if well-being is distributed equally? The most plausible answer to this question appeals to the value of a kind of fairness.[13] The inequalities in *Inequality* and *Inequality 2*, in other words, may be said to be unfair: in those outcomes some people do worse than others, through no fault of their own. And unfairness in an outcome may be said to count against it. Since this

---

[10] Parfit calls these 'same people choices' (*Reasons and Persons*, 356).

[11] This version of the restriction differs from that in my 'Equality, Priority, and Compassion', which would in certain cases have permitted features to count in favour or against if they had no grounding in well-being. As previously, I am assuming that issues of desert are bracketed.

[12] It is sometimes said that egalitarianism should be assumed to be the default position. That may be true, but the levelling down objection appears sufficient to dislodge it from that position.

[13] See Broome, *Weighing Goods*, 193; Temkin, *Inequality*, 13.

conception of fairness depends only on the comparative positions of individuals to one another, we may call it *comparative fairness*.[14]

I have two doubts about comparative fairness, one concerning its source, and another concerning its confusion with another, more plausible, principle. First, consider the source of the notion. I have already offered in Chapter 1 some general arguments to the conclusion that we should seek to avoid stating ultimate reasons in principles which rest normative weight on moral notions such as fairness. Here I wish to suggest in connection with fairness in particular a genealogical hypothesis of a kind similar to that offered by Mill to explain the origin of the notion of justice.[15] According to Mill on my reading of him, our 'sentiment of justice', which might otherwise be taken to constitute insight into a non-utilitarian moral principle, has emerged out of two natural tendencies: towards self-defence and towards sympathy with others. The essential idea is that the sentiment of justice has developed out of a natural desire that harm be done to those who harm others. This genealogy is meant to throw doubt on the self-standing normative status of principles of justice, on the ground that they have emerged through a non-rational process from natural and non-rational desires (though of course Mill accepts that they are extremely important 'secondary principles', whose place in our 'customary morality' is justified by the utilitarian principle). What I want to suggest is that a similar story may be told about comparative fairness, based on the natural disposition human beings have towards envy and—once again—on the tendency to sympathize. Envy involves, at its heart, the desire that the good in question be removed from the person envied for their possession of that good and anger at that possession. Generalized through sympathy, it becomes anger at anyone's doing better than any other.[16] Note that I am suggesting not that appeals to comparative fairness rest on envy,

---

[14] See Temkin, 'Egalitarianism Defended', 767.

[15] Mill, *Utilitarianism*, ch. 5. For further exegesis and discussion, see my *Mill on Utilitarianism*, ch. 7.

[16] Partly because of the appeal to sympathy, my account differs from Freud's neo-Hobbesian or Humean account, in which the principle of equality is adopted by envious individuals for self-interested reasons, to prevent hostile depredation. The two accounts need not of course be mutually exclusive. For a helpful discussion of Freud's account, see Rawls, *A Theory of Justice*, 539–40. Freud plausibly suggests that we can see envy developing into a sense of justice in the nursery. Rawls comments (ibid. 540): 'Certainly children are often envious and jealous; and no doubt their moral notions are so primitive that the necessary distinctions are not grasped by them. But waiving these difficulties, we could equally well say that their social feeling arises from resentment, from a sense that they are unfairly treated.' I suspect we could say this only of older children, whose sense

but that they have their ultimate source in envy, generalized through sympathy. The idea is that generalized envy may have become, through a process of cultural evolution, the principle that it is bad if, through no fault of their own, one individual does worse than another. Comparative fairness, so adapted, need involve no ill will to the better off and may indeed function in cases in which ill will would be quite out of place (such as, for example, when one is considering inequalities in societies in the distant past, or inequalities between oneself and those who are worse off than oneself).[17] Further, it may be tied to notions such as self-respect or rational consistency or be limited by other principles, such as those of desert. But the question is whether, once appropriate moral weight has been given to these other notions, the origin of comparative fairness in generalized envy throws it into doubt as a moral notion with its own independent weight. There may, of course, be much to be said in favour of keeping the notion, as in the case of justice in Mill. And it may be that, despite its origin, comparative fairness is ultimately something to which we should be prepared to subscribe. My point is merely that the envy hypothesis requires answering and does throw some doubt on comparative fairness.

But it is a mere hypothesis. And, it may be suggested, people's relative positions surely do appear to matter to us in distributions. Consider the following case. Anya, through no fault of her own, has had a really miserable childhood so far which has resulted in a low level of well-being overall; Bikhu, again independently of any efforts on his part, has had a wonderful childhood so far and a consequently high level of well-being. If I have some indivisible good to distribute—a holiday in Disneyland, for example—is there not a case for giving it to Anya, even if I am sure that Bikhu would enjoy it just as much? And were I to give the holiday to Bikhu, would Anya not have a justified claim based on comparative fairness, not envy?

If one believes that Anya would have a justified claim to the holiday, on the ground that she, through no fault of her own, has had a worse childhood than Bikhu, this is merely to accept that people's relative positions may matter in the distribution of some good (or indeed some unavoidable bad); this position—which we may call the principle of

---

of justice has already developed. When my daughters and their friends were 2 years old, they had no moral notions I could discern; but they were certainly envious.

[17] I owe these examples to Temkin and am indebted to him for discussion of this topic.

the relevance of relativity in distribution (principle R)—is quite different from mere comparative fairness. It implies not that equality is a good in itself, or inequality a bad, merely that relative positions of potential recipients of goods and bads may be relevant in distribution.

The egalitarian may ask why someone should be concerned with relative positions in distribution if they are not concerned with comparative fairness per se. Why should anyone want to attend to the relative positions of Anya and Bikhu if they do not think that their being in an unequal relation is bad, and thus something to be removed? Well, why not? There is a deep difference here between egalitarianism, on the one hand, and the combination of principle R with the welfarist restriction on the other. And, I want to suggest, the appeal of a view which allows us to take note of relative position but forbids levelling down has more going for it than egalitarianism, and it is likely that at least some of the attraction of egalitarianism arises from its being confused with the combination in question.

2. PRIORITY

Principle R allows us to attend to the relative positions of recipients in any distribution, but does not commit us to the idea that inequality in itself is bad. It thus allows us to avoid the levelling down objection, while preferring *Equality* to *Inequality* in my original pair of outcomes. Let me now discuss that version of principle R which has recently been presented, by Parfit, as a response to the levelling down objection.[18] According to Parfit, those known as political egalitarians have been concerned often not with mere equality, but with the plight of the worse off, and have wished to give the worse off priority. Thus he advocates:

> *The Priority View.* Benefiting people matters more the worse off those people are.

The difference between a concern for comparative fairness on the one hand and the priority view on the other can be brought out by noting that the priority view is not comparative.[19] The egalitarian is

[18] See Parfit, 'Equality and Priority', 12. Parfit himself refers to Scanlon and others.
[19] See ibid. 13. This point brings out an important difference between comparative fairness and principle R: principle R does not require one to believe that relative position matters *in itself*, allowing merely that facts about relative position may be relevant.

concerned with the position of the worse off only in so far as their position compares unfavourably with that of the better off, whereas the prioritarian is concerned with the worse off proportionally in relation to their absolute level of well-being.

Let me now attempt to find the most plausible version of the priority view. Consider first Nagel's suggestion that we might see ourselves as seeking a kind of 'unanimity' in assessing outcomes:

> The essence of such a criterion is to try in a moral assessment to include each person's point of view separately, so as to achieve a result which is in a significant sense acceptable to each person involved or affected . . . it is possible to assess each result from each point of view to try to find the one that is least unacceptable to the person to whom it is most unacceptable. This means that any other alternative will be more unacceptable to someone than this alternative is to anyone. The preferred alternative is in that sense the least unacceptable, considered from each person's point of view separately. A radically egalitarian policy of giving absolute priority to the worst off, regardless of numbers, would result from always choosing the least unacceptable alternative, in this sense.[20]

On this conception, the priority view may be stated as:

> *The Absolute Priority View.* When benefiting others, the worst-off individual (or individuals) is (or are) to be given absolute priority over the better off.

Consider the following distributions, where WP is the worst-off person and each group contains 1,000 people:

	WP	*Group 1*	*Group 2*
Status Quo	8.9	9.1	100
Absolute Priority	9	9.1	100
Expanded Concern	8.9	100	100

---

[20] Nagel, 'Equality', 123. McKerlie ('Egalitarianism and the Separateness of Persons', 219–21) suggests that unanimity is not really Nagel's concern, since the prioritarian outcome may well be one which only the worst-off person accepts. Parfit has suggested to me that the unanimity in question might consist in maximizing the degree of acceptability to everyone. Since the worst-off person will be worst off *even* in the outcome which is best for her, by choosing this outcome we are thereby choosing the outcome whose degree of acceptability to everyone is as high as it could be. But the fact remains that the better off might still not accept the prioritarian outcome, and I would suggest that the core notion here is the availability of a justification of a policy to each individual concerned, there being a justification available to the better off for benefiting the worse off at their expense but not the other way around. See also McKerlie, 'Egalitarianism', 224–7.

The absolute priority view in this case favours moving from *Status Quo* to *Absolute Priority* rather than *Expanded Concern*. The key notion in Nagel's elucidation is the contractualist view that we must consider each person's point of view *separately*.[21] Imagine that WP is in quite serious pain, and that in *Absolute Priority* Group 1 is in pain almost as serious. All that will happen in *Absolute Priority* is that WP will be given a chocolate (her pain is bad but not so bad that she cannot enjoy a chocolate). The absolute priority view favours giving her the chocolate over alleviating the serious pain of 1,000 others. Because the absolute priority view is an 'innumerate' maximin principle, it will like Rawls's 'difference principle' allow the smallest benefit to the smallest number of worst off to trump any benefit, however large, to any but the worst off, even the next worst off. And this, it may be thought, is almost as absurd as levelling down.[22]

What is required, then, is a principle that allows us to give priority to the worse off but in giving priority to take into account the size of benefits at stake and the numbers of people who will benefit. So understood, the priority view is essentially a non-lexical weighting principle:[23]

> *The Weighted Priority View.* Benefiting people matters more the worse off those people are, the more of those people there are, and the greater the benefits in question.

The weighted priority view, then, will permit us to benefit those who are better off if the benefit to them is significantly greater than to the worse off or if they are greater in number. One might wonder how the factors of absolute position, size of benefit, and number of beneficiaries are to be weighted. But I now want to suggest that whatever weights are attached to these factors the weighted priority view allows too much weight. Consider the following proposal:

---

[21] For discussion of this conception of contractualism, see Scanlon, *What we Owe*, 229–41.

[22] Nagel himself suggests ('Equality', 125) that one may accord greater urgency to larger benefits to those better off than to smaller benefits to the worst off. But this amounts to giving up on his conception of selecting the outcome that is least unacceptable to the person to whom it is most unacceptable, in the sense that, if acceptability is not tied closely to the position of the person in question, theories such as utilitarianism can meet the unanimity test (see also n. 20, above). Further, Nagel suggests that numbers do count and admits both that his unanimity criterion cannot account for this, and that no alternative criterion suggests itself to him.

[23] Cf. here Temkin's 'weighted additive principle' (*Inequality*, 41).

Improvement in level	Weight	Overall value
1 → 2	100	100
2 → 3	99	99
3 → 4	98	98
...		
98 → 99	3	3
99 → 100	2	2
100 → 101	1	1

This table represents the weights attached to improvements in the position of any individual.[24] If, for example, I can offer one unit of the good to be distributed to P, who already possesses one unit, two units to Q, who has two units, or three units to R, who has 98, the overall value of my so doing will be:

P (has 1, gets 1): 100
Q (has 2, gets 2): 99 + 98 = 197
R (has 98, gets 3): 3 + 2 + 1 = 6

Attention to the size of benefits, then, requires me to benefit Q in this case. But if we imagine that there is *another* person, P′, in P's position to whom I may also give one unit when benefiting P, and that everything else remains the same, the overall value of benefiting P and P′ will be:

P + P′(have 1 each, get 1 each) : 100 + 100 = 200.

In this case the number of beneficiaries outweighs the importance of the amount of benefit available to any particular individual.

The weighted priority view will judge *Expanded Concern* clearly superior to *Absolute Priority*. But because it allows for straightforward aggregation across persons the following problem now arises, regardless of the weighting.[25] Consider the following situations, involving ten people doing pretty badly and 15,000 pretty well:[26]

	10 Poor	15,000 Rich
Status Quo	1	98
Pain-Relief	51	98
Chocolates	1	99

---

[24] We should assume that 101 represents the highest possible level of well-being a person may attain.

[25] Compare here Temkin's 'Repellent Conclusion' (*Inequality*, 218).

[26] I am of course assuming my 'Rich' to be well-being-rich, my 'Poor' to be well-being-poor.

In *Pain-Relief,* each Poor person gains *fifty* units and there are ten such people. The value of increasing the level of the Poor in this outcome is thus:

$$(100 + 99 + 98 + 97... + 53 + 52 + 51 = 3,775)$$
$$\times\ 10 = 37,750.$$

The value of giving a chocolate (a really *good* chocolate!) to the Rich is:

$$3 \times 15,000 = 45,000.$$

In other words, the weighted priority view, though it may avoid requiring us to give the smallest benefits to the smallest number of worst off at the largest costs to the largest number of those only slightly better off, does require us to give tiny benefits to those who are very well off at huge costs to the worst off. Its readiness to aggregate straightforwardly 'all the way up' leads it to fail to attach the appropriate significance to size of benefits and numbers of recipients. This seems if anything an even less palatable position than the absolute priority view, since that view at least always skews distributions in favour of the worst off.

It will not solve the problem to allow the weighting to operate only at lower levels. For as long as the number of the rich is large enough, priority may be given to benefiting them to a small degree rather than benefiting the worse off to a large degree. The problem is arising from straightforward aggregation, so one possible solution here would be to decrease the weight attached to numbers of individuals.[27] Consider:

> *The Number-Weighted Priority View.* Benefiting people matters more the worse off those people are, the more of those people there are, and the larger the benefits in question. But the number of beneficiaries matters less the better off they are.

It may be claimed, for example, that the importance of numbers asymptotically approaches zero as they become large. Thus a weighting could easily be devised which ensured that, in the *Pain-Relief–Chocolates* case, when aggregating, one weighted the second rich person's contribution to the sum at somewhat less than 3, the third at even less, and so on, in such a way that the total was lower than 37,750, thus respecting our intuitions.

---

[27] For this suggestion I am indebted to McMahan.

But now consider what I shall call the *Beverly Hills case*, in which you can offer fine wine to different groups of well-off individuals:[28]

	10 Rich	10,000 Super-Rich
Status Quo	80	90
Lafite 1982	82	90
Latour 1982	80	92

The value of giving Lafite 1982 to each of the ten Rich is:

$$(20 + 19) \times 10 = 390.$$

Now let me assume that a number-weighting has been devised such that the value of giving the Latour 1982 to the 10,000 Super-Rich comes out as less than 390 (how the figures might be calculated is not important for the purposes of this example). Once again, I suggest, a modification of the priority view has taken us from one extreme to another—from allowing that numbers count straightforwardly to denying them appropriate relevance. It seems somewhat absurd to think that the Rich should be given priority over the Super-Rich to the extent that aggregation is entirely forbidden in the case of the latter. Indeed, what the *Beverly Hills* case brings out is that, once recipients are at a certain level, any prioritarian concern for them disappears entirely. This implies that any version of the priority view must fail: when people reach a certain level, even if they are worse off than others, benefiting them does *not* in itself matter more.[29] And this seems true even if, in a *Beverly Hills* case, the improvements in well-being are equal. That is, even if the benefits to each of the Rich and the Super-Rich are identical, and their numbers are the same, there still seems to me nothing to be said for giving priority to the 'worse off'. At this level only well-being matters, so there would be nothing to choose between the two distributions. Let me now outline an alternative to the priority view based on the lessons learned so far.

---

[28] I am assuming that the wine is supplied in some quantity, and does not constitute a trivial good. If you think it is trivial, then think of some non-trivial good instead.

[29] Note Anderson's complaints about modern egalitarians' concerns with the lazy, surfers, *et al.*, in her 'What is the Point of Equality?', 287–8.

3. SUFFICIENCY

Egalitarianism failed because comparative fairness is not a value; the priority view failed because, since priority is not always a value, it cannot explain why we think priority should be given in those cases in which we think it should. So we must look elsewhere for an appealing account of why in my original pair of distributions we should favour *Equality* over *Inequality* (on the assumption that this is not itself a *Beverly Hills* case).

What is required is an account that incorporates a threshold above which priority does not count, but below which it does—and we may assume that it will be priority that takes into account both size of benefits and numbers of recipients, so as to avoid the problems of the absolute priority view, as well as how badly off those below the threshold are.[30] What is to happen above the threshold? The placing of the threshold is best understood as a tempering of act-utilitarian accounts of distribution, so above the threshold goods and bads should be distributed so as to maximize well-being impartially.[31] The threshold need not be seen as an absolute one, such that those below the threshold should be given absolute priority over those above. Rather the well-being of those below the threshold is to be given some extra weighting.

An obvious question to ask is where the threshold at which special concern gives out is situated, and at this point I shall merely sketch some of the issues and arguments involved. One suggestion might be that it is closely tied to needs. When we see someone in need, we should give them some special priority over those who are not in need.

A problem with this proposal is that on any plausible distinction between needs and other components of well-being, needs give out before special concern. Imagine a society which includes among a large number of very wealthy and flourishing individuals a group which is very poor but whose basic and indeed non-basic needs are met.[32] Concern for the badly off speaks in favour of at least some transfers from the rich to the poor, even if the poor use any resources gained to purchase goods which they could not be said to need. Of course, the notion of need

---

[30] In 'Equality, Priority, and Compassion', I sought to show how such a principle could emerge from an impartial spectator model. But it seems to me sufficiently plausible also to stand on its own.

[31] See Temkin, *Inequality*, 187.

[32] I leave it to the reader to give their own content to 'basic' and 'non-basic' here.

may be expanded to cover the area in which concern is appropriate. But this still leaves the question of the boundaries of that area itself.

One obvious move is to attempt to set the threshold at some absolute level of well-being. Consider, however, the following scenario, which includes many human beings in some considerable pain and a contented dog:

	1,000 Humans	Dog
Status Quo	6	3
Pain-Relief 2	20	3
Biscuits	6	4

Any plausible threshold is likely to require us to give priority to small though non-trivial increases in the well-being of any number of perfectly contented non-human animals over large increases in the well-being of any number of human beings.[33] If we assume that the threshold is, say, 5, in this case it appears that the threshold view requires us to give better-quality biscuits to the dog (over his lifetime) in preference to relieving the pain of many human beings (again, perhaps, over their lifetime).

It may be claimed that any such result would demonstrate a flaw not in the notion of an absolute threshold, but in the theory of well-being in play. On the most plausible and widely held views of well-being, however, the lives of non-human animals are less valuable than the lives of most humans.[34] According to hedonism, well-being consists in the balance of enjoyable mental states over those involving suffering. It is clear that many human lives contain a greater such balance than any non-human life, not just because of the different kinds of enjoyment available to humans, but because of the length of human life. As the hedonist J. S. Mill famously said, 'It is better to be a human being dissatisfied than a pig satisfied.'[35] The same is true of the comparison between humans and non-humans on so-called 'desire accounts' of well-being. Human desires are more numerous and more complex than those of non-humans. Finally, consider the 'objective list' theory of well-being, according to which the value of a life consists in its instantiating certain goods such as knowledge or friendship. Once again, most humans do a lot better than most non-humans.

---

[33] Cf. McMahan, 'Cognitive Disability, Misfortune, and Justice', 8–9.

[34] In the previous chapter, of course, I defended a particular account of well-being. But I do not wish my argument here to depend on any particular account.

[35] *Utilitarianism*, 2. 6.

Now it is undoubtedly true that *we* feel concern for the suffering human beings, and not for the contented dog. But the question we have to ask is whether that concern is itself impartial. Most human beings feel greater concern for other human beings than for other animals. Compare, for example, our attitudes, generally, to slavery with those towards factory-farming. But a benefit is a benefit, whoever or whatever receives it. The impartial view, then, is the most reasonable. If this approach seems too counter-intuitive, one alternative would be to correlate compassion with what McMahan calls 'fortune', that is, how well the individual is faring relative to some appropriate standard.[36] McMahan rejects the view that the standard is species-specific, in favour of an account which assesses the fortune of any individual in the light of both the possible lives open to them given their own psychological capacities, and the lives of others in certain relevant comparison classes. But against this someone who wishes to advocate that concern be proportionate to well-being might claim that concern may be appropriate for some being (such as, say, a dog) just because it has only relatively meagre psychological capacities to begin with. True, it makes little sense to say of a highly contented dog that it is 'unfortunate', since it is not clear how things could have gone better *for it*. But the a priori appeal of the notion that concern correlates with levels of well-being may be enough to make the introduction of the notion of fortune unnecessary.

What does seem to be important, on whatever model one adopts, is that the threshold is tied to the notion of a *lack*. Where the individual in question has *enough*, special concern seems to give out—though of course their well-being will play its part in the overall good. This gives us

> *The Sufficiency Principle.* Special concern for any being B is appropriate up to the point at which B has a level of well-being such that B can live a life which is sufficiently good.[37]

The obvious question is again 'How much is enough?' Might my suggestion that those in the *Beverly Hills* case have enough itself be based

---

[36] *Ethics of Killing*, ch. 5.

[37] The idea that political egalitarians have been concerned with individuals' getting enough is illuminatingly discussed in Frankfurt, 'Equality as a Moral Ideal'. I take it that the sufficiency principle is person-affecting, and that there is a further analogy here with the sufficiency threshold in the case of the reason to promote one's own good. That is to say, though there are reasons to have children, these rest entirely on the promotion of the good per se, and not on any principle of distribution.

on too narrow a conception of well-being? Imagine that the universe contains trillions of beings whose lives are at a much higher level of well-being than even those of the best off on this planet. Does that mean we should set the threshold of concern high relative to levels of human well-being on earth? It is hard to know how to answer such questions, but despite this the *Beverly Hills* case suggests that there is *some* threshold or other, even if we may have to revise our immediate judgements of sufficiency in the light of further reflection upon imagined scenarios such as that described.

A further important question is whether well-being should be judged globally, across the relevant being's life as a whole, or at the time of assessment.[38]

There are cases which speak in favour of either:

> *Cinema Ticket.* You have a spare cinema ticket. You can give it either to Rich, who is usually at level 100 but today has a very bad headache and is at 10, or to Poor, who is, as always, at 10. In either case, it will raise the present level of the recipient by 1.
>
> *Painful Death.* Rich is enduring a painful death, over the course of several days. You can buy her pain-relief, or give the money to Poor. Rich's global level is 99, but now she is at 5. The pain-relief would bring her present level up to 25, and her global level up to 100. Poor's present and global level is 30. Any benefit given to Poor will be distributed equally over the rest of her life, raising its level to 31.

There seems to be a case based on special concern for benefiting Poor in the first case and Rich in the second. In particular, it seems that present suffering is particularly salient when it comes to at-a-time assessments.[39] I used to believe that both global and at-a-time assessments of well-being are required to decide whether priority is appropriate. But I now think that I was attaching too much weight to our natural sympathetic responses to those who suffer. On reflection, it now seems to me that what matters to a person is the amount of well-being in their life as a

[38] For good discussions of this issue, see McKerlie, 'Equality and Time'; Temkin, *Inequality*, ch. 8; Kappel, 'Equality, Priority, and Time'. A similar question arises for the threshold discussed in the previous section limiting the force of other-regarding reasons.

[39] This would have implications for intrapersonal rationality: see Kappel, 'Equality, Priority, and Time', 227. It may be thought reasonable, for example, to avoid some severe suffering here and now even though it will result in one's life as a whole being less valuable overall.

whole, and the significance of any episode of suffering rests entirely on that. So it is only global assessments that count.

4. CONCLUSION

I began this book with the suggestion that a fundamental, perhaps *the* fundamental, question in philosophical normative or practical ethics concerns what reasons—in particular, what grounding reasons—a person has to act. I went on to propose self-interest as a source of such a reason, and defended the general idea that we have such reasons against various Humean and Kantian objections. In the third chapter I outlined how we might have intuitive knowledge of such reasons, though the limits of knowledge are closely drawn by the large degree of disagreement that exists in ethics. The notion of self-interest raises the question what that self-interest or well-being consists in. I defended hedonism, before going on to claim that the well-being of others can provide us with reasons to act. There is a dualism of practical reason, consisting in the self-interest principle on the one hand and a principle of impartiality on the other. In this final chapter, I have argued that the most plausible principle of impartiality will attach special weight to those whose well-being is below some threshold, that weight being greater the further below the threshold the individuals in question are. How to decide on the balance of reasons is a matter for reflective judgement.[40]

[40] See Sect. 5.2.

Bibliography

ALSTON, W. P., 'Pleasure', in Paul Edwards (ed.), *The Encyclopedia of Philosophy* (Macmillan, 1967), s.v.

ANDERSON, E., 'What is the Point of Equality?', *Ethics*, 109 (1999), 287–337.

ANSCOMBE, G. E. M., 'Modern Moral Philosophy', repr. in R. Crisp and M. Slote (eds.), *Virtue Ethics* (Oxford University Press, 1997), 26–44.

ARISTOTLE, *Ethica Nicomachea*, ed. I. Bywater (Clarendon Press, 1894).

—— *De Arte Poetica*, ed. R. Kassel (Clarendon Press, 1964).

—— *Nicomachean Ethics*, ed. and tr. R. Crisp (Cambridge University Press, 2000).

AUDI, R., 'Intuitionism, Pluralism, and the Foundations of Ethics', in W. Sinnott-Armstrong and M. Timmons (eds.), *Moral Knowledge? New Readings in Moral Epistemology* (Oxford University Press, 1996), 101–36.

—— 'Prospects for a Value-Based Intuitionism', in P. Stratton-Lake (ed.), *Ethical Intuitionism: Re-evaluations* (Clarendon Press, 2002), 29–55.

—— *The Good in the Right* (Princeton University Press, 2004).

AUSTIN, J., *The Province of Jurisprudence Determined*, ed. W. Rumble (Cambridge University Press, 1995).

BACON, F., *Novum Organum*, ed. T. Fowler (Clarendon Press, 1888).

BAIER, K., *The Moral Point of View* (Cornell University Press, 1958).

—— 'Radical Virtue Ethics', in P. French, T. Uehling, and H. Wettstein (eds.), *Midwest Studies in Philosophy*, 13: *Character and Virtue* (University of Notre Dame Press, 1988), 126–35.

BEALER, G., 'The A Priori', in J. Greco and E. Sosa (eds.), *The Blackwell Guide to Epistemology* (Blackwell, 1999), 243–70.

BENACERRAF, P., 'Mathematical Truth', repr. in P. Benacerraf and H. Putnam (eds.), *Philosophy of Mathematics: Selected Readings*, 2nd edn. (Cambridge University Press, 1983), 403–20.

BENGTSSON, D., 'Pleasure and the Phenomenology of Value', in W. Rabinowicz and T. Rønnow-Rasmussen (eds.), *Patterns of Value: Essays on Formal Axiology and Value Analysis*, ii (Department of Philosophy, Lund University, 2004), 21–35.

BENTHAM, J., *Introduction to the Principles of Morals and Legislation*, ed. J. Burns and H. L. A. Hart (Clarendon Press, 1996).

BERNARDETE, S., 'XRH and DEI in Plato and Others', *Glotta*, 43 (1965), 285–98.

BERNSTEIN, M., *On Moral Considerability: An Essay on Who Morally Matters* (Oxford University Press, 1998).

BLACKBURN, S., *Spreading the Word* (Blackwell, 1984).

BLACKBURN, S., 'Moral Realism', repr. in *Essays on Quasi-Realism* (Oxford University Press, 1993), 111–29.

—— 'Supervenience Revisited', repr. in *Essays on Quasi-Realism* (Oxford University Press, 1993), 130–48.

—— 'Errors and the Phenomenology of Value', repr. in *Essays on Quasi-Realism* (Oxford University Press, 1993), 149–65.

—— 'How to be an Ethical Anti-Realist', repr. in *Essays on Quasi-Realism* (Oxford University Press, 1993), 166–81.

BLAKE, R. M., 'Why Not Hedonism? A Protest', *International Journal of Ethics*, 37 (1926), 1–18.

BLUM, L. A., *Friendship, Altruism, and Morality* (Routledge & Kegan Paul, 1980).

BOEHM, C., *Hierarchy in the Forest* (Cambridge University Press, 1999).

—— 'Conflict and the Evolution of Social Control', in L. D. Katz (ed.), *Evolutionary Origins of Morality: Cross-Disciplinary Perspectives* (Imprint Academic, 2000), 79–101.

BOGHOSSIAN, P., 'Knowledge of Logic', in P. Boghossian and C. Peacocke (eds.), *New Essays on the A Priori* (Clarendon Press, 2000), 229–54.

—— 'Inference and Insight', *Philosophy and Phenomenological Research*, 63 (2001), 633–41.

—— and C. PEACOCKE, 'Introduction', in Boghossian and Peacocke (eds.), *New Essays on the A Priori* (Clarendon Press, 2000), 1–10.

BONJOUR, L., *In Defense of Pure Reason: A Rationalist Account of A Priori Justification* (Cambridge University Press, 1998).

—— 'Replies', *Philosophy and Phenomenological Research*, 63 (2001), 673–93.

BOYD, R., and P. J. RICHERSON, *The Origin and Evolution of Cultures* (Oxford University Press, 2005).

BRANDT, R., 'The Concept of Welfare', in S. R. Krupp (ed.), *The Structure of Economic Science* (Prentice-Hall, 1966), 257–76.

BRENTANO, F., *The Origin of our Knowledge of Right and Wrong*, ed. O. Kraus; Eng. edn., ed. R. Chisholm, tr. R. Chisholm and E. H. Schneewind (Routledge, 1969).

BRINK, D., *Moral Realism and the Foundations of Ethics* (Cambridge University Press, 1989).

—— 'Mill's Deliberative Utilitarianism', *Philosophy and Public Affairs*, 21 (1992), 67–103.

BROAD, C. D., *Five Types of Ethical Theory* (Kegan Paul, Trench, & Trubner, 1930).

—— 'Emotion and Sentiment', *Journal of Aesthetics and Art Criticism*, 13 (1954), 203–14.

BROOME, J., *Weighing Goods* (Blackwell, 1991).

—— 'Normative Requirements', repr. in J. Dancy (ed.), *Normativity* (Blackwell, 2000), 78–99.

—— 'Practical Reasoning', in J. Bermúdez and A. Millar (eds.), *Reason and Nature: Essays in the Theory of Rationality* (Oxford University Press, 2002), 85–112.

—— 'Reasons', in R. J. Wallace, P. Pettit, S. Scheffler, and M. Smith (eds.), *Reason and Value: Themes from the Moral Philosophy of Joseph Raz* (Clarendon Press, 2004), 28–55.

BURGE, T., 'Individualism and the Mental', in P. French, T. Uehling, and H. Wettstein (eds.), *Midwest Studies in Philosophy*, 4: *Metaphysics* (University of Minnesota Press, 1979), 73–121.

CARSON, T., *Value and the Good Life* (Notre Dame University Press, 2000).

CHANG, R., 'Can Desires Provide Reasons for Action?', in R. J. Wallace, P. Pettit, S. Scheffler, and M. Smith (eds.), *Reason and Value: Themes from the Moral Philosophy of Joseph Raz* (Clarendon Press, 2004), 56–90.

CICERO, *De Finibus Bonorum et Malorum*, ed. L. Reynolds (Clarendon Press, 1998).

CRISP, R., 'Utilitarianism and the Life of Virtue', *Philosophical Quarterly*, 42 (1992), 139–60.

—— 'Motivation, Universality and the Good: A Critical Notice of Jonathan Dancy, *Moral Reasons*', *Ratio*, 6 (1993), 181–90.

—— 'The Dualism of Practical Reason', *Proceedings of the Aristotelian Society*, 96 (1996), 53–73.

—— *Mill on Utilitarianism* (Routledge, 1997).

—— 'Particularizing Particularism', in B. Hooker and M. Little (eds.), *Moral Particularism* (Clarendon Press, 2000), 23–47.

—— 'Utilitarianism and Accomplishment', *Analysis*, 60 (2000), 264–8.

—— 'Sidgwick and the Boundaries of Intuitionism', in P. Stratton-Lake (ed.), *Ethical Intuitionism* (Clarendon Press, 2002), 56–75.

—— 'Equality, Priority, and Compassion', *Ethics*, 113 (2003), 745–63.

—— 'Egalitarianism and Compassion', *Ethics*, 114 (2003), 119–26.

—— 'Does Modern Moral Philosophy Rest on a Mistake?', in A. O'Hear (ed.), *Modern Moral Philosophy*, Royal Institute of Philosophy, suppl. 54 (2004), 75–93.

—— 'Deontological Ethics', in T. Honderich (ed.), *Oxford Companion to Philosophy*, 2nd edn. (Oxford University Press, 2005).

—— 'Value, Reasons and the Structure of Justification: How to Avoid Passing the Buck', *Analysis*, 65 (2005), 80–5.

—— 'Well-Being', in E. N. Zalta (ed.), *Stanford Encyclopedia of Philosophy* (Winter 2005 edn.). <http://plato.stanford.edu/archives/win2005/entries/well-being/>.

—— 'Ethics without Reasons?', *Journal of Moral Philosophy* (forthcoming).

—— 'Hedonism Reconsidered', *Philosophy and Phenomenological Research* (forthcoming).

CULLITY, G., *The Moral Demands of Affluence* (Clarendon Press, 2004).

DANCY, J., *Moral Reasons* (Blackwell, 1993).

—— *Practical Reality* (Oxford University Press, 2000).

—— 'Should we Pass the Buck?', in A. O'Hear (ed.), *The Good, the True, and the Beautiful* (Cambridge University Press, 2000), 159–73.

—— *Ethics without Principles* (Clarendon Press, 2004).

DAVIS, W., 'Pleasure and Happiness', *Philosophical Studies*, 39 (1981), 305–17.

DE SOUSA, R., *The Rationality of Emotion* (MIT Press, 1987).

DIOGENES LAERTIUS, *Lives of Eminent Philosophers*, ed. and tr. R. Hicks, rev. H. Long (Harvard University Press and Heinemann, 1972).

DONNER, W., *The Liberal Self* (Cornell University Press, 1991).

DOVER, K., *Greek Popular Morality in the Time of Plato and Aristotle* (repr. Hackett, 1994).

DREIER, J., 'The Supervenience Argument against Moral Realism', *Southern Journal of Philosophy*, 30 (1992), 13–38.

DUNCKER, K., 'On Pleasure, Emotion, and Striving', *Philosophy and Phenomenological Research*, 1 (1941), 391–430.

EDWARDS, R. B., *Pleasures and Pains* (Cornell University Press, 1979).

EWING, A. C., 'Reason and Intuition', *Proceedings of the British Academy*, 27 (1941), 67–107.

—— *The Definition of Good* (Macmillan, 1947).

—— *Ethics* (Macmillan, 1947).

—— *The Fundamental Questions of Philosophy* (Routledge & Kegan Paul, 1951).

FELDMAN, F., *Utilitarianism, Hedonism, and Desert* (Cambridge University Press, 1997).

—— *Pleasure and the Good Life* (Clarendon Press, 2004).

FESSLER, D., 'The Evolution of Human Emotions', in M. Pagel (ed.), *The Oxford Encyclopedia of Evolution* (Oxford University Press, 2002), 296–9.

FIELD, H., *Realism, Mathematics and Modality* (Blackwell, 1989).

—— 'Recent Debates about the A Priori', in T. S. Gendler and J. Hawthorne (eds.), *Oxford Studies in Epistemology*, i (Clarendon Press, 2005), 69–88.

FINDLAY, J. N., *Values and Intentions* (Allen & Unwin, 1961).

FLEW, A., *The Politics of Procrustes* (Temple Smith, 1981).

FOOT, P., 'Utilitarianism and the Virtues', repr. in S. Scheffler (ed.), *Consequentialism and its Critics* (Oxford University Press, 1988), 224–42.

FRANKENA, W. K., *Ethics*, 2nd edn. (Prentice-Hall, 1973).

—— 'Sidgwick and the History of Ethical Dualism', in B. Schultz (ed.), *Essays on Henry Sidgwick* (Cambridge University Press, 1992), 175–98.

FRANKFURT, H., 'Equality as a Moral Ideal', repr. in *The Importance of What we Care About* (Cambridge University Press, 1988), 134–58.

FRAZIER, R., 'Intuitionism', in E. Craig (ed.), *Routledge Encyclopedia of Philosophy* (Routledge, 1998), s.v.

FREUD, S., *Civilization and its Discontents*, in *The Standard Edition of the Complete Psychological Works of Sigmund Freud*, ed. and tr. J. Strachey and A. Freud, xxi (Hogarth Press, 1961).

GALLAGHER, S., *How the Body Shapes the Mind* (Clarendon Press, 2005).

GAUT, B., 'Justifying Moral Pluralism', in P. Stratton-Lake (ed.), *Ethical Intuitionism: Re-evaluations* (Clarendon Press, 2002), 137–60.

GERT, J., *Brute Rationality* (Cambridge University Press, 2004).

GIBBARD, A., *Wise Choices, Apt Feelings* (Clarendon Press, 1990).

—— 'Knowing What to Do, Seeing What to Do', in P. Stratton-Lake (ed.), *Ethical Intuitionism: Re-evaluations* (Clarendon Press, 2002), 212–28.

GLASSEN, P., 'A Fallacy in Aristotle's Argument about the Good', *Philosophical Quarterly*, 7 (1957), 319–22.

GLOVER, J., *What Sort of People should there Be?* (Penguin, 1984).

GOLDIE, P., *The Emotions: A Philosophical Exploration* (Clarendon Press, 2000).

GOLDSTEIN, I., 'Why People Prefer Pleasure to Pain', *Philosophy*, 55 (1980), 349–62.

—— 'Hedonic Pluralism', *Philosophical Studies*, 48 (1985), 49–55.

GOODELL, T. D., 'XRH and DEI', *Classical Quarterly*, 8 (1914), 91–102.

GOSLING, J. C. B., *Pleasure and Desire: The Case for Hedonism Reviewed* (Clarendon Press, 1969).

GRECO, J., 'Introduction: What is Epistemology?', in J. Greco and E. Sosa (eds.), *The Blackwell Guide to Epistemology* (Blackwell, 1999), 1–31.

GREEN, T. H., *Prolegomena to Ethics* (Clarendon Press, 1883).

GREENSPAN, P. S., *Emotions and Reasons: An Inquiry into Conceptual Justification* (Routledge, 1988).

GRIFFIN, J., *Well-Being: Its Meaning, Measurement, and Moral Importance* (Clarendon Press, 1986).

—— *Value Judgement* (Clarendon Press, 1996).

HALE, B., *Abstract Objects* (Blackwell, 1987).

HARE, R. M., *The Language of Morals* (Oxford University Press, 1952).

—— *Freedom and Reason* (Oxford University Press, 1963).

—— *Moral Thinking: Its Methods, Levels, and Point* (Clarendon Press, 1981).

HART, H. L. A., *The Concept of Law* 2nd edn. (Oxford University Press, 1997).

HAYBRON, D. M., 'Happiness and Pleasure', *Philosophy and Phenomenological Research*, 62 (2001), 501–28.

HESIOD, *Opera et Dies*, ed. F. Solmsen, 3rd edn. (Clarendon Press, 1990).

HOBBES, T., *Human Nature: or The Fundamental Elements of Policy*, in *The English Works of Thomas Hobbes*, ed. W. Molesworth, iv (1839).

HOLTUG, N., 'In Defence of the Slogan', in W. Rabinowicz (ed.), *Preference and Value* (Department of Philosophy, Lund University, 1996), 64–89.

HOOKER, B., *Ideal Code, Real World: A Rule Consequentialist Theory of Morality* (Clarendon Press, 2000).

HUME, D., *An Enquiry concerning the Principles of Morals*, ed. T. L. Beauchamp (Clarendon Press, 1998).

—— *A Treatise of Human Nature*, ed. D. F. Norton and M. F. Norton (Oxford University Press, 2000).

HURKA, T., ' "Good" and "Good For" ', *Mind*, 96 (1987), 71–3.

HURLEY, S., 'Animal Action in the Space of Reasons', *Mind and Language*, 18 (2003), 231–56.

IRWIN, T., 'Eminent Victorians and Greek Ethics', in B. Schultz (ed.), *Essays on Henry Sidgwick* (Cambridge University Press, 1992), 279–310.

—— *Plato's Ethics* (Oxford University Press, 1995).

JOACHIM, H. H., *Aristotle, The Nicomachean Ethics: A Commentary*, ed. D. A. Rees (Clarendon Press, 1951).

JOYCE, R., *The Myth of Morality* (Cambridge University Press, 2001).

KAGAN, S., 'The Additive Fallacy', *Ethics*, 99 (1988), 5–31.

—— *The Limits of Morality* (Clarendon Press, 1989).

—— 'The Limits of Well-Being', in E. F. Paul, F. D. Miller, Jr., and J. Paul (eds.), *The Good Life and the Human Good* (Cambridge University Press, 1992), 169–89.

KAHNEMAN, D., 'Objective Happiness', in D. Kahneman, E. Diener, and N. Schwartz, *Well-Being: The Foundations of Hedonic Psychology* (Russell Sage Foundation, 1999), 3–25.

KAMM, F., 'Non-Consequentialism, the Person as an End-in-Itself, and the Significance of Status', *Philosophy and Public Affairs*, 21 (1992), 354–89.

—— *Morality, Mortality*, ii: *Rights, Duties, and Status* (Oxford University Press, 1996).

KANT, I., *The Metaphysics of Morals*, ed. and tr. M. Gregor (Cambridge University Press, 1996).

—— *Groundwork for the Metaphysics of Morals*, ed. T. E. Hill, Jr., and A. Zweig, tr. Zweig (Oxford University Press, 2002).

KAPPEL, K., 'Equality, Priority, and Time', *Utilitas*, 9 (1997), 203–25.

—— 'Challenges to Audi's Ethical Intuitionism', *Ethical Theory and Moral Practice*, 5 (2002), 391–413.

KAWALL, J., 'The Experience Machine and Mental States of Well-Being', *Journal of Value Inquiry*, 33 (1999), 381–7.

KORSGAARD, C., 'Skepticism about Practical Reason', repr. in *Creating the Kingdom of Ends* (Cambridge University Press, 1996), 311–34.

—— *The Sources of Normativity* (Cambridge University Press, 1996).

—— 'The Normativity of Instrumental Reason', in G. Cullity and B. Gaut (eds.), *Ethics and Practical Reason* (Clarendon Press, 1997), 215–54.

KYMLICKA, W., *Contemporary Political Philosophy* (Clarendon Press, 1990).

LACEWING, M., 'Emotional Self-Awareness and Ethical Deliberation', *Ratio*, 18 (2005), 65–81.

LIDDELL, H. G., and R. Scott, *Greek–English Lexicon*, 9th edn. (Clarendon Press, 1940).

LILLEHAMMER, H., 'Smith on Moral Fetishism', *Analysis*, 57 (1997), 187–95.

LLOYD-JONES, H., *The Justice of Zeus*, rev. edn. (University of California Press, 1983).

LOCKE, D., 'The Trivializability of Universalizability', *Philosophical Review*, 78 (1968), 25–44.

LOCKE, J., *An Essay concerning Human Understanding*, ed. P. Nidditch (Clarendon Press, 1975).

LUCAS, J. R., 'Intuitionism II', *Philosophy*, 46 (1971), 1–11.

McCLOSKEY, H. J., 'An Examination of Restricted Utilitarianism', *Philosophical Review*, 66 (1957), 466–85.

McKERLIE, D., 'Egalitarianism', *Dialogue*, 23 (1984), 223–37.

——'Egalitarianism and the Separateness of Persons', *Canadian Journal of Philosophy*, 18 (1988), 205–26.

——'Equality and Time', *Ethics*, 99 (1989), 475–91.

MACKIE, J. L., *Ethics: Inventing Right and Wrong* (Penguin, 1975).

McMAHAN, J., 'Cognitive Disability, Misfortune, and Justice', *Philosophy and Public Affairs*, 25 (1996), 3–35.

——*The Ethics of Killing: Problems at the Margins of Life* (Oxford University Press, 2002).

McTAGGART, J. M. E., *The Nature of Existence*, 2 vols. (Cambridge University Press, 1921).

MADDY, P., *Realism in Mathematics* (Clarendon Press, 1990).

MILL, J. S., *Utilitarianism*, ed. R. Crisp (Oxford University Press, 1998).

MILLER, A., 'An Objection to Smith's Argument for Internalism', *Analysis*, 56 (1996), 169–74.

MILLER, G., *The Mating Mind* (Doubleday, 2000).

MITCHELL, B., *Old English Syntax* (Clarendon Press, 1985).

MOORE, A., and R. CRISP, 'Welfarism in Moral Theory', *Australasian Journal of Philosophy*, 74 (1996), 598–613.

MOORE, G. E., *Principia Ethica* (Cambridge University Press, 1903).

——*Principia Ethica*, ed. T. Baldwin, rev. edn. (Cambridge University Press, 1993).

MULGAN, T., *The Demands of Consequentialism* (Clarendon Press, 2001).

NAGEL, T., *The Possibility of Altruism* (Princeton University Press, 1970).

——'Equality', repr. in *Mortal Questions* (Cambridge University Press, 1979), 106–27.

——*The View from Nowhere* (Oxford University Press, 1986).

NARVESON, J., 'Moral Problems of Population', *Monist*, 57 (1973), 187–95.

NICHOLS, S., *Sentimental Rules* (Oxford University Press, 2004).

NIETZSCHE, F., *On the Genealogy of Morals*, tr. D. Smith (Oxford University Press, 1996).

NORMAN, R., *Reasons for Action: A Critique of Utilitarian Rationality* (Blackwell, 1971).

NOWELL-SMITH, P., *Ethics* (Penguin, 1954).

NOZICK, R., *Anarchy, State, and Utopia* (Blackwell, 1974).

——*The Examined Life: Philosophical Meditations* (Simon & Schuster, 1989).

NUSSBAUM, M., *Love's Knowledge: Essays on Philosophy and Literature* (Oxford University Press, 1990).

—— *Upheavals of Thought* (Cambridge University Press, 2001).

OWEN, G. E. L., 'Aristotelian Pleasures', *Proceedings of the Aristotelian Society*, 72 (1971–2), 135–52.

Oxford English Dictionary Online, <http://dictionary.oed.com/>.

PANKSEPP, J., *Affective Neuroscience: The Foundations of Human and Animal Emotions* (Oxford University Press, 1998).

PARFIT, D., *Reasons and Persons* (Clarendon Press, 1984).

—— 'Reasons and Motivation', *Proceedings of the Aristotelian Society*, suppl. vol. 71 (1997), 99–130.

—— 'Equality and Priority', in A. Mason (ed.), *Ideals of Equality* (Blackwell, 1998), 1–20.

—— 'Rationality and Reasons', in D. Egonsson, J. Josefsson, B. Petersson, and T. Rønnow-Rasmussen (eds.), *Exploring Practical Philosophy: From Action to Values* (Ashgate, 2001), 17–39.

PEACOCKE, C., 'Explaining the A Priori: The Programme of Moderate Rationalism', in P. Boghossian and C. Peacocke (eds.), *New Essays on the A Priori* (Clarendon Press, 2000), 255–85.

—— *The Realm of Reason* (Clarendon Press, 2004).

PHILLIPS, H., 'The Pleasure Seekers', *New Scientist*, 2416 (11 Oct. 2003), 36–40.

PIGDEN, C., 'Anscombe on "Ought" ', *Philosophical Quarterly*, 38 (1988), 20–41.

PILLER, C., 'Normative Practical Reasoning', *Proceedings of the Aristotelian Society*, suppl. vol. 75 (2001), 195–216.

PLANTINGA, A., 'Reformed Epistemology', in P. L. Quinn and C. Taliaferro (eds.), *A Companion to the Philosophy of Religion* (Blackwell, 1997), 383–9.

PLATO, *Euthyphro*, in *Platonis Opera*, i, ed. E. Duke *et al.* (Clarendon Press, 1995).

—— *Philebus*, in *Platonis Opera*, ii, ed. J. Burnet (Clarendon Press, 1901).

—— *Protagoras*, in *Platonis Opera*, iii, ed. J. Burnet (Clarendon Press, 1903).

—— *Protagoras*, tr. and annot. C. C. W. Taylor (Clarendon Press, 1976).

PUGMIRE, D., *Sound Sentiments: Integrity in the Emotions* (Clarendon Press, 2005).

PUTNAM, H., 'The Meaning of "Meaning" ', in K. Gunderson (ed.), *Minnesota Studies in the Philosophy of Science*, 7: *Language, Mind, and Knowledge* (University of Minnesota Press, 1975), 131–93.

QUINN, W., 'Putting Rationality in its Place', repr. in *Morality and Action* (Cambridge University Press, 1993), 228–55.

RABINOWICZ, W., and T. RØNNOW-RASMUSSEN, 'The Strike of the Demon: On Fitting Pro-Attitudes and Value', *Ethics*, 114 (2004), 391–423.

RACHELS, S., 'Is Unpleasantness Intrinsic to Unpleasant Experiences?', *Philosophical Studies*, 99 (2000), 187–210.

—— 'Six Theses about Pleasure', *Philosophical Perspectives*, 18 (2004), 247–67.

RAILTON, P., 'Alienation, Consequentialism, and the Demands of Morality', *Philosophy and Public Affairs*, 13 (1984), 134–71.

—— 'Naturalism and Prescriptivity', *Social Philosophy and Policy*, 7 (1989), 151–74.

RAKZIK, L., 'A Normative Regress Problem', *American Philosophical Quarterly*, 36 (1999), 35–47.

RASHDALL, H., *The Theory of Good and Evil* (Clarendon Press, 1907).

RAWLS, J., *A Theory of Justice*, rev. edn. (Oxford University Press, 1999).

RAZ, J., *Practical Reason and Norms* (Hutchinson, 1975).

—— *The Morality of Freedom* (Clarendon Press, 1986).

—— 'Authority, Law, and Morality', repr. in *Ethics in the Public Domain* (Clarendon Press, 1994), 210–37.

RIDGE, M., 'Moral Non-Naturalism', in E. N. Zalta (ed.), *Stanford Encyclopedia of Philosophy* (Spring 2003 edn.), <http://plato.stanford.edu/archives/spr2003/entries/moral-non-naturalism/>.

ROBINSON, J., *Deeper than Reason* (Clarendon Press, 2005).

ROSS, W. D., *The Right and the Good* (Clarendon Press, 1930).

—— *Foundations of Ethics* (Clarendon Press, 1939).

SCANLON, T. M., *What we Owe to Each Other* (Belknap Press, 1998).

SCHEFFLER, S., *The Rejection of Consequentialism* (Clarendon Press, 1982).

—— 'Prerogatives without Restrictions', *Philosophical Perspectives*, 6 (1992), 377–97.

SCHNEEWIND, J., *Sidgwick's Ethics and Victorian Moral Philosophy* (Clarendon Press, 1977).

SCHROEDER, T., *Three Faces of Desire* (Oxford University Press, 2004).

SELIGMAN, M. E. P., *Authentic Happiness* (Free Press, 2002).

—— A. C. PARKS, and T. STEEN, 'A Balanced Psychology and Full Life', in F. A. Huppert, N. Baylis, and B. Keverne (eds.), *The Science of Well-Being* (Oxford University Press, 2005), 275–83.

SEXTUS EMPIRICUS, *Outlines of Scepticism*, tr. J. Annas and J. Barnes (Cambridge University Press, 1994).

SHAFER-LANDAU, R., *Moral Realism: A Defence* (Clarendon Press, 2003).

SIDGWICK, H., *The Methods of Ethics*, 7th edn. (Macmillan, 1907).

SILVERSTEIN, M., 'In Defense of Happiness: A Response to the Experience Machine', *Social Theory and Practice*, 26 (2000), 279–300.

SINGER, P., *The Expanding Circle: Ethics and Sociobiology* (Oxford University Press, 1981).

—— *How are we to Live? Ethics in an Age of Self-Interest* (Prometheus Books, 1995).

SINNOTT-ARMSTRONG, W., 'Moral Relativity and Intuitionism', *Philosophical Issues*, 12 (2002), 305–28.

SKORUPSKI, J., 'Reasons and Reason', in G. Cullity and B. Gaut (eds.), *Ethics and Practical Reason* (Clarendon Press, 1997), 345–67.

—— 'Irrealist Cognitivism', *Ratio*, 12 (1999), 436–59.

SMITH, M., 'The Humean Theory of Motivation', *Mind*, 96 (1987), 36–61.

—— 'Realism', in P. Singer (ed.), *A Companion to Ethics* (Blackwell, 1991), 399–410.

—— *The Moral Problem* (Blackwell, 1994).

—— 'The Argument for Internalism: Reply to Miller', *Analysis*, 56 (1996), 175–83.

—— 'In Defense of *The Moral Problem*: A Reply to Brink, Copp, and Sayre-McCord', *Ethics*, 108 (1997–8), 84–119.

SOBEL, D., 'Pleasure as a Mental State', *Utilitas*, 11 (1999), 230–4.

—— 'Varieties of Hedonism', *Journal of Social Philosophy*, 33 (2002), 240–56.

SOLOMON, R., *In Defense of Sentimentality* (Oxford University Press, 2004).

SOPHOCLES, *Antigone*, in *Fabulae*, ed. H. Lloyd-Jones and N. G. Wilson (Clarendon Press, 1990).

SPRIGGE, T. L. S., *The Rational Foundations of Ethics* (Routledge & Kegan Paul, 1988).

STOCKER, M., 'The Schizophrenia of Modern Ethical Theories', *Journal of Philosophy*, 73 (1973), 453–66.

—— 'How Emotions Reveal Value and Help Cure the Schizophrenia of Modern Ethical Theories', in R. Crisp (ed.), *How Should One Live?* (Clarendon Press, 1996), 173–90.

STRATTON-LAKE, P. (ed.), *Ethical Intuitionism: Re-evaluations* (Clarendon Press, 2002).

—— and B. HOOKER, 'Scanlon versus Moore on Goodness', in T. Horgan and M. Timmons (eds.), *Metaethics after Moore* (Clarendon Press, 2006), 149–68.

STREUMER, B., 'Reasons and Impossibility', unpub.

STRIKER, G., 'Historical Reflections on Classical Pyrrhonism and Neo-Pyrrhonism', in W. Sinnott-Armstrong (ed.), *Pyrrhonian Scepticism* (Oxford University Press, 2004), 13–24.

STURGEON, N., 'Ethical Intuitionism and Ethical Naturalism', in P. Stratton-Lake (ed.), *Ethical Intuitionism: Re-evaluations* (Clarendon Press, 2002), 184–211.

SUMNER, L. W., 'The Evolution of Utility', in B. Hooker (ed.), *Rationality, Rules, and Utility: New Essays on the Philosophy of R. B. Brandt* (Westview Press, 1993), 97–114.

—— *Welfare, Happiness, and Ethics* (Clarendon Press, 1996).

SVAVARSDÓTTIR, S., 'Moral Cognitivism and Motivation', *Philosophical Review*, 108 (1999), 161–219.

TÄNNSJÖ, T., *Hedonistic Utilitarianism* (Edinburgh University Press, 1998).

TAYLOR, G., *Pride, Shame, and Guilt* (Clarendon Press, 1985).

TEMKIN, L., 'Intransitivity and the Mere Addition Paradox', *Philosophy and Public Affairs*, 16 (1987), 138–87.

—— 'Harmful Goods, Harmless Bads', in R. G. Frey and C. W. Morris (eds.), *Value, Welfare, and Morality* (Cambridge University Press, 1993), 290–324.

—— *Inequality* (Oxford University Press, 1993).

—— 'Rethinking the Good, Moral Ideals and the Nature of Practical Reasoning', in J. Dancy (ed.), *Reading Parfit* (Blackwell, 1997), 290–345.

—— 'Egalitarianism Defended', *Ethics*, 113 (2003), 764–82.

—— 'Rethinking the Good, Moral Ideals and the Nature of Practical Reasoning', unpub. TS.

THOMSON, J. J., *Goodness and Advice* (Princeton University Press, 2001).

Vision 2020 Eye Disease Information: Cataract, <http://www.v2020.org/Eye_disease/cataract.asp>.

WALZER, M., *Spheres of Justice* (Blackwell, 1985).

WHITE, N., *Individual and Conflict in Greek Ethics* (Clarendon Press, 2002).

WIGGINS, D., *Needs, Values, Truth* (Blackwell, 1987).

WILLIAMS, B., 'A Critique of Utilitarianism', in J. Smart and B. Williams, *Utilitarianism For and Against* (Cambridge University Press, 1973), 75–155.

—— 'Morality and the Emotions', repr. in *Problems of the Self* (Cambridge University Press, 1973), 207–29.

—— 'Persons, Character and Morality', repr. in *Moral Luck* (Cambridge University Press, 1981), 1–19.

—— 'Moral Luck', repr. in *Moral Luck* (Cambridge University Press, 1981), 20–39.

—— 'Internal and External Reasons', repr. in *Moral Luck* (Cambridge University Press, 1981), 101–13.

—— *Ethics and the Limits of Philosophy* (Fontana, 1985).

—— *Shame and Necessity* (University of California Press, 1993).

—— 'Internal Reasons and the Obscurity of Blame', repr. in *Making Sense of Humanity* (Cambridge University Press, 1995), 35–45.

—— 'What Does Ethical Intuitionism Imply?', repr. in *Making Sense of Humanity* (Cambridge University Press, 1995), 182–91.

WOODS, M., 'Reasons for Action and Desire', *Proceedings of the Aristotelian Society*, suppl. vol. 46 (1972), 189–201.

WRIGHT, C., *Frege's Conception of Numbers as Objects* (Aberdeen University Press, 1983).

XENOPHON, *Memoirs of Socrates*, in *Libri Socratici*, ed. E. Marchant, 2nd edn. (Clarendon Press, 1963).

ZANGWILL, N., 'Moral Supervenience', in P. French, T. Uehling, and H. Wettstein (eds.), *Midwest Studies in Philosophy*, 20: *Moral Concepts* (Notre Dame University Press, 1995), 240–59.

Index